US CONSTITUTION

FOR BEGINNERS

STEVEN BACHMA...

ILLUSTRATED BY

JOEL PETT

...ION AND

THE CONSTITUTION

Writers and Readers

WRITERS AND READERS PUBLISHING, INCORPORATED
One West 125th Street
Dr. Martin Luther King, Jr. Blvd.
New York, N.Y. 10027

ACKNOWLEDGEMENTS

The Constitution is the product of the efforts of many people beyond the Founding Fathers, and so too is this book. Special thanks to Naomi Rosenblatt for designing, Dan Simon for editing, and Patrick Scherer for translating Mr. Otto. And, for general help and inspiration, additional thanks to Robert and Ruth Bachmann, Morty Horwitz, Kim Huff, Alexander Nagy, Ann Shields, Dan Snow, and Glen Thompson. Finally, thanks to the men and women of ACORN and Local 100, SEIU—and those of like mind and efforts—for teaching us that if there is anything more beautiful than a painting by Mondrian, it is the sight of ordinary people rising off their knees.

Mondrian Collage by Stephen Bachmann

TABLE OF CONTENTS

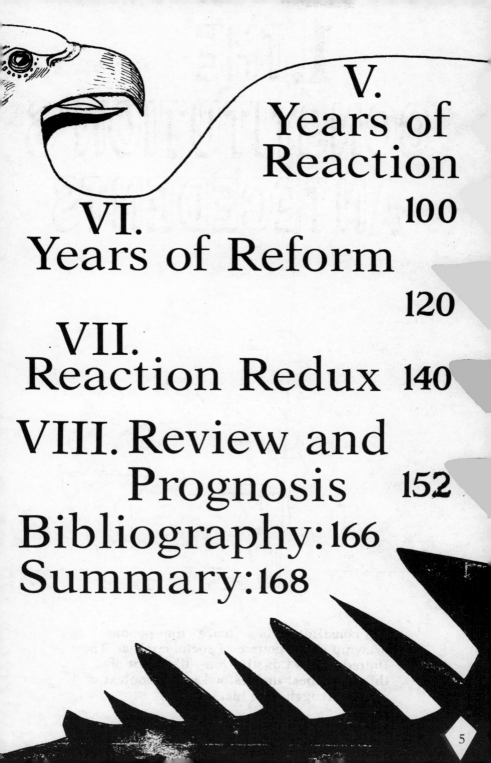

1. THE CONSTITUTION'S ANTECEDENTS

'TRUCE' IS BORING.... LET'S CALL IT A CONSTITUTION!

A constitution is a "truce" that people draw up in the course of social conflict. The United States Constitution—like a lot of things—is best understood in the context of people struggling in history.

Magna Carta

The first constitution in the English speaking world was the **Magna Carta.** It appeared in Eng. and when a group of barons finally got tired of the way that King John was ruling the realm.

YOU WORK YOUR
WAY UP THROUGH
THE RAT RACE, YOU
FINALLY MAKE KING,
AND EVERYBODY GETS
BENT OUT OF SHAPE
OVER A FEW LOUSY
RIDICULOUS MILITARY
ADVENTURES!

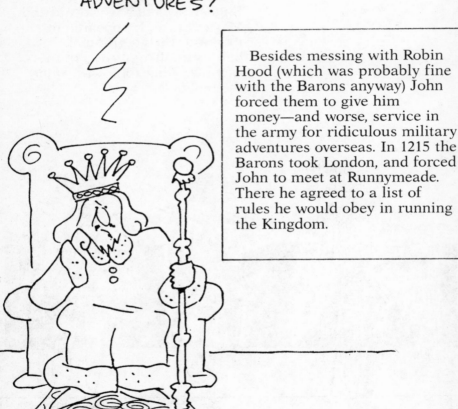

Besides messing with Robin Hood (which was probably fine with the Barons anyway) John forced them to give him money—and worse, service in the army for ridiculous military adventures overseas. In 1215 the Barons took London, and forced John to meet at Runnymeade. There he agreed to a list of rules he would obey in running the Kingdom.

38. *Henceforth no bailiff shall put anyone on trial by his own unsupported allegation, without bringing credible witnesses to the charge.*

39. *No free man shall be taken or imprisoned or disseized or outlawed or exiled or in any way ruined, nor will we go or send against him, except by the lawful judgment of his peers or by the law of the land.*

40. *To no one will we sell, to no one will we deny or delay right or justice.*

It appears that John intended to break the Magna Carta agreement as soon as he had the power to do so. However, he died the next year, and his young son Henry (the Third) was in no position to fight with the barons over Magna Carta. The English came to see Magna Carta as the primary list of rules for living in the kingdom.

Early Constitutions

WHICH SOUNDS BETTER...
"WITHIN EVERY OR ANY OF THE SAID SEVERAL COLONIES" OR DOMINIONS", OR "IN THESE HERE PARTS"?

When English people started living in North America, they set up rules for living in the new land. Usually they did this on the basis of a charter granted by the King, like the **Virginia Charter.** Or they would make one up themselves, if they could, which is what the Pilgrims did in Massachusetts. Documents like the Virginia Charter and the **Mayflower Compact** were early constitutions.

FIRST CHARTER OF VIRGINIA, April 10, 1606: Also we do, for Us, our Hiers, and Successors, DECLARE, by these Presents, that all and every Persons being our Subjects, which shall dwell and inhabit within every or any of the said several Colonies and Plantations, and every of their children, which shall happen to be born within any of the Limits and Precincts of the said several Colonies and Plantations, shall HAVE and enjoy all Liberties, Franchises, and Immunities, within any of our other Dominions, to all Intents and Purposes, as if they had been abiding and born, within this our Realm of ENGLAND, or any other of our said Dominions.

MAYFLOWER COMPACT, NOV. 11, 1620: We, whose names are underwritten . . . Do by these Presents, solemnly and mutually, in the Presence of God and one another, covenant and combine ourselves together into a civil Body Politick, for our better Ordering and Preservation, and Furtherance of the Ends aforesaid: And by Virtue hereof do enact, constitute, and frame, such just and equal Laws, Ordinances, Acts, Constitutions, and Officeres, from time to time, as shall be thought most meet and convenient for the general Good of the Colony . . .

Reasons For Emigration

English people were leaving merrie olde England to live in North America because England wasn't so merrie anymore.

The centuries after Magna Carta had seen your regular array of royal assassinations, baronial rebellions, and peasant riots. The Magna Carta was seldom an issue, though, either because people had other things to fight over, or because there weren't enough strong groups to create a stalemate.

PEASANT RIOTS, ROYAL ASSASINATIONS, BARONIAL REBELLIONS... I TELL YOU, THIS IS GETTING OLDE!

In the 1600s, however, all this began to change, particularly when the Stuart family assumed the throne of England after Elizabeth's death.

Queen Elizabeth would have been a hard act to follow for anybody, but the Stuarts made it even harder. Elizabeth was a feisty but popular old bird. She had impeccable Protestant credentials. More importantly, she knew how to treat Catholic Spaniards. (Remember the Armada?) By contrast, James I and his son Charles I were snots. They liked their religion with a certain degree of pomp (which outraged the Puritans). They sucked up to Catholic powers like Spain and France.

English people started leaving England in droves. A lot of them went to North America.

FORGET LEAVING IN DROVES... HOW MUCH IS THE CONCORDE?

"NATIONAL SECURITY" IS A CLASSIC... REMEMBER IT WHEN WE GET TO NIXON!

Revolution in England

Not every malcontent left England. As fast as they left, King Charles created more of them. Not only did he marry a Catholic wife. He was even more aggressive telling the Puritans that they could not worship like Puritans. Worse, he began levying taxes without the consent of Parliament, which was the body of the well-to-do in the Kingdom. Finally, he started throwing people into jail who did not pay his illegal taxes.

Much of what Charles did seemed to violate the provisions of Magna Carta. When Parliament protested, Charles stopped calling Parliament. When people tried to take these issues to court, the judges (appointed by the King) said that what Charles did was OK because of national security, his highnessness, and so forth:

The law is of itself an old and trusty servant of the King's; it is his instrument or means which he useth to govern his people by.

Charles managed well enough until 1639 when he tried to tell the Scots how to worship. They raised an army which overran Charles' forces. Charles had to call Parliament in order to raise money and better troops. Parliament was more interested in talking about Magna Carta. The King tried to arrest some of the Parliamentarians in the House of Commons, and they raised their own troops. England was plunged into Civil War.

Parliament's army beat the pants off Charles' troops because they were willing to let ordinary people serve in positions normally filled by aristrocrats. By 1647 some of the more politically active commoners in the army thought it was time for them to determine how the country would be run after the revolution. A group of them began drafting a series of documents which would have been the first official constitution for England.

THE FIRST AGREEMENT OF THE PEOPLE, 28 Oct. 1647:

1. That matters of religion and the ways of God's worship are not at all entrusted by us to any human power . . .

2. That the matter of impressing and constraining any of us to serve in the wars is against our freedom . . .

3. That after the dissolution of the present parliament no person be at any time questioned for anything said or done in reference to the late public differences . . .

4. That in laws made or to be made every person may be bound alike . . .

5. That as the laws ought to be equal, so they must be good, and not evidently destructive to the safety and well-being of the people.

This group was called the **Levellers,** because they wanted a more equal ("levelled") distribution of power.

Revolutionary Colonist Constitutions

In the meantime the English people in the colonies were not sitting idle. They too drafted various declarations of rights.

Maryland Toleration Act, 1649: . . . noe person or persons whatsoever within this Province . . . professing to believe in Jesus Christ, shall from henceforth bee any waies troubled, Molested or discountenanced for or in respect of his or her religion.

AT LEAST UNTIL PAT ROBERTSON ARRIVETH!

MARYLAND TOLERATION ACT

MASS. BODY OF LIBERTIES, DEC. 10, 1641:

1. No mans life shall be taken away, no mans honor or good name shall be stayned, no mans person shall be arested, restrayned, banished, dismembered, nor any ways punished . . . unlesse it be by vertue or equitie of some expresse law of the Country warranting the same . . .

2. Every person within this Jurisdiction, whether Inhabitant or forreiner shall enjoy the same justice and law . . .

47. No man shall be put to death without the testimony of two or three witnesses or that which is equivalent thereunto.

48. Every Inhabitant of the Country shall have free libertie to search and veewe any Rooles, Records, or Regesters of any Court or office except the Councell . . .

80. Everie married woeman shall be free from bodilie correction or stripes by her husband, unless it be in his owne difence upon her assalt . . .

89. If any people of other Nations professing the true Christian Religion shall flee to us from the Tiranny or oppression of their persecutors, or from famyne, warres, or the like necessary and compulsarie cause, They shall be entertayned and succoured amongst us, according to that power and prudence god shall give us.

Counter-Revolution to Glorious Revolution

NONE OF MY BUSINESS, BUT THERE'S A RUMOR ABOUT THAT YOU'VE LOST THE CONSENT OF THE GOVERNED!

The Revolution in England did not last. The Levellers were squished. Without popular support, the English Revolution slid into a "protectorate" under the charge of Oliver Cromwell. When he died, the son of Charles I was called from France to return to England and become King. (His father had been executed for treason by a revolutionary court.) Charles II was given the throne on the condition that he listen to the well-to-do in Parliament, pay the army, allow some freedom of religion, and sanction land transactions that had occurred during the Revolution.

When the new Parliament met, the well-to-do started "taking care" of the less-well-to-do. During the revolution ordinary people had begun exercising a number of democratic rights, including the right to print local news, and the right to gather signatures in a petition and present them to Parliament. After the "Restoration", Parliament squelched these rights.

Charles II generally steered clear of any confrontation with Parliament. His brother and successor James II was less circumspect, appointing Catholics to every post he could, and allowing freedom of religion to Catholics and religious dissenters. When he jailed some protesting Anglican bishops for seditious libel, seven rich Englishmen invited William of Orange to invade England. He did. James ran.

This was called the **Glorious Revolution of 1688–9.** Some people consider it "glorious" because James did not have his head cut off. Others consider it glorious because it was during this period that Parliament re-established the right to petition. It also allowed the censorship laws to lapse. It formalized the right to *habeas corpus*, which forced jailors to give legal grounds for holding prisoners and valid information as to prisoners' whereabouts.

WHAT DO YOU MEAN YOU DON'T HABEUS THE CORPUS?

In 1689 it passed a Bill of Rights.

BILL OF RIGHTS
Dec. 16, 1689:

6. That the raising or keeping of a standing army within the kingdom in time of peace, unless it be with consent of parliament, is against law.

9. That the freedom of speech, and of debates or preceedings in parliament, ought not to be impeached or questioned in any court or place out of parliament.

10. That excessive bail ought not to be required, nor excessive fines imposed; nor cruel and unusual punishments inflicted.

STANDING ARMY MY FOOT... I'M BEAT!

Transition

After 1702 the English had about done with charter drafting and rights declarations. If everyone was not totally satisfied, dissatisfaction did not raise people to revolutionary levels as it had in the middle 1600s. Additionally, the English people in America were as worried about the nearby and hostile French and the Indians as they were about their rulers across the sea.

In 1763 things changed again. England had just won a war with France. It decided it was time to run an empire. For the colonists this meant, among other things, that they could not steal the Indians' lands beyond the Appalachians. Worse, they had to start buying British goods, instead of any goods they fancied. Worse still, they had to pay taxes that Parliament imposed on them without their consent.

IT CAN'T BE TIME TO RUN AN EMPIRE ALREADY....

Declaration of Independence

The colonists did not like any of this empire stuff. They threw British tea into the Boston Harbor.

The British closed the port of Boston, revoked privileges in some colonial charters, and forced colonists to house British soldiers. The colonists started protesting in the streets. They burnt effigies. They boycotted British goods. They set up committees to keep themselves informed of local political and military developments. In 1775 some British soldiers and some American farmers began shooting at each other in Lexington, Massachusetts. George Washington traveled from Virginia to Massachusetts to raise a people's army. American revolutionaries had been meeting in "continental congresses" to talk about their problems with the British.

THE BRITISH ARE COMING! FILM AT ELEVEN!

In their third meeting in 1776 they issued a **Declaration of Independence,** declaring themselves free from Britain:

> We hold these truths to be self-evident, that all men are created equal, that they are endowed by their Creator with certain unalienable Rights, that among these are Life, Liberty and the pursuit of Happiness.—That to secure these rights, Governments are instituted among Men, deriving their just powers from the consent of the governed,—That whenever any Form of Government becomes destructive of these ends, it is the Right of the People to alter or to abolish it, and to institute new Government, laying its foundation on such principles and organizing its powers in such form, as to them shall seem most likely to effect their Safety and Happiness.

Britain's answer was to send more troops, and seven years of fighting began.

State Constitutions

The Declaration of Independence meant that each colony was suddenly a new nation. The states began drafting constitutions which set up the principles of government they would follow.

- *PA: Nor can any man who is conscientiously scrupulous of bearing arms, be justly compelled thereto, if he will pay such equivalent, nor are the people bound by any laws, but such as they have in like manner assented to, for their common good.*
- *MD: that a long continuance, in the first executive departments of power or trust, is dangerous to liberty; a rotation, therefore, in those departments, is one of the best securities of permanent freedom.*
- *NC: That general warrants—whereby an officer or messenger may be commanded to search suspected places, without evidence . . . ought not to be granted.*

MASS: The end of the institution, maintenance, and administration of government, is to secure the existence of the body politic, to protect it, and to furnish the individuals who compose it with the power of enjoying in safety and tranquility their natural rights, and the blessings of life; and whenever these great objects are not obtained, the people have a right to alter the government, and to take measures necessary for their safety, prosperity, and happiness.

Revolution & Rights

While the colonists began governing themselves, they also set to work ridding themselves of counterrevolutionaries. **Loyalists** (those who remained sympathetic to King George) were purged from college faculties, tortured, intimidated, imprisoned, deprived of arms, property and voting rights. On a proportional basis more people were driven from revolutionary America than from revolutionary France (1789) or revolutionary Cuba (1961).

Articles, Pro

In the meantime the new states wanted to remain united. In 1777 they drafted a document called the **Articles of Confederation** which gave certain limited authority to a national Congress.

> *II. Each state retains its sovereignty, freedom, and independence, and every power, jurisdiction, and right, which is not by this Confederation expressly delegated to the United States, in Congress assembled.*

Under the Articles the new nation beat the British and won the war (1783). It created a post office and a bureau for foreign affairs. It ended the squabbling between the states over the Western lands and created a policy for the establishment of democratic institutions there. It demobilized troops that might have toyed with the idea of a coup d'état.

THEY GOT HERE JUST IN TIME... WE'D NEVER HAVE DISPOSED OF OUR LAND WITHOUT 'EM!

Articles, Con

According to the system established by the Articles of Confederation, the national government depended upon the good graces of the states for its income.

The weakness of the national government was fine with those who preferred to have the primary sources of power situated nearby in their state capitals. However, there were a number of groups in American society who were not so happy with things as they stood. Manufacturers wanted a stronger national government that could pass protective tariffs and create a protected market in all thirteen states. Merchants wanted a stronger national government to establish uniform trade laws. Owners of western lands thought their holdings would be more secure with a stronger federal power. Financiers preferred a uniform national financial system, and did not want the payment of the national debt to depend on the whims of the several states. Creditors were afraid that state legislatures would start printing reams of paper money, and so cheapen the value of their holdings.

Shay's Rebellion and Rhode Island

While creditors dreaded the printing of paper money, debtors welcomed it, especially the farmers, who were consistently short of cash.

"The want of a circulating medium subjects the inhabitants to the greatest inconveniences, the people in general are extremely embarrassed with publick and private debts—no money can be obtained either by the sale or mortgage of real estate."
28 Sept. 1786, from a county convention petition.

Some states tried issuing paper money, but creditors either refused to accept it; or they would take it and give credit for only part of its value.

Then in 1786 Rhode Island passed a law requiring creditors to accept its paper money at full value. That same year angry farmers in Western Massachusetts took up arms and began closing the courts to prevent creditors from foreclosing on their lands. The wealthy raised money to help the state government raise an army. This army squished **Shays' Rebellion** (named after one of the farmers' leaders, a revolutionary war veteran unable to pay a $12 debt). Defeated with guns, the farmers went to the ballot box and elected a governor (John Hancock) and a legislature sympathetic to their cause.

Reaction to Shays' Rebellion

The rising of the Shaysites and others in New England shocked a number of "respectable" Americans.

Henry Knox to George Washington: Their [the Shaysites'] creed is 'That the property of the United States has been protected from the confiscations of Great Britain by the joint exertions of all, and therefore ought to be the common property of all ... This dreadful situation has alarmed every man of principle and property in New England ... Our government must be braced, changed, or altered to secure our lives and property.

George Washington to Henry Lee: You talk, my good sir, of employing influence to appease the present tumults in Massachusetts ... Influence is no government. Let us have one by which our lives, liberties, and properties will be secured, or let us know the worst at once ...

And thrilled others:

Thomas Jefferson, in Paris: I hold it that a little rebellion now and then is a good thing. ... It is a medicine necessary for the sound health of government. ... God forbid that we should ever be twenty years without such a rebellion. ... The tree of liberty must be refreshed from time to time with the blood of patriots and tyrants. It is its natural manure.

2. MAKING THE CONSTITUTION

Convention Preludes

The "respectable" Americans were so shocked that they started taking their class interests seriously. Delegates from Virginia and Maryland had met in 1785 to discuss navigation of the Potomac River and the Chesapeake Bay. They called for a more general meeting to take place in 1786 in Annapolis, ostensibly to discuss commercial matters. In the end only five states attended the gathering. The Annapolis delegates called for another convention to take place in 1787.

In the meantime the national Congress argued over possible amendments to the Articles of Confederation. In early 1787 it called for the states to send delegates to a new convention to consider revisions to the national system.

Had it not been for the eruptions in Rhode Island and Massachusetts, it is not clear that the 1787 convention would have received any more attention than any of the prior meetings. However, the "respectable" Americans were worried. Except for Rhode Island, delegates from every state showed up in Philadelphia.

In the meantime, the French charge d'affaires was writing to his superiors in Paris, giving them his own perspective on events as they were developing:

Even though there are not patricians in America, there can be found certain men known under the label "gentlemen" who, by their rules, by their talents, by their education, by their families or by their position, aspire to a pre-eminence that the people refuse to let them have; and although several of these men have betrayed the interest of their kind to acquire popularity, there exists among them a rapport made stronger by the fact that they all fear the people's efforts to deprive them of their riches, and also by the fact that they are creditors who have thus an interest in making the government stronger and in overseeing the administering of the law. These men ordinarily pay the highest taxes, whereas poor owners escape the vigilance of the collectors. Most of them being merchants, it is important for them that the United States establish a good credit history with Europe by paying back its debts in full, and that they give Congress enough powers to force the people to contribute.

The necessity has now been felt for a long time, my Lord, to give to the Federal Government more energy and vigor, but one can feel as well that the excessive independence granted to the citizens vis-a-vis the states, and the states vis-a-vis Congress, is much too dear to the individuals to be taken away from them without great precautions. The people do not ignore that the natural consequences of a greater power granted to Congress would be a regular collecting of taxes, a severe administering of justice, extraordinary rights on imports, rigorous actions against debtors, and lastly a marked preponderance of rich men and property owners.

Convention Opens

The "reformists" who attended the Philadelphia Convention consisted of a number of types. There were people like James Madison and Alexander Hamilton, who knew how to get things done.

James Madison, Operative. Delegate to Continental Congress, Virginia House of Delegates, and Annapolis Convention. Helped to draft Virginia Constitution. In constant contact with nearly everyone during this period.

Alexander Hamilton, Operative. Ill-born, well-married, ambitious and cynical. John Adams called him "the bastard brat of a Scotch peddlar." Thomas Jefferson described him as being "Of acute understanding, disinterested, honest, and honorable in all private transactions, amiable in society, and duly valuing virtue in private life, yet so bitched by the British example as to be under thorough conviction that corruption was essential to the government of a nation."

There were national celebrities like George Washington and Benjamin Franklin who were expected to lend their prestige to the gathering.

George Washington, Star. Commander in Chief of the victorious revolutionary army. Possibly the wealthiest man in North America.

Benjamin Franklin. Best selling author (POOR RICHARD'S ALMANAC). Inventor (Franklin stove, lightning rod). Scientist, diplomat, postmaster, librarian, revolutionary.

There were also members of the Society of Cincinnati, a national fraternity of revolutionary army veterans. A number of Americans (including Franklin, Jefferson, and Adams) were concerned that this group might want to establish itself as a new hereditary aristocracy. Twenty-seven of the 55 delegates to the convention were members of this organization.

Not attending the Convention were John Adams, who was representing the United States in England; Thomas Jefferson, who was representing the United States in France; and Patrick Henry, who refused to attend because he "smelt a rat."

I WASN'T THERE, BECAUSE I SMELLED PATRICK HENRY!

CONDUCTING DEMOCRACY IN SECRET! WHAT AN ORIGINAL CONCEPT!

Virginia Plan, Checks and Balances

The delegates chose to meet in secret. They did not want the press reporting to their constituents back home the frank discussions they intended to have.

After the convention opened, the representatives from Virginia presented a plan for a new government, drafted by Madison. Borrowing on ideas from the French philosopher Montesquieu, Madison conceived of having three separate branches of government: the legislature to make the laws, the executive to enforce the laws, and the judiciary to interpret the laws. The aim was to parcel the power out into three distinct branches of government, so that each one might serve as a check on the other.

Arguments Over Democracy

Under the **Virginia Plan** (as it came to be called) the legislature was to consist of two houses, with representatives from each state according to population. Madison included this feature in hopes of securing popular support. The delegates immediately began arguing about democracy.

Roger Sherman: The people immediately should have as little do as may be about the government.

Elbridge Gerry: the evils we experience flow from the excess of democracy.

Gouverneur Morris: Men don't unite for liberty or life ... They unite for protection of property.

NO WONDER THEY WANTED TO KEEP THINGS SECRET!!

George Mason: We had been too democratic but were afraid we should incautiously run into the opposite extreme.

James Wilson: No government could long subsist without the confidence of the people.

Madison: No agrarian attempts have yet been made in this country, but symptoms of a levelling spirit, as we have understood, have sufficiently appeared in certain quarters to give notice of the future danger. How is the danger to be guarded against on republican principles?

Alternatives
===================

MEN DON'T UNITE FOR LIBERTY, BUT FOR PROPERTY!

NOWADAYS WHAT YOU CALL YOUR JOISEY PLAN!

Of course another problem with the Virginia Plan was that the small states would be overwhelmed by the bigger states. The smaller states organized together, and on June 15 presented what came to be known as the **New Jersey Plan**. The New Jersey plan called for a single legislative body comprised of representatives selected by the state legislatures, with each state having an equal voice.

WHAT SAY WE PROMISE NEW HAMPSHIRE THE FIRST PRIMARY, WITH ALL THE MEDIA HYPE?

A few days later Alexander Hamilton presented a plan of his own, based on the British model, offering a "distinct and permanent share in the government" to the "rich and well born" so that they would be able to "check the unsteadiness" of the people. According to Hamilton, "Nothing but a permanent body can check the imprudence of democracy."

Great Compromise

At bottom Hamilton wanted to resurrect the British King and House of Lords in an American version. His plan was so far off in right field that nobody took it seriously. Indeed, some observers think the moderates asked Hamilton to proffer such a crazy plan in order to encourage every one to settle down and compromise.

However, neither the large states nor the smaller states were in any mood for compromise. For weeks the delegates wrangled. They leaked reports to the press suggesting that everything was going wonderfully within the guarded halls of the convention:

> *So great is the unanimity, we hear, that prevails in the Convention, upon all great federal subjects, that it has been proposed to call the room in which they assemble, UNANIMITY HALL.*

This, of course, was patently false. Various individuals threatened to pack up and go home. Finally, on July 16 the delegates reached what has come to be known as **THE GREAT COMPROMISE.**

IMPRESSIVE HUH?
GREAT COMPROMISE!

The Great Compromise borrowed ideas from both the Virginia and New Jersey plans. (Hamilton's plan was in the trash bin.) Principles of the New Jersey plan were embodied in the provision that the states would be represented equally in one house of the national legislature. The principles of the Virginia plan were embodied in provisions stating that representation according to population would take place in the other house of the national legislature. To placate the Virginia supporters the delegates also agreed that taxes could originate only in the popular house, a census should be taken every 10 years, and one slave equalled 3/5 of a person.

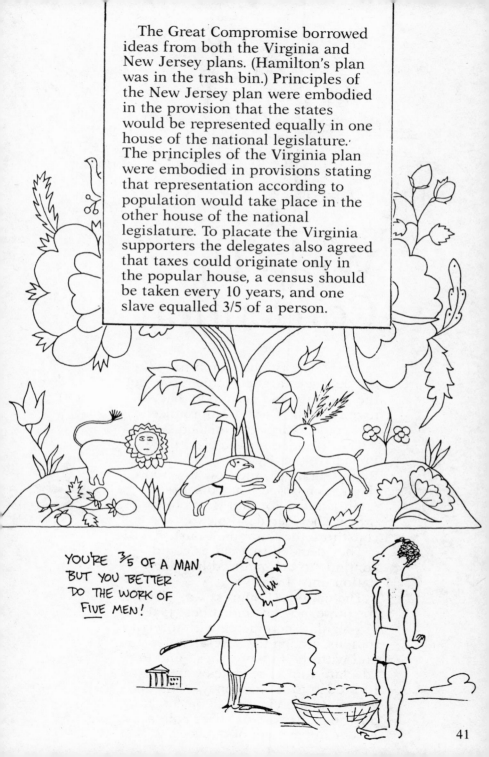

YOU'RE 3/5 OF A MAN, BUT YOU BETTER DO THE WORK OF FIVE MEN!

NOWHERE DOES IT SAY THAT THE CONGRESS CAN LAY AROUND AND COLLECT TAXES!

Wrap Up Convention

After "The Great Compromise" the delegates argued some more, but the intensity and acrimony that preceded The Great Compromise had considerably diminished.

They decided how to elect the President, the Senators, and Representatives, and how to remove them from office. They discussed qualifications for and terms of office. They decided how to constitute the Supreme Court.

They decided that slaves could continue to be imported into the nation until 1808.

The national Congress was given the power to "lay and collect taxes," "to regulate commerce with foreign nations, among the several states and with the Indian tribes," and to "declare war." The states were forbidden to "coin money," "impair contractual obligations," or "make anything but gold or silver coin a tender in payment of debts."

Some delegates asked whether or not the constitution should enumerate a **Bill of Rights,** but everybody was tired, and they decided there was no need for a list.

By September 17, 1787 the delegates had completed their final draft of the U.S. CONSTITUTION. Franklin says, "It's a Republic, if you can keep it."

After Signing

IT'S NOT VERY LONG...
MAYBE I SHOULD
PAD IT WITH
CHARTS....

The Constitution that the **Framers** finally drafted was only a few pages long, consisting of just seven articles. Articles One, Two and Three dealt with the Legislature, the Executive, and the Judiciary. Article Four covered relations between the states. Article Five dealt with amending the Constitution, and Article Six covered miscellaneous provisions like debts owed by the Confederation, foreign treaties, and qualifications for office. Article Seven stated that only nine states had to ratify the Constitution to bring it into effect. (The delegates did not want to have to wait for states like Maryland, which didn't ratify the Articles of Confederation until 1781—or Rhode Island, which might never ratify as long as its people believed in paper money.)

QUALIFICATIONS FOR OFFICE?...
... WELL, IT SHOULD BE
SPACIOUS, NICE
CARPETING,
FIREPLACE.....

I THINK YOU'LL LIKE IT....
WE'RE TALKING WICKED
PROJECT HERE!

THE CONSTITUTION SHALL BE FLEXIBLE, SO AS TO KEEP PACE WITH PROGRESS!

YOU KNOW, PROGRESS... LIKE DISPOSABLE BOTTLES, DRIVE-THRU FUNERAL HOMES...

One reason the document was so concise was that the Framers wanted a flexible instrument that would hold good in the long term. They knew that things changed with time, and they wanted the Constitution to be able to be responsive to change. Thus Edmund Randolph, one of the five men charged with drafting the Constitution, observed that "In the draught of a fundamental constitution," it was necessary to "insert essential principles only, lest the operations of government should be clogged by rendering those provisions permanent and unalterable, which ought to be accommodated to times and events . . . "

Constitution supporter John Marshall (who later sat on the Supreme Court) would write in a famous opinion that "[The Constitution is] intended to endure for ages to come, and, consequently, to be adapted to the various CRISES of human affairs."

For his part Thomas Jefferson did not always agree with the **Federalists** (as supporters of the Constitution came to be called called). But he did agree with them that "... laws and institutions must go hand in hand with the progress of the human mind. As that becomes more developed, more enlightened, as new discoveries are made, new truths disclosed, and manners and opinions change with the change of circumstances, institutions must advance also, and keep pace with the times."

In short, the reality of the Constitution would be found within the practice of history, and not within words set out on paper.

The Federalists

Of course before the Constitution could develop any meaning in history, it first had to be adopted by the states. As we have seen, the Framers decided that only 9 states would be needed to ratify. Additionally, they stated that ratification should issue from specially called state conventions, and not state legislatures. Legislatures might have a vested interest in the old ways of doing things, and general elections might be harder to influence than a smaller body of selected delegates.

Having set the ground rules out according to their satisfaction, the Federalists then put together one of history's most impressive political campaigns. They issued a number of propaganda pamphlets that came to be known as **THE FEDERALIST,** where Hamilton, Madison and John Jay elaborated politial arguments designed to support the new Constitution:

EFFICIENCY: Those who have been conversant in the proceedings of popular assemblies . . . will readily conceive how impossible it must be to induce a number of such assemblies, deliberating at a distance from each other, at different times, and under different impressions, long to co-operate in the same views and pursuits."
#15 [Hamilton]

PRECLUSION OF TYRANNY: Among the numerous advantages promised by a well-constructed Union, none deserves to be more accurately developed than its tendency to break and control the violence of faction . . . A rage for paper money, for an abolition of debts, for an equal division of property, will be less apt to pervade the whole body of the Union than a particular member of it . . .
#10 [Madison]

STABILITY: [A]n institution [such as the national Senate] may sometimes be necessary as a defence to the people against their own temporary errors and delusions . . .
#63

And when asked about the legality of the Constitution (which had come from a convention asked only to recommend amendments to the Articles of Confederation), Madison simply adverted to the right of Revolution:

. . . in all great changes of established governments, forms ought to give way to substance; that a rigid adherence in such cases to the former, would render nominal and nugatory the transcendant and precious right of the people to 'abolish or alter their governments as to them shall seem most likely to effect their safety and happiness', since it is impossible for the people spontaneously and universally to move in concert towards their object; and it is therefore essential that such changes be instituted by some INFORMAL AND UNAUTHORIZED PROPOSITIONS, made by some patriotic and respectable citizen or number of citizens. #40.

Anti Federalists

Not everyone had unqualified enthusiasm for the Constitution.

> *I had rather be a free citizen of the small republic of Massachusetts, than an oppressed subject of the great American empire...*

> *These violent partisans... consist generally, of the NOBLE order of C[incinnatu]s, holders of public securities, men of great wealth and expectations of public office, B[an]k[er]s and L[aw]y[er]s: these with their train of dependents from the Aristocratick combination. [from a pamphlet]*

What then are we to think of the motives and designs of those men who are arguing the implicit and immediate adoption of the proposed government; are they fearful, that if you exercise your good sense and discernment, you will discover the masqued aristocracy, that they are attempting to smuggle upon you under the suspicious garb of republicanism? [from a pamphlet]

NO MILITARY KING..?
ISN'T THAT RATHER
RADICAL?

Before MARTIAL LAW is declared to be the supreme law of the land, and your character of free citizens be changed to that of the subjects of a MILITARY KING, which are necessary consequences of the adoption of the proposed constitution, let me admonish you in the name of SACRED LIBERTY, to make solemn pause. ... There is not a tincture of democracy in the proposed constitution. [ditto]

More Reservations

Jefferson's response was mixed:

"I like much the general idea of framing a government which should go on of itself peaceably, without needing continual recurrence to the state legislatures. . . . There are other good things of less moment.

I will now add what I do not like. First, the omission of a bill of rights providing clearly and without the aid of sophisms for freedom of religion, freedom of the press, protection against standing armies, restriction against monopolies, the eternal and unremitting force of the habeas corpus laws, and trials by jury in all matter of fact triable by the laws of the land and not by the law of Nations. . . . Let me add that a bill of rights is what the people are entitled to against every government on earth, general or particular, and what no just government should refuse, or rest on inference. The second feature I dislike, and greatly dislike, is the abandonment in every instance of the necessity of rotation in office, and most particularly in the case of the President."

Patrick Henry's response was not mixed at all. Believing that individual liberty and not material advantage should be the goal of government, he feared that:

"the American spirit, assisted by the ropes and chains of consolidations, is about to convert this country into a powerful and mighty empire . . . I dread the operation of it on the middling and lower classes of people: it is for them I fear the adoption of this system . . . "

I SMELL A RATIFICATION!

Ratification I

While the arguments went on, the struggle for
ratification proceeded. Delaware, New Jersey, Georgia
and Connecticut were all small states with limited
resources. They had everything to gain by joining a
national union. All four of them ratified the Constitution
by mid-January, 1788.

Pennsylvania had ratified a month earlier, but under
less auspicious circumstances. There an assembly with a
majority sympathetic to calling a ratifying convention
had been due to adjourn on September 29. By hiring a
special courier, the Federalists managed to have a copy
of the new Constitution delivered to the assembly by
September 28. The following day Antifederalist
legislators vanished from the scene, preventing the
assembly from holding a quorum. Undaunted, the
Federalists organized a mob of supporters which scoured
Philadelphia. Two Antifederalist representatives were
found and forced back into the assembly. Provisions for
a ratifying convention were "duly" enacted. The
Constitution was ratified by its first large state on
December 12, 1787.

Ratification II

In February, the ratification movement began to hit snags. In Massachusetts, the Federalists secured an affirmative vote, but not without some upfront and backroom deals. Upfront the convention recommended that a Bill of Rights be appended to the new Constitution. In the back rooms, the Federalists swayed John Hancock (elected by Shaysites) with the promise that he could be Vice President of the new union; and, if Virginia did not join, he might expect the Presidential office.

GOUVERNEUR MORRIS:
"Loaves and fishes must bribe the demagogues. They must be made to expect higher offices under the general than the state government."

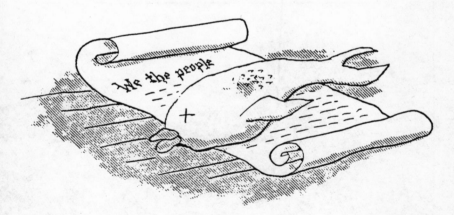

Antifederalist feeling was more intense in New Hampshire, despite its small size. The Federalists found the ratifying convention filled with opponents to the new Constitution. The best they could do for the time being was maneuver an adjournment before any decision was made.

In May, Rhode Island chose to hold a democratic plebiscite instead of a republican convention. To no one's surprise, the constitution was rejected outright.

Ratification III

While they were losing in New Hampshire and Rhode Island, in April and May the Federalists secured the weak states of Maryland and South Carolina. (In the latter state nearly half the delegates were related to the delegates sent to Philadelphia.)
In June a new convention was held in New Hampshire. This time the delegates ratified the Constitution, although they followed Massachusetts' example and also recommended amendments.
With New Hampshire, the requisite nine states had ratified. However, without the states of New York and Virginia the new nation would be a sham.

Virginia debated the constitution for the entire month of June, and finally ratified with the provision that "the liberty of Conscience and of the Press cannot be cancelled."

New York's delegates were initially opposed to the Constitution. However, the ratification by Virginia, the promise of a Bill of Rights, and the threat that New York City might secede to join the new union brought New York State into the ratifying column.

North Carolina rejected the Constitution in August.

Legitimation

The precarious success of the Constitution was not lost on the politicians who supported the new government. As the returns showed, those who were asked to give an opinion concerning the Constitution ratified it by only the slimmest of margins. And of course those who were female, black, or poor, had even less to say. Support for the new order was by no means certain, and there were calls for a second convention. Thus, even while the politicans were prepared for a transfer of power from the Confederation to the constitution, they took steps to insure that the new system might receive the greatest support possible.

1.

First, they selected the nation's officers from the two key states, north and south. George Washington from Virginia was made President. Massachusetts was placated by having one of its own elected Vice President—but this individual was John Adams, a fellow more conservative than the Shaysite-supported John Hancock.

2.

Second they insured that as many interests as possible would be represented in the new government. Representatives from all over the nation were appointed to the Supreme Court. George Washington included both the right-wing Alexander Hamilton and the left-wing Thomas Jefferson in his cabinet.

3.

Third, and most importantly, they passed the first ten amendments to the Constitution, which came to be known as the **Bill of Rights.** These included a list of rights for citizens, and limits on governments. The lack of such a list in the original Constitution had provided a great source of controversy during the ratification struggle, and it had not abated. It was a major issue in James Madison's district, and it had almost defeated him in his bid for a seat in the House of Representatives. When Congress began sitting, he quickly went to work to draft and pass a list of rights which the federal government could not abrogate.

Bill of Rights

The objective of the Bill of Rights was to stop governments from the abuses of power that English speaking people had known ever since King John.

The First Amendment was to prevent the government from telling people what they should say or print, or how they were to organize, or complain to their rulers. It also prevented the government from imposing religious beliefs on people.

The Second Amendment was to prevent the government from taking the ultimate source of political power from the people: their guns. In feudal society ordinary citizens were not allowed to bear arms. The Second Amendment reflects the fundamental political insight that a society built on consent (instead of oppression) can afford to have an armed citizenry.

The Third Amendment was designed to prevent the government from forcing citizens to give their homes to soldiers. (This had been a common way of housing troops for a number of centuries.)

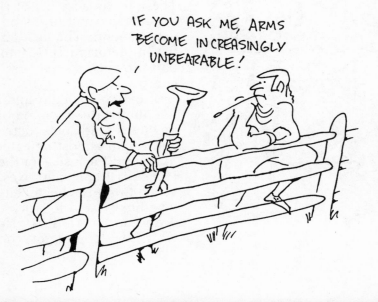

IF YOU ASK ME, ARMS BECOME INCREASINGLY UNBEARABLE!

AS SEARCHES AND SEIZURES GO, THAT WAS QUITE REASONABLE!

The Fourth Amendment was to prevent the government from sticking its nose into the personal affairs of people. It stated that before government officials could start arresting people or going through their things, they would have to have a warrant, based on "probable cause, supported by oath or affirmation, and particularly describing the place to be searched, and the persons or things to be seized."

The Fifth Amendment was to prevent the government from using its powers to harass political opponents. If the government wanted to accuse someone of a big crime, it first had to secure the consent of a group of ordinary citizens (the **Grand Jury**). If the government lost a trial, it couldn't try again (i.e., an accused could not be placed into **double jeopardy**). Nor could the government force an accused to testify against himself. Nor could the government take any citizen's "life, liberty, or property," without some sort of legal proceeding. And if the government needed somebody's property for public use, it would have to pay them "just compensation."

NOBODY ACTUALLY SAW ME DO IT, SO I'M TAKING THE FIFTH!

The Sixth Amendment set out additional checks on the powers of government, particularly those that related to its capacity to jail people, accuse them, and haul them into court. The Sixth Amendment required that an accused person receive a speedy trial; that he not be tried away from the place where the crime was supposed to have been committed; that he be told why he was being tried; that he be allowed to confront his accusers; that he be allowed to have witnesses presented at the trial to speak for him; and that he be allowed to have a lawyer help him defend himself. In the Sixth Amendment the American people were looking back to show trials of Levellers' leaders (and looking forward to show trials of future politial dissidents).

The Seventh Amendment was to prevent the government from using establishment-minded judges for railroading people. It guaranteed the right to have a jury trial, so that if somebody was going to be railroaded, it would be with the consent of some ordinary citizens. (This Amendment has had both its happy and adverse affects. In California, a jury acquitted Angela Davis of various charges invented by government prosecutors. In Mississippi a jury of whites acquitted Klansmen of murdering civil rights workers.)

The Eighth Amendment was to prevent the government from squishing people once it had jailed them, or secured a guilty plea. It forbade "excessive bail," "excessive fines," and "cruel and unusual punishment." (What the Supreme Court thinks of the Eighth Amendment is still open to question, since it allows corporal punishment for children, and capital punishment for certain felons.)

The Ninth Amendment wanted to make sure that nobody thought that the preceding list ended the rights that citizens had against the government: "The enumeration in the Constitution, of certain rights, shall not be construed to deny or disparage others retained by the people." Obviously the American people were concerned about the extent to which those in power could be corrupted by power.

The Tenth Amendment was another insurance clause. Powers not given to the central government were reserved "to the States respectively, or to the people." In short, the American people didn't trust the political propriety of government any further than they could spit.

Congress began work on the Bill of Rights in 1789. By 1791, the states had ratified it. During this time North Carolina and Rhode Island finally decided they would join the new system.

3. ARGUING OVER THE CONSTITUTION

How To Interpret?

SHALL THE LAW PREVAIL? OR THE CONSTITUTION?

OR SHOULD WE GO WITH ROCK, PAPER, SCISSORS?

The constitutional system was now in place, but many specific meanings and practical workings had yet to be elucidated. Perhaps the most controversial question at this point in the nation's history was whether the Constitution should be interpreted broadly or narrowly.

On the broad side of the issue was Alexander Hamilton, who thought that the government should be able to do anything "necessary and proper" to fulfilling its functions. For Hamilton this meant, among other things, that the new national government could assume the debts of the states, charter a national bank, and pursue an economic policy designed to encourage manufacturers at home. Hamilton's following came to be known as Federalists to their friends, and Monarchists to their enemies.

On the narrow side of the issue were individuals like Thomas Jefferson who preferred a society with more farmers and less government. Some of his worst fears were confirmed when speculators lined up behind Hamilton's program; and later, when Washington called up an army larger than any he had commanded during the Revolution to crush a tax protest by Pennsylvania farmers (known as the Whiskey Rebellion). Jefferson's following came to be known as Republicans to their friends. Their enemies called them Jacobins, after the groups committing violent revolution in France.

The question of how to properly interpret the Constitution naturally led to a second: Who finally decided what the Constitution meant if different people in the government disagreed?

For a while the question was answered by bald practice. Washington usually listened to Hamilton, and Washington was too popular to oppose. This went on for eight years.

The States Respond

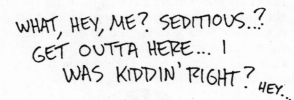

In 1796 John Adams was elected President, and in 1798 he and his Federalists were concerned about winning the next election. They passed the **Alien and Sedition Acts,** which made it a crime to criticize the government. The statute was used to convict various Republican newspapermen; a congressman from Vermont; and one worthy citizen who was heard voicing the hope that a cannon salute might blast John Adams from behind, or something like that.

While various Federalist judges were sustaining these acts, Jefferson and Madison induced the legislatures of Virginia and Kentucky to pass resolutions claiming for the states the right to invalidate unconstitutional legislation. (The Eleventh Amendment, ratified during this period, further increased state power by refusing the right of citizens from one state to sue another state directly.) In response to Virginia and Kentucky Resolutions many Northern states passed their own declarations, stating that authority to pass on federal laws lay with the Supreme Court.

The Revolution of 1800

In the end the question was resolved, like so many in the past (and future), by political struggle. In 1800 the Republicans won the election, but the choice for President had to be made in the House of Representatives because they hadn't gotten their candidates straight. (The Twelfth Amendment was passed to care for this problem henceforth.)

After Jefferson was elected, he did what he could to abrogate the Alien and Sedition Acts. They had been designed to dissolve on the day of the next President's inauguration anyway, and Jefferson ensured that those who had been imprisoned were released and those who had been fined received refunds.

REFUND MAYBE, BUT WHAT ABOUT INTEREST!

The Republicans' **Revolution of 1800** included an assault on the Federalist judiciary, whose interpetations of the Constitution had proven so noxious.

JEFFERSON:
The Federalists "have retired into the Judiciary as a stronghold . . . and from that battery all the works of Republicanism are to be beaten down and erased."

The Republicans repealed the Federalists' Judiciary Act of 1801, which would have allowed for the appointment of more Federalist judges, and they redefined the Supreme Court's term so as to prevent it from holding hearings as to the repeal's constitutionality until 1803. The Republicans also began impeachment proceedings against a notorious Federalist judge who was more guilty of drunkenness and insanity than he was of treason, bribery, or high crimes and misdemeanors. They dumped him anyway, and then moved against Supreme Court Justice Samuel Chase who had howled against the Jefferson's "mobocracy." This impeachment effort failed, but Chase watched his mouth ever after.

In an attempt to thwart the Republicans, some Federalists tried filing various test cases in hopes of securing judicial invalidation of the Republicans' measures. Their hopes were disappointed by John Marshall, a Federalist recently appointed by John Adams to head the Supreme Court. Yet while Marshall yielded battles to the Republicans, he was laying the groundwork for winning the war.

Marbury V. Madison

For Marshall, winning the war did not mean returning all political power to the Federalists. Given the state of the country, that would be impossible. What was possible, though, was an increase in power for the federal judiciary. Since its members were appointed for life—and since most of them at that point were Federalists—the federal judiciary held the potential for serving as a conservative brake on Jefferson and his "radicals".

PROFILE: John Marshall: Distant cousin and political foe of Thomas Jefferson, who called him "that gloomy malignity." Marshall explained that his nationalist sentiments derived from his experience as a youth during the Revolution: "I had grown up at a time when love of the union and resistance to the claims of Great Britain were the inseparable inmates of the same bosom . . . when the maxim united we stand, divided we fall was the maxim of every orthodox American; and I had imbibed these sentiments so thoroughly that they Constituted a part of my being."

The question, though, was how to assert the judiciary's power without inviting more reprisals from the Republicans in the legislative and executive branches. The case of MARBURY V. MADISON provided John Marshall with his opportunity. As every law student knows, MARBURY V. MADISON involved the first time the Supreme Court asserted it could declare an act of Congress to be unconstitutional. As every law student may not know, MARBURY V. MADISON also constituted a shrewd political ploy.

The case grew out of the Federalists' last ditch efforts to cram judicial offices with Federalists before they lost power in 1801. William Marbury was one Federalist appointed by John Adams to fill a justice of the peace slot in the District of Columbia. However, the appointment had been made so late that John Marshall (at that time Adams' Secretary of State) did not have time to deliver to Marbury his papers of commission.

The new Secretary of State was the Republican James Madison, and when Marbury came for his papers Madison told Marbury to go jump in the lake. Marbury sued.

The Decision

In 1803 the Supreme Court had its first chance to rule on Marbury's case. Marshall—who probably shouldn't have heard the case to begin with, because Marbury's plight was partially Marshall's fault—wrote a decision that gave with one hand and took with another. On the one hand, he said that Marbury could not get his commission, and this suited the Republicans just fine. On the other hand, he laced his opinion with snide remarks about the Republican administration. Most importantly, Marshall said that Marbury could not get his papers because he had come to the Supreme Court on the basis of a Congressional law which contravened the constitution. Of course to do this Marshall had to assert the Supreme Court's power to place its interpretation of the Constitution over Congress':

> *"So if a law be in opposition to the Constitution . . . the court must determine which of these conflicting rules govern the case. This is of the very essence of judicial duty."*

Thus, while Marshall managed to avoid a confrontation with the Republicans, he also managed to reserve power in the judicial branch which might eventually use MARBURY V. MADISON to restrain Republican excesses. Some Republicans might not have worried, but Jefferson did:

> *I long wished for a proper occasion to have the gratuitous opinion in MARBURY V. MADISON brought before the public, and denounced as not law . . . (Jefferson, 1807)*

THE PROVIDENTIAL DETECTION

Marshall I

When **MARBURY V. MADISON** was rendered, it was probably more significant for the judicial power it preserved than any new judicial power it created. As we shall see, neither the Presidents nor the states nor the people gave up their rights to determine what the Constitution meant.

Nevertheless, through the next 34 years that he sat on the bench, Marshall quietly but decisively enhanced the Supreme Court's power to interpret the Constitution.

THE POWER TO TAX IS THE POWER TO DESTROY!

AND NO DESTRUCTION WITHOUT ʃ REPRESENTATION!

Procedurally, he encouraged the Court to speak through only one Justice (usually himself), which lent more force to Court opinion. Jefferson remarked:

"Another most condemnable practice of the supreme court to be corrected is that of cooking up a decision in Caucus & delivering it by one of their members as the opinion of the court, without the possibility of our knowing how many, who, and for what reasons each member concurred.

An opinion is huddled up in conclave perhaps by a majority of one, delivered as if unanimous, and with the silent acquiescence of lazy or timid associates, by a crafty chief judge, who sophisticates the law to his own mind."

Marshall II

Substantively, Marshall's Court sustained the Federalist vision of rights of contract, property, and national power.

FLASHBACK:

JUNE, 1788:

" I HOPE THAT NO GENTLEMAN WILL THINK THAT A STATE WILL BE CALLED AT THE BAR OF A FEDERAL COURT "
—— MARSHALL

1810: FLETCHER V. PECK.
U.S. Supreme Court asserts the right to invalidate state laws.

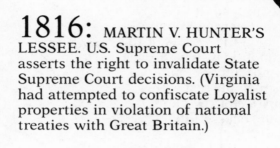

1816: MARTIN V. HUNTER'S LESSEE. U.S. Supreme Court asserts the right to invalidate State Supreme Court decisions. (Virginia had attempted to confiscate Loyalist properties in violation of national treaties with Great Britain.)

1819: DARTMOUTH COLLEGE V. WOODWARD. Supreme Court invalidates the State of New Hampshire's attempts to alter the Charter granted to Dartmouth College in 1769 by King George III, on the basis of the contracts clause. (The fact that a Republican legislature was trying to take over a Federalist dominated Board of Trustees had nothing to do with the outcome of this case.)

1819: MCCULLOCH V. MARYLAND. U.S. Supreme Court prevents Maryland from taxing the U.S. Bank, and upholds Hamilton's broad interpretation of the Constitution by sustaining the constitutionaltiy of the National Bank.

1823: JOHNSON V.
M'INTOSH. The authority of the
national government to dispose of
Indian lands is upheld. In his
decision Marshall wrote: "Conquest
gives a title which the Courts of the
conqueror cannot deny, whatever
the private or speculative opinions
of individuals may be, respecting
the original justice of the claim
which has been successfully
asserted...

The title by conquest is acquired
and maintained by force. The
conqueror prescribes its limits..."

POLITICAL POWER
ISSUES FROM
THE MOUTH OF
A GUN
— MAO

As Mao once wrote, "Political
power issues from the mouth of a
gun."

1824: GIBBONS V. OGDEN.
Supreme Court sustains Congress'
power to regulate interstate
commerce. (Aaron Ogden had a
monopoly to navigate the Hudson
granted by New York, and this
conflicted wth a federal navigating
license granted Thomas Gibbons.)

Alternatives To Marbury

While Marshall was setting the terms for constitutional debate in years to come, other parties continued asserting their rights to deal with constitutional interpretation.

For example, Jefferson ignored Marshall when Marshall demanded documents from Jefferson for the Aaron Burr treason trial, citing the basis of separation of powers between executive and judiciary. (Jefferson wanted Burr convicted, and Marshall responded by giving a narrow construction to "treason" which let Burr go free.)

As they served the country in various political offices, both Jefferson and Madison continued to insist on the rights of other parties than the Supreme Court to interpret the Constitution.

JEFFERSON:
You seem to think it devolved on the judges to decide on the validity of the sedition law. But nothing in the Constitution has given them a right to decide for the Executive, more than to the Executive to decide for them . . . the co-ordinate branches [of government] should be checks on each other. Letter to Abilgail Adams, Sept. 11, 1804.

MADISON, from Report on
Virginia Resolutions, 1800:
However true, therefore, it may be, that the judicial department is, in all questions submitted to it by the forms of the Constitution, to decide in the last resort, this resort must necessarily be deemed the last in relation to the authorities of the other departments of the government; not in relation to the rights of the parties to the constitutional compact, from which the judicial, as well as the other departments, hold their delegated trusts.

The New England states took a leaf from the books of Virginia and Kentucky when, in 1814–1815 they met in Hartford, and declared that they should "adopt all such measures as may be necessary effectually to protect the citizens of said states from the operation and effects of all acts which have been or may be passed by the Congress of the United States, . . . not authorized by the Constitution of the United States."

Jackson

Some of the greatest controversies over who had what say over the U.S. Constitution occurred during the Presidency of Andrew Jackson (1829–1837).

PROFILE: Andrew Jackson. An incarnation of frontier energy at its most extreme. A law unto himself. A gambler, duelist, prankster, and wooer of at least one married woman. Left poverty through speculation in slaves, cotton, and land. Became a war hero by beating the British in New Orleans, and the Spanish in Florida. Removed the Indians from the Southeastern United States through a policy of fraud and violence which presaged 20th century genocide. Now sits on the $20 bill.

Jackson was quite clear about his independent role as an expositor of the Constitution.

JACKSON:
The opinion of the judges has no more authority over Congress than the opinion of Congress has over the judges, and on that point the President is independent over both.

Jackson quickly put theory into practice. When a second U.S. Bank Bill was passed and justified on the basis of MCCULLOCH V. MARYLAND, Jackson vetoed it anyway. When South Carolina claimed the rights to nullify tariff legislation (borrowing a leaf from the books of Virginia, Kentucky, Connecticut, Massachusetts, Rhode Island, Vermont and New Hampshire), Jackson threatened to invade South Carolina with an army. When the Marshall Court invalidated a Georgia statute passed in line with Jackson's Indian removal policy, Jackson is said to have remarked in private: "John Marshall has made his decision, now let him enforce it." When South Carolina cited Georgia's rejection of national authority, Jackson changed his mind. (He pushed the litigants to settle, and so organized a united front against South Carolina.)

79

Judicial Retreat

Though he rejected nullification doctrines, Jackson was more a states' righter than he was a centralizing Federalist. (For example, when South Carolina "nullified" a Supreme Court decision validating the rights of freed Negro seamen in Charleston, he did not threaten with another invasion.) His policies enjoyed sufficient ratification at the polls so that even John Marshall had to take notice. During his last years on the bench, the Marshall Court began to accord greater deference to the power of the individual states.

A year after Jackson's election, the right of the states to have some say in commerce was affirmed in WILSON V. BLACK BIRD CREEK MARCH COMPANY. (GIBBONS had been ambivalent on this point.)

In BARRONS V. BALTIMORE (1832) the Bill of Rights was held to have no application to the State governments. This allowed the States to ignore at least some of the Constitution.

Marshall was succeeded by Jackson's Attorney General, Roger B. Taney.

PROFILE: Taney. Maryland hack, Jackson henchman. As provisional Secretary of the Treasury he helped destroy the second Bank of the United States by withdrawing its government funds. In response the Senate refused to confirm him as Treasurer. Jackson later rewarded Taney for his loyalty by forcing the Senate to take him as Supreme Court Chief Justice.

Under Taney the Court took further steps to sanction state powers. BRISCOE V. BANK OF KENTUCKY (1837) all but abrogated Marshall's CRAIG V. MISSOURI (1830), which had disallowed a state from issuing notes of credit.

Perhaps the most controversial decision was CHARLES RIVER BRIDGE V. WARREN BRIDGE CO. (1837). Massachusetts had granted a group of investors a charter to build a second bridge over the Charles River, which would have put them in competition with an older bridge company with an earlier charter. Federalist Justice Story said Massachusetts had violated its contract with the earlier group. Jacksonian Justice Taney (with the majority), said Massachusetts could take these measures to promote economic progress. The fact that Federalists (and Whigs) had an old money constituency and the Jacksonians had a new money constituency had nothing to do with the outcome of this case.

Transition

Some of the biggest battles in these years were fought not over people's rights, but states' rights. In general the people felt better about having political power closer to home, although in many cases these "states' rights" arguments reflected conflicts between local and national elites. While some of the Taney Court's decisions engendered protests when they were initially issued, the controversy did not last. In general the nation supported a mixture of national and local political power. Moreover, the decision from the Taney court tended to encourage economic initiative on a number of fronts, and Americans have seldom opposed that. For example, BANK OF AUGUSTA V. EARLE (1839) allowed corporations to go national, and SWIFT V. TYSON (1842) helped to establish a national commerical law.

Politics and economy also brought on the next significant constitutional crisis, and that was SLAVERY!!

4. WARRING OVER THE CONSTITUTION

I AM I NOT A MAN AND A BROTHER?

Slavery

Slavery had made problems for the United States that every party had tried to solve. Congress tried to solve them by passing various statutes. Southern states like South Carolina thought they could solve them by advocating doctrines like **nullification**, which asserted that a state could invalidate laws of congress which it thought were unconstitutional. For their parts free states like California, Ohio, and Wisconsin thought they could solve them by ignoring slave enforcement laws that they didn't like. Slaves like Nat Turner and visionaries like John Brown tried to solve them by revolting. Stephen Douglas thought he could solve the problem in the territories with local elections. Henry David Thoreau came closer to the solution when he said it was up to the American people.

> *The authority of government, even such as I am willing to submit to . . . is still an impure one: to be strictly just, it must have the sanction and consent of the governed. It can have no pure right over my person and property but what I concede to it . . . Thoreau, in CIVIL DISOBEDIENCE (1849).*

Dred Scott

Then there was Dred Scott.

Dred Scott had been a slave who had spent time in free territory before he was taken back into the slave holding state of Missouri. Some sorry fools decided that through his situation the Supreme Court might solve the problem of slavery. These fools included Scott's owners, the President of the United States, and the Justices of the U.S. Supreme Court. Scott's Missouri master sent ownership papers to his brother-in-law in New York to insure that a federal court could hear the case. When President Buchanan (1857–1861) heard that the Supreme Court members were discussing a narrowly based decision, he encouraged them instead to render a broad ranging opinion.

85

Some Justices agreed, and 6 of them (5 of them southerners) decided that not only could Scott not sue because he was not a citizen, they also decided that the Constitution said that Congress could not regulate slavery in U.S. territories:

> ... Dred Scott was not a citizen of Missouri within the meaning of the Constitution of the United States, and not entitled as such to sue in its courts ...
> ... the right of property in a slave is distinctly and expressly affirmed in the Constitution.
>
> "A Black man has no rights which a white man is compelled to respect."

The **DRED SCOTT** decision upset a number of Americans.

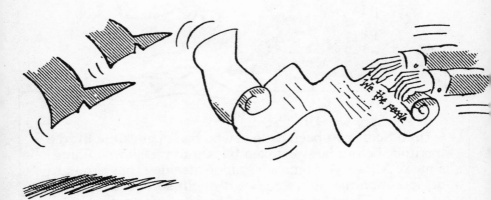

LINCOLN:
> ... if the policy of the Government upon vital questions affecting the whole people is to be irrevocably fixed by decisions of the Supreme Court, ... the people will have ceased to be their own rulers ...

War Issues

The nation had depended upon Congress to juggle a balance between slave and free states. The SCOTT decision undercut Congress' ability to juggle any longer.

When Lincoln was elected President (1860), one last minute compromise proposal was offered in Congress, which would have created a 13th amendment to the Constitution guaranteeing slavery in the Southern states (but not in the territories). This measure failed.

Lincoln PROFILE: From backwoods rube to corporation lawyer. Under a homespun exterior operated one of the shrewdest political minds the nation has witnessed. According to his law partner, "his ambition was a little engine that knew no rest." Master of English prose with the vision of a tragic poet. Seldom has anyone expressed so much profundity with so few words: "as Labor is the common BURTHEN . . . so the effort of SOME to shift their share of the burthen on to the shoulders of OTHERS, is the great, durable, curse of the [human] race."

AND THE BEST THEY COULD GET ME WAS THE FIVE-SPOT!

The Southern states seceded, many of them through dubiously organized conventions. The arguments they used asserted that the Constitution was a compact between sovereign states; since the Northern states' approach to slavery violated this compact, the Southern states had the right to leave.

For his part Lincoln maintained that the Constitution was a compact of the sovereign people.

> *This country, with its institutions, belongs to the people who inhabit it. Whenever they shall grow weary of the existing government, they can exercise their constitutional right of amending it or their revolutionary right to dismember or overthrow it. ... Why should there not be a patient confidence in the ultimate justice of the people? (March 4, 1861)*

War

Jefferson Davis, president of the Confederacy, expressed the Southern point of view:

> *An organization created by the States ... has been gradually perverted into a machine for their control in their domestic affairs. The creature has been exalted above its creators; the principals have been made subordinate to the agent appointed by themselves. ... so utterly have the principles of the Constitution been corrupted in the Northern mind that, in the inaugural address delivered by President Lincoln in March last, he asserts as an axiom, which he plainly deems to be undeniable, that the theory of the Constitution requires that in all cases the majority shall govern; ... This is the lamentable and fundamental error on which rests the policy that has culminated in his declaration of war against these Confederate States ... (April 29, 1861)*

This was one argument the Supreme Court could not resolve.

War ensued.

Resolution

LINCOLN:

This is essentially a people's contest. On the side of the Union it is a struggle for maintaining in the world that form and substance of government whose leading object is to elevate the condition of men—to lift artificial weights from all shoulders; to clear the path of laudable pursuit for all; to afford all an unfettered start, and a fair chance in the race of life.

Our popular government has often been called an experiment. Two points in it our people have already settled—the successful establishing and the successful administering of it. One still remains—its successful maintenance against a formidable internal attempt to overthrow it. It is now for them to demonstrate to the world that those who can fairly carry an election can also suppress a rebellion ... Such will be a great lesson of peace: teaching men that what they cannot take by an election, neither can they take it by war ... (July 4, 1861)

After 600,000 deaths, Lincoln's interpretation won.

HEY, I KNOW YOU HAVE POLITICAL REASONS, BUT THANKS ANYWAY...

Emancipation

After the Civil War the problem of slavery seemed solved. The Southern states were TOLD to ratify a **Thirteenth Amendment** different from the one offered 5 years earlier, and in December of 1865 the Constitution had a new provision abolishing slavery:

(Lincoln's famous **Emancipation Proclamation** had freed slaves only in territory held by Confederate troops.)

> *Neither slavery nor involuntary servitude, except as a punishment for crime whereof the party shall have been duly convicted, shall exist within the United States or any place subject to their jurisdiction ...*

Reconstruction

However, if the problems of slavery were resolved, the problems of racism were not. Neither were questions of constitutional balance.

In 1865 Lincoln had a plan for "reconstructing" the Southern states, and bringing them back into the Union. However, he was assassinated by a Southern sympathizer. Lincoln's successor Andrew Johnson attempted to implement Lincoln's program. It proceeded to backfire. Southern states sent ex-Confederate military commanders to Congress, including a Confederate Vice President. They passed "black codes" which made blacks something more than slaves, but something less than real citizens.

Mississippi penal code: All penal and criminal laws now in force describing the mode of punishment of crimes and misdemeanors committed by slaves, free negroes, or mulattoes are hereby re-enacted, and decreed to be in full force against all freedmen, free negroes and mulattoes."

Northern congressmen were outraged. They threw the representatives from the Southern state out of Congress and passed measures designed to aid and protect blacks. When President Johnson resisted a number of these measures, the battle lines were drawn. The election of 1866 sent overwhelming majorities to Congress supporting the "radicals".

Impeaching Johnson

NG THE VOTE ON THE IMPEACHMENT OF PRESIDENT JOHNSON, SENATE CHAMBER, WASHINGTON, D. C., MAY 16TH, 1868.—SENATOR ROSS, OF KANSAS, VOTING "NO

   With the new majorities the "radical" congress implemented its own version of **"Reconstruction."** It put the Southern states under military rule. Under the leadership of Representative Thad Stevens and Senator Charles Sumner, it passed a number of civil rights acts, the constitutionality of which it insured by passing the **14th and 15th amendments** to the Constitution.

XIV: All persons born or naturalized in the United States, and subject to the jurisdiction thereof, are citizens of the United States and of the State wherein they reside. No State shall make or enforce any law which shall abridge the privileges or immunities of citizens of the United States; nor shall any State deprive any person of life, liberty, or property, without due process of law; nor deny to any person within its jurisdiction the equal protection of the laws . . .

XV: The right of citizens of the United States to vote shall not be denied or abridged by the United States or by any State on account of race, color or previous condition of servitude.

When Johnson attempted to resist this, the House of Representatives voted to impeach him. However, the Senate failed to convict him, by one vote. Though Johnson had resisted laws passed by Congress, he was not found guilty of "high crimes and misdemeanors."

Supreme Court Tap Dances

During these tumultuous years the Supreme Court did more tap dancing over what was "really" constitutional than Congress ever had to do over slavery. In periods of intense political struggle, the law's supposed stability frequently gives way to expediency.

In 1861 the Supreme Court had told Lincoln he could not suspend habeas corpus (EX PARTE MERRYMAN). Lincoln told the Supreme Court that he was sorry, but he was busy fighting a civil war.

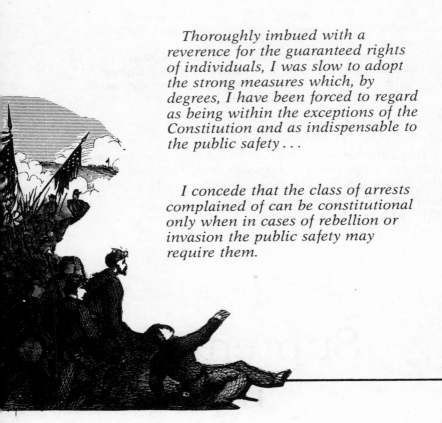

Thoroughly imbued with a reverence for the guaranteed rights of individuals, I was slow to adopt the strong measures which, by degrees, I have been forced to regard as being within the exceptions of the Constitution and as indispensable to the public safety . . .

I concede that the class of arrests complained of can be constitutional only when in cases of rebellion or invasion the public safety may require them.

So in 1863 the Supreme Court refused to hear a case involving the holding of a civilian by a military court (**EX PARTE VALLANDIGHAM, 1864**). After the war, however, the Court reversed a case of a civilian convicted by a military court (**EX PARTE MILLIGAN, 1866**).

During the war the Court refused to hear a case challenging the government's authority to issue paper money (ROOSEVELT V. MEYER, 1863). In HEPBURN V. GRISWOLD (1870), however, it held that a creditor could refuse paper money as payment for debt. Within 15 months President Grant (elected in 1869) appointed two new Justices, and the HEPBURN decision was reversed.

During Reconstruction the Court invalidated some restrictions on ex-Confederate officers as being in violation of the ex post facto clause. CUMMINGS V. MISSOURI (1867), EX PARTE GARLAND (1867). When Congress imposed military rule over the Southern states it denied the Supreme Court jurisdiction to review the habeas corpus act it passed in conjunction with that legislation. In general the Supreme Court sustained Congress' Reconstruction laws. MISSISSIPPI V. JOHNSON (1867), GEORGIA V. STANTON (1867), EX PARTE MCCARDLE (1869), TEXAS V. WHITE (1869).

Supreme Court Guts the 14th Amendment

Originally the 14th Amendment was passed to force state governments to respect human rights just like the Bill of Rights forced the federal government to respect human rights. (Recall that in BARRON V. BALTIMORE John Marshall said the Bill of Rights did not apply to the states.) What the state governments did in the 19th century was very important to individual citizens, because they frequently exercised more power over everybody's day to day affairs than did the federal government.

TOUGH DAY... TOOK US ALL MORNING TO GUT THE 14TH AMENDMENT.

But whatever the American people wanted from the 14th Amendment when they ratified it in 1868, in 1873 the Court refused to use it to overrule BARRON V. BALTIMORE, and hold the states accountable to a broad list of individual rights. Louisiana had granted one group of butchers a monopoly to pursue their trade. In the SLAUGHTERHOUSE CASES (1873) the Court told the butchers left out in the cold that the 14th Amendment protected only federally secured rights, not state secured rights. This gutting of the 14th Amendment was also used to sustain state statutes which prohibited women from voting (MINOR V. HAPPERSETT, 1875), and engaging in the practice of law:

" . . . *in view of the peculiar*
characteristics, destiny and mission of
women, it is within the province of the
Legislature to ordain what offices, positions
and callings shall be filled and discharged
by men . . . " (BRADWELL V. ILLINOIS,
1873)

WHAT, PRACTICE LAW, AND GIVE UP ALL THIS?

Though the 14th Amendment was undercut for the sake of state governments in the cases of women and blacks, in a few years it would be used liberally against state governments for the sake of the wealthy . . .

5. YEARS OF REACTION

The Compromise of 1877

The Civil War's constitutional issues which centered on human rights climaxed and faded with the presidential election of 1876. When the returns came in, Democrat Tilden had 184 certain electoral votes and Republican Garfield Hayes had only 165. However, 185 votes were needed to win and 20 electoral votes remained contested and uncounted. There were questions as to whether this election would have to be settled like the one 16 years before—that is, by military force.

A commission selected to resolve the crisis "elected" Hayes when 8 Republicans outvoted 7 Democrats. Instead of using guns and appeals to human rights, the Republicans secured acceptance of this decision by bribing Southern Democrats with (a) an end to the army's occupation of the South; (b) a cabinet post replete with patronage; (c) support for capital improvements in the South; and (d) a southern transcontinental railroad.

This arrangement came to be known as the **Compromise of 1877.** What it salvaged in terms of political quietude it lost in terms of principled decency. Concern for human rights was giving way to racism and greed.

The Lawyers Take Over

At bottom the Compromise politicians were doing only what the rest of the country was doing, i.e, grabbing at everything. These were the days of the Gilded Age, when Robber Barons used corporations to produce profits by any means necessary, including monopoly, thuggery and bribery.

The order of the day was avarice, and to protect this order various ideologues justified it with words like "personal liberty", "freedom", "nature," "individualism," "survival of the fittest," and so on.

Lawyers (and judges) representing the very rich banded together in conferences and organizations to encourage one another to use these words to translate the Constitution. Indeed, they began to assert that interpreting the Constitution was such a specialized science that only they could do it. The result was a string of Supreme Court decisions designed to suppress anyone who got in the way of the free, white and wealthy.

101

Memory Lane (i)

1875: Supreme Court Justice Samuel Miller: "It is vain to contend with Judges who have been at the bar the advocates for forty years of railroad companies, and all forms of associated capital"

1877: National Railroad strike; general strike in St. Louis.

1878: American Bar Association formed.

1879: ABA President Phelps tries to use professionalism to squelch democracy: " . . . it is too true that [the Constitution] has become more and more a subject to be hawked about the country," by those "who have never found leisure for the graces of English grammar".

1883: Reconstruction Act (designed to protect blacks) held not to apply to Ku Klux Klan terrorism or white discrimination in the absence of state action. STATES V. HARRIS, CIVIL RIGHTS CASES.

Joseph P. Bradley, for majority: "Mere discrimination on account of race or color were not regarded as badges of slavery."

John Marshall Harlan, dissent: "I cannot resist the conclusion that the substance and spirit of the recent [14th] amendment of the Constitution have been sacrificed by a subtle and ingenious verbal criticism."

1886: Corporation recognized as a "person" enjoying all the rights that human persons enjoy. SANTA CLARA COUNTY V. SOUTHERN PACIFIC RAILROAD COMPANY. During this year the Court invalidates 230 state laws designed to regulate corporations.

Memory Lane (ii)

1892: Homestead Strike in Pennsylvania, General Strike in New Orleans. Populists adopt **Omaha Platform**, calling for popular control of the currency, support for the Knights of Labor, a graduated income tax, nationalization of the railroads, eight hour work day, and popular election of Senators.

1893: Supreme Court Justice David Brewer addresses New York State Bar Association: "It is the unvarying law that the wealth of the community will be in the hands of the few ... "

1894: Pullman Strike. Led by future socialist Eugene Debs, railroad workers stop midwestern railroad traffic.

1895: Ignoring years of precedent, POLLOCK V. FARMERS LOAN AND TRUST CO. responds to corporate lawyer Joseph Choate's appeal to halt the "communist march," and holds income tax laws unconstitutional. Basically, the government is forbidden to force the rich to pay a fair share of society's expenses.

U.S.V.E.C. KNIGHT CO. holds that a Sugar Trust manufacturing 90% of the nation's sugar does not violate the **Sherman Anti-Trust Act** because such involves local manufacture and not interstate commerce. (The Sherman Anti-Trust Act had been passed to curtail monopoly in American business, although after KNIGHT it was hard to tell WHAT the Surpreme Court would consider a monopoly.)

In IN RE DEBS the Supreme did find one use for the Sherman Anti-Trust Act: union busting. It held that the Act could be used to enjoin union activity during a strike.

A N.Y. banker toasts Supreme Court: "I give you, gentlemen, the Supreme Court of the United States— guardian of the dollar, defender of private property, enemy of spoilation, sheet anchor of the Republic."

1896: The Supreme Court sanctions Louisiana segregation laws in PLESSY V. FERGUSON.

Henry Billings Brown, majority: "If one race be inferior to the other socially, the Constitution of the United States cannot put them upon the same plane . . ."

Harlan, dissent: "The destinies of the two races, in this country, are indissolubly linked together, and the interests of both require that the common government of all shall not permit the seeds of race hate to be planted under the sanction of law."

AND IF WE WERE ON THE SAME PLANE, GUESS WHO'D SIT IN THE BACK!

1897: In DAVIS V. MASSACHUSETTS the Supreme Court upholds the conviction of William Davis for preaching on the Boston Common without a permit.

Oliver Wendell Holmes: "For the Legislature absolutely or conditionally to forbid public speaking in a highway or public park is no more an infringement of the rights of a member of the public than for the owner of a private house to forbid it in his house."

1905: The Supreme Court invalidates state legislation limiting bakers' working hours to 60 per week in LOCHNER V. NEW YORK.

1908: Supreme Court allows legislation regulating work hours for women in MULLER V. OREGON, invalidates legislation making it a crime for an employer to fire an employee because of union membership (ADAIR V. U.S.); and awards treble damages against a union for a secondary boycott under the Sherman Anti-Trust Act (LOEWE V. LAWLOR).

The People Fight Back

The number of statutes that the Supreme Court invalidated indicates that the people were not idle in trying to protect themselves. In 1913 they finally forced Congress and the state legislatures to pass two amendments to the constitution, theoretically beyond the bite of the Supreme Court (although we have already seen what the Supreme Court managed to do with the Fourteenth Amendment).

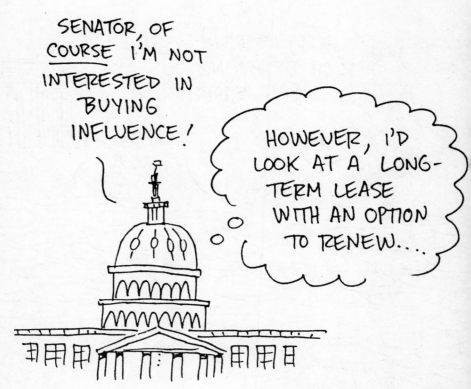

The Sixteenth Amendment was designed to overrule POLLOCK V. FARMERS LOAN AND TRUST CO., and give power to the government to force the rich to give some of their wealth back to society:

XVI: The Congress shall have power to lay and collect taxes on incomes, from whatever source derived, without apportionment among the several States, and without regard to any census or enumeration.

The Seventeenth Amendment gave the people the right to elect their own Senators. Heretofore Senators had been elected by state legislatures. (It's a lot easier to buy one state legislature than it is to buy the whole state!)

XVII: The Senate of the United States shall be composed of two Senators from each State, elected by the people thereof . . .

HELL, WE DIDN'T <u>GET</u> RICH BY PAYING OUR FAIR SHARE!

World War One

The 16th and 17th Amendments constituted some of the achievements of the Progressive Movement, which was the middle class remainder of the nation's reform forces after the farmer and factory worker components of Populism had been co-opted and smashed.

"We refused to take up the gun [and] so we lost..." —Hardy Brian, Louisiana Populist newspaper editor, 1899.

Whatever additional hopes that Progressivism might have held for the nation were soon wiped out by

WORLD WAR ONE

President Wilson knew what would happen if he led the nation into war:

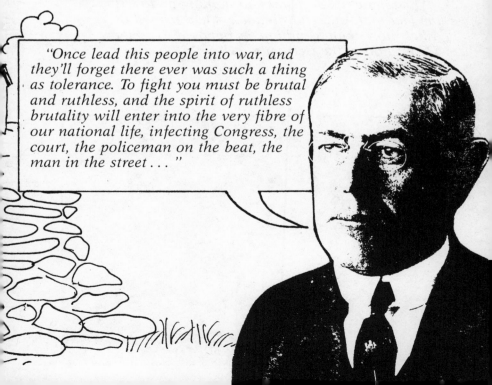

"Once lead this people into war, and they'll forget there ever was such a thing as tolerance. To fight you must be brutal and ruthless, and the spirit of ruthless brutality will enter into the very fibre of our national life, infecting Congress, the court, the policeman on the beat, the man in the street..."

In spite of the fact that the British violated American neutrality rights as much as the Germans, Wilson used the latter's unrestricted submarine warfare as a means of leading the nation into war.

"I suppose his decision had nothing to do with the fact that American financiers had loaned the Allies more than $2 billion, as opposed to a mere $27 million to the Germans . . . "

"Democracy" at Home is Killed to "Save Democracy" Abroad

Wilson was quite right about what would happen to America should it go to war. With his Espionage Act (1917) and Sedition Act (1918) Wilson surpassed the Alien and Sedition Act of 1798 in both quantity and quality:

QUANTITY:
1798 and after:
25 prosecutions,
10 convictions
1917 and after:
more than 1500 prosecutions,
more than 1000 convictions

SO, YOU CAN STILL SAY WHAT'S ON YOUR MIND...

...BUT YOUR MIND MIGHT WIND UP IN JAIL!

QUALITY:

—Socialist Congressman Berger gets 20 years for calling war a capitalist conspiracy;

—Socialist Presidential candidate Debs gets 20 years for statements having a "tendency" to encourage draft resistance;

—Over 100 Chicago IWW members convicted for opposing war effort;

—Film producer sentenced to 10 years for film celebrating American Revolution, because of its implied criticism of British;

—Farmer gets 21 months for comparing Germans in Belgium to Americans in Philippines;

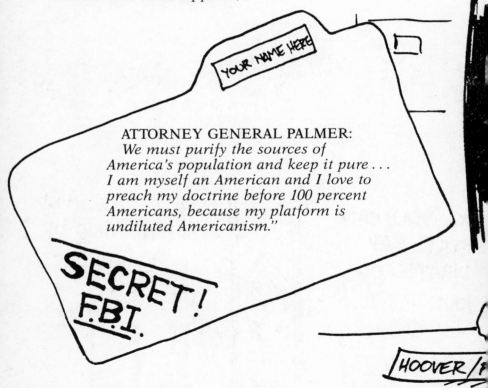

YOUR NAME HERE

ATTORNEY GENERAL PALMER:
We must purify the sources of America's population and keep it pure . . . I am myself an American and I love to preach my doctrine before 100 percent Americans, because my platform is undiluted Americanism."

SECRET! F.B.I.

HOOVER /

The Supreme Court held these acts constitutional as soon as it was able. SCHENCKS V. U.S., ABRAMS V. U.S. (1919).

The War encouraged repression in America and revolution in Russia, which in turn encouraged even more repression in America. In New York 5 duly elected Socialist officials were expelled from the state legislature. Under Attorney General A. Mitchell Palmer, over 200 persons were deported to Russia without a hearing. Thousands of homes and offices were raided. People were held without warrants. (Among them were Sacco and Vanzetti who were later convicted and executed.) J. Edgar Hoover got his start heading the new General Intelligence division, keeping files on various radicals.

More Amendments

Immediately after World War One the Constitution was amended twice.

With a million dollar grant from a woman's magazine publisher, coupled with conscientious organizing, women finally secured the right to vote with the **Nineteenth Amendment.** Appeals to race, class, and ethnic hatred also made their contributions to this otherwise decent cause.

Suffragist leader
CARRIE CHAPMAN CATT:
"this government is menaced with great danger. That danger lies in the slums of the cities, and the ignorant foreign vote. ... There is but one way to avert the danger ... cut off the vote of the slums and give it to women ... the usefulness of woman suffrage [is] a counterbalance to the foreign vote, and is a means of legally preserving white supremacy in the South ... "

Other women pressed for farther reaching reforms.

HELEN KELLER:
Our democracy is but a name. We vote? What does that mean? It means that we choose between two bodies of real, though not avowed, autocrats. We choose between Tweedledum and Tweedledee.

EMMA GOLDMAN:
Our modern fetish is universal suffrage. The women of Australia and New Zealand can vote, and help make the laws. Are the labor conditions better there?

Additionally, **Prohibition** ascended to constitutional status, having been elevated in a war atmosphere which (a) emphasized eating grain instead of drinking it; (b) hated Germans and their occupations (like brewing) and (c) demanded conformity. (That saloons frequently served as meeting places for labor unions and urban ward bosses mobilizing the "foreign" vote had nothing to do with the passage of this amendment . . .)

Laws passed under Prohibition's Eighteenth Amendment were consistently violated until 1933, when two new amendments were added to the Constitution. The Twenty-first Amendment amended prohibition, and the Twentieth adjusted some dates for certain terms of office: the President now starts his term in January; it used to be March.

As for women, they began working on something called the **Equal Rights Amendment** (first introduced into Congress in 1923).

113

114

Supreme Court Backs Reaction

In the meantime the Supreme Court continued to promote the normalcy that Americans had begun to know, if not love.

It invalidated laws that attempted to regulate child labor. HAMMER V. DAGENHART (1918), BAILEY V. DREXEL FURNITURE (1922).

It held unions liable for treble damages under the Sherman Act. UMW V. CORONADO COAL CO. (1922).

It held that courts might issue injunctions if unions (a) picketed; (b) attempted to organize employees who had signed non-union contracts; (c) or engaged in secondary boycotts. AMERICAN STEEL FOUNDRIES V. TRI-CITY CENTRAL TRADES COUNCIL (1921), TRUAX V. CORRIGAN (1921), HITCHMAN COAL AND COKE CO. V. MITCHELL (1917), DUPLEX PRINTING PRESS CO. V. DEERGIN (1921), BEDFORD CUT STONE COMPANY V. JOURNEYMEN STONE CUTTERS ASSOCIATION (1927).

Between 1880 and 1930 the injunction was used 1,845 times against labor, 921 times during 1920–30.

"Since 1920, the Court has invalidated more legislation than in fifty years preceding. Views that were antiquated twenty-five years ago have been resurrected in decisions nullifying:

—minimum wage laws for women in industry,

—a standard-weight bread law to protect buyers from short weights and honest bakers from unfair competition,

—a law fixing the resale price of theater tickets by ticket scalpers in New York,

—laws controlling exploitation of the unemployed by employment agencies,

—and many tax laws . . .

Merely as a matter of arithmetic, this is an impressive mortality rate."

—Felix Frankfurter, 1930, future S.Ct. Justice

116

Taft and Hughes

The court was guided in its course by the steady right hand of former President William Howard Taft.

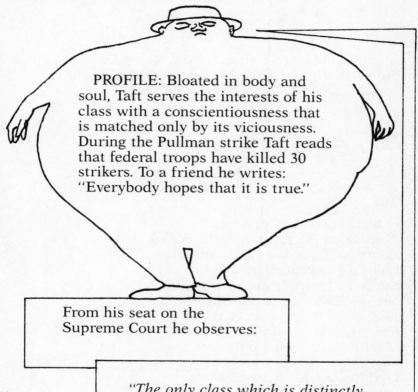

PROFILE: Bloated in body and soul, Taft serves the interests of his class with a conscientiousness that is matched only by its viciousness. During the Pullman strike Taft reads that federal troops have killed 30 strikers. To a friend he writes: "Everybody hopes that it is true."

From his seat on the Supreme Court he observes:

"The only class which is distinctly arrayed against the Court is a class that does not like the Courts at any rate, and that is organized labor. That faction we have to hit every little while, because they are continually violating the law and depending on threats and violence to accomplish their purpose."

Taft knew why he took the office of Chief Justice. Shortly after being appointed (1921), he told his fellow justices that he had been chosen "to reverse a few decisions." He also knew why he stayed on the bench:

> As long as things continue as they are, and I am able to answer in my place, I must stay on the Court in order to prevent the Bolsheviki from getting control . . .

The Supreme Court's stranglehold on the Constitution seemed secure when Charles Evan Hughes replaced Taft in 1930.

PROFILE: Child prodigy, governor of New York, GOP presidential candidate, Secretary of State, World Court judge, ex-Associate Supreme Court Justice. Scammed out of Chief Supreme Court Justice position in 1910 by Taft, who, while suggesting to Hughes the post was his, nevertheless appointed another, older man, so Taft would have a chance to take the seat later (which he did). Populist Senator Norris: "No man in public life so exemplifies the influence of powerful combinations in the political and financial world as does Mr. Hughes."

However, all this was changed by . . . .

HUGHES:
"We are under a Constitution, but the Constitution is what the judges say it is.

The Depression

With the stock market crash of 1929 the economy fell into an abyss that traumatized the nation. Between 1929 and 1932 thousands of banks and more than 100,000 businesses failed. Capital investment fell from $10 billion in 1929 to $1 billion in 1932, and unemployment skyrocketed from 4 to 11 million people, almost ¼ of the labor force. Industrial production and personal incomes halved.

Many Americans were very upset with this situation. They took over buildings, like state capitols and city banks. In the farmland lawyers and judges who processed mortgage foreclosures were beaten and killed. Working people joined unions, held strikes, took over factories, and halted almost everything in Minneapolis, Toledo and San Francisco.

NOT EVERYONE'S INCOME WAS CUT IN TWO... THERE WERE THE HALVEDS AND THE HALVED-NOTS!

6. YEARS OF REFORM

In the meantime the Supreme Court continued to invalidate laws establishing railroad pensions, state minimum wage laws, and federal regulations concerning coal and farm production. Many of the Court's reactionary decisions rested on votes of 6-3 or 5-4.

A crisis of constitutional if not revolutionary proportions was brewing.

The New Deal

In 1932 the country elected a new Congress and a new President (Franklin Roosevelt). In 1933 they took office and began searching for legislative solutions to the economic mess. In the words of Huey Long, some programs like the **National Recovery Administration** had "every fault of socialism . . . without one of its virtues." Other programs like the **Tennessee Valley Authority** showed that public control over public resources could generate tremendous benefits.

This array of attacks on economic disaster was known as FDR's **New Deal**. The "new" part was the fact that government now actually worried about capitalism's awful effect on individual human beings, and sometimes tried to do something to ameliorate those effects.

"The deal is that capitalism was going to be preserved, whether it deserves it or not."

For its part the Supreme Court was more interested in preserving its jurisprudence than in solving the Depression. In 1935 it began invalidating major pieces of New Deal legislation. Roosevelt and Congress responded with the "Second New Deal" which included measures concerning Social Security and labor relations.

The Judicial Revolution of 1937

For better or worse the so-called **Judicial Revolution of 1937** resolved the crisis. Part of the story is told by its chronology:

Nov. 1936: FDR enjoys landslide victory

Feb. 7, 1937: FDR

announces his "Court packing plan". Based on ideas originally proposed by Supreme Court Justice J.C. McReynolds when he had been attorney general, FDR proposes that he be allowed to appoint additional judges for benches where judges of retirement age are sitting. This would have allowed him to appoint enough new justices to the Supreme Court to outnumber the reactionary majority.

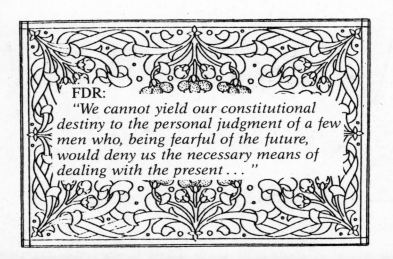

FDR:
"We cannot yield our constitutional destiny to the personal judgment of a few men who, being fearful of the future, would deny us the necessary means of dealing with the present..."

March 29, 1937: Hughes and
Roberts join 3 progessive Justices to sustain a
state minimum wage law for women in WEST
COAST HOTEL V. PARISH, reversing 1936's
MOREHEAD V. TIPALDO.

April 12. Another 5-4 decision sustains
the **National Labor Relations Act.**

May 18. Eldest of the conservative bloc
of four (Justice Willis Van Devanter) announces
that he will retire from the Court on June 1.

May 24. Provisions of **Social Security
Act** upheld by votes of 5-4 (HELVERING V. DAVIS)
and 7-2 (STEWARD MACHINE CO. V. DAVIS).

The other part of the story is that the critical swing vote
seems to have been ready to change its mind before FDR
announced his court packing scheme. Owen Roberts shifted
gears in 1937. Judges rarely tip their hands, but in 1951 Roberts
gave his explanation as to why he began switching his votes:

> *Looking back, it is difficult to see how
> the Court could have resisted the popular
> urge for uniform standards throughout
> the country—for what in effect was a
> unified economy . . .*
>
> *An insistency by the court on holding
> federal power to what seemed its
> appropriate orbit when the Constitution
> was adopted might have resulted in even
> more radical changes in our dual
> structure than those which have been
> gradually accomplished through the
> extension of the limited jurisdiction on
> the federal government.*

In other words, either we change our
minds to agree with what the people
want, or the people will revolt.

The New Court: Closures

After the "switch in time that saved nine" (as some wags called it), the conservative justices began to retire. Roosevelt replaced them with individuals sympathetic to his New Deal, and in the end FDR appointed a total of eight new Justices.

The new court did a number of things to promote a new order based on FDR's vision of a more equitable capitalism. In addition to ratifying the concept of national regulations for a national economy, it also began reigning in the power of labor where it counted most, viz., at the site of the means of production. In NLRB V. FANSTEEL (1939) the Court declared factory "sit-ins" to be illegal. (In a "sit-in", workers would occupy their factory by "sitting in" at their posts, thereby preventing the bosses from sending in scabs (who might take their jobs); or goons (who might damage them—or the factory property). Sitting in was not only effective, it was also safe.) By forbidding this powerful but non-violent recourse to management violence, FANSTEEL made it clear that the Supreme Court was more worried about worker illegalities than management illegalities, and that capitalism was more important to the American order than equity. Limiting power was fine if you talked about it in terms of constitutional rhetoric, as long as you didn't try to apply it to managerial prerogatives.

The New Court: Openings

Yet while the Court did its best to check labor's advances into its most critical arena, it conceded the power to organize to ordinary people in a number of other significant areas. It began rendering a number of decisions which constituted important turning points in the development of American civil liberties. From one perspective these decisions might be seen simply as means of enhancing the political capacity of individuals potentially sympathetic to the New Deal. From another perspective they can be viewed as attempts to raise the Constitution to a level of minimal decency:

The new Court began to re-instate the right to picket in SENN V. TILE LAYERS UNION (1937) AND THORNHILL V. ALABAMA (1940).

It opened the way for the Bill of Rights to be applied to the States in PALKO V. CONNECTICUT (1937).

It overturned DAVIS V. MASSACHUSETTS and declared that the parks and streets were the property not of the state, but of the people, in HAGUE V. CIO (1939).

In a number of cases the Court restricted the right of government to interfere with leafletting and doorknocking. LOVELL V. GRIFFIN (1938), SCHNEIDER V. IRVINGTON (1939), CANTWELL V. CONNECTICUT (1940), MARTIN V. STRUTHERS (1943).

In SMITH V. ALLWRIGHT (1944) the Court reversed a 1935 decision which had sanctioned all-white primaries.

In the case of a company town it limited the owning corporation's capacity to restrict the rights of free speech. MARSH V. ALABAMA (1946).

War Again

Of course it seems that whenever individual rights begin to make progress in the United States, some war comes along. World War Two might have solved the economic problems of the Depression, but it did little to improve political circumstances in the United States.

Under President Roosevelt the executive branch assumed more and more power. While some of these measures might have helped finally defeat Hitler, others set precedents with noxious repercussions for the years to come. Without congressional authorization Roosevelt sent ships to Britain, and instituted undeclared naval warfare against Germany. To cover himself he declared a limited state of national emergency in September of 1939, and in May 1941 "unlimited" that state. At one point he threatened to "nullify" a provision of an Act of Congress (the **Emergency Price Control Act**) if it failed to repeal it (which it did, for better or worse). Some of Roosevelt's actions were particularly problematic, like when he seized a steel mill in order to stop workers from striking; or when he sent thousands of Japanese into detention camps. The Congress belatedly sanctioned the former with the War **Labor Disputes Act,** and the Supreme court sanctioned the latter in KOREMATSU V. U.S. (1944).

Truman

The trend towards concentration of power in the executive branch was somewhat slowed when FDR died in 1945, and was replaced by Harry Truman. In 1951 Republicans helped passed the **Twenty-second Amendment** to the Constitution, in hopes of controlling any FDRs of the future. Roosevelt had been elected to four terms, and this Amendment restricted any future President to only two terms.

For its part, in 1952 the Supreme Court told Truman that Korean war or no, he had to go to Congress before he could begin seizing steel mills to stop a labor dispute. YOUNGSTOWN SHEET AND TUBE CO. V. SAWYER (1952).

Nevertheless, executive power continued to grow. On his own initiative Truman had dropped atomic bombs on Japan, sent troops to Korea, and desegregated the armed forces. During his tenure executive agencies like the Council of Economic Advisors, the National Security Council, and the Bureau of Budget (now the OMB) were created. In addition, Truman established a loyalty board which evaluated over 4¼ million federal employees during 1947–1953.

Red Scares

One reason why Americans accepted this employment of power passed under the phrase "national emergency." World War Two had ended in 1945. But with Hitler gone, Stalin soon took his place as the international bogeyman. It was during this period that Americans began to accept the notion that Congresspeople could not engage in controversies over foreign policy during periods of undeclared war without being called traitors. "Bipartisanship" was the label used to describe this phenomenon. Both parties were expected to line up behind the President no matter what he wanted to do with the country in foreign affairs.

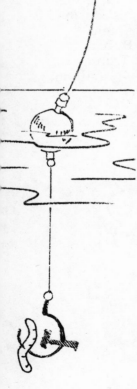

In addition to being cited as a justification for growing presidential power, these various shibboleths were also used to justify many congressional actions that would have delighted the most dedicated totalitarian. In 1950 the **Internal Security Act** established a Subversive Activities Control Board, along with six concentration camps for political undesirables in case of an "internal security emergency." In 1954 the Communist Party was outlawed. Senator Joseph McCarthy and the **House** on **UnAmerican Activities Committee** used congressional investigating power (along with their congressional immunity) to create self-serving publicity and destroy the lives and careers of many people.

The Supreme Court generally did little to interpose the Bill of Rights between the witch hunters and their victims. AMERICAN COMMUNICATION ASSOCIATION V. DOUDS (1950), DENNIS V. U.S. (1951), BAILEY V. RICHARDSON (1951), contrast JOINT ANTI-FASCIST COMMITTEE V. MCGRATH (1951).

It was not until the second half of the decade that this trend changed. QUINN V. U.S. (1955), PETERS V. HOBBY (1956), COLE V. YOUNG (1956), YATES V. U.S. (1957), WATKINS V. U.S. (1957).

There were at least two reasons underlying the Court's eventual shift. First, the nation's appetite for Joe McCarthy proved limited, and after the Senate's censure of him (Dec. 2, 1954) the Supreme Court felt safer to oppose redbaiting. Second, Earl Warren had been appointed Chief Justice.

Earl Warren

The good news about Earl Warren was that he promulgated a vision of the Constitution which insured that it would be interpreted as a guarantor of democracy and human rights. The bad news was that he was so effective that many people began to look to the Court as the source of their political good fortunes, instead of to themselves. They started giving their problems to lawyers, asking them to solve things in courtrooms, instead of looking to themselves and taking to the streets. In any case, the impact of the Warren court on America's constitutional order is impossible to deny.

Warren was a Republican from California appointed to the Chief Justice position by Dwight Eisenhower. In part the appointment was a reward for Warren's help in securing Ike the presidential nomination in 1952. In part it was an attempt to kick Warren upstairs, and get him out of California so that Vice President Nixon's minions could enjoy more power in that state's GOP.

Whatever Eisenhower might have expected of Warren, he was unpleasantly surprised.

I MADE TWO MISTAKES, AND THEY'RE BOTH ON THE SUPREME COURT!

One of the most significant cases was U.S. V. CAROLENE PRODUCTS. Though it dealt with adulterated milk, the decision contained a footnote intimating that the Court was ready to look as rigorously at laws affecting the rights of ordinary people as it had for the past 50 years scrutinized the laws that affected the rights of the super rich. It put litigants on notice that if a law could be viewed as unduly restrictive or discriminatory, the Supreme Court would be more disposed to invalidate it.

When asked if he had made any mistakes during his administration, Eisenhower replied "Yes, two, and they are both sitting on the Supreme Court." [The other "mistake" was William Brennan.]

One of the first things that Warren did when he assumed his seat was to engineer possibly the most significant decision of his 16 years on the Court, viz. BROWN V. BOARD OF EDUCATION.

In BROWN, black schoolchildren challenged the "separate but equal" educational facilities that the state of Kansas was supposedly giving them. BROWN held that not only was Kansas being unequal; the separation of the races itself was inherently unequal:

"We conclude that in the field of public education, the doctrine of 'separate but equal' has no place. Separate educational facilities are inherently unequal."

The short term significance of the BROWN decision lay in its explicit repudiation of PLESSY V. FERGUSON, which had sanctioned state-sponsored racism for over half a century. The long term significance of BROWN lay in the constitutional upheavals which it unleashed.

Brown V. Board of Education

JUSTICE FOR ALL, GIVE OR TAKE A FEW

Warren assumed his seat on the Court when the BROWN case was already before the Court. The justices could not agree whether to overrule PLESSY outright, or simply to enforce the equal part of the separate but equal doctrine. Four justices preferred the latter course, in part because they had been doing that for years, and in part because they feared the political uproar that was bound to follow if they overruled.

According to Justice William O. Douglas, Warren's skillful organizing transformed a potentially divisive 5-4 vote into a 9-0 unanimous vote:

> *The fact that a worldly and wise man like Warren would stake his reputation on this issue not only impressed Frankfurter but seemed to have a like influence on Reed and Clark. Clark followed shortly, Reed finally came around somewhat doubtfully, and only Jackson was left.*

Warren visited Jackson who was recuperating from a heart attack in the hospital.

> *Jackson had said to count him in, which made the opinion unanimous. We could present a solid front to the country, and it was a brilliant diplomatic process which Warren had engineered.*

131

Reactions

The political turmoil anticipated by the more conservative justices was not long in coming. Many southern states passed resolutions and laws defying the Supreme Court. In 1957 President Eisenhower had to send federal troops into Little Rock to keep order. In the litigation following the Little Rock crisis the Supreme Court cited **MARBURY V. MADISON** to the effect that "this decision declared the basic principle that the federal judiciary is supreme in the exposition of the law of the Constitution." More dubiously it asserted that "that principle has ever since been respected by this Court and the Country as a permanent and indispensable feature of our constitutional system."

Whatever words the Supreme Court might write in its decisions, the fact is that by the early '60s it had achieved only limited success in eliminating institutionalized racism in the south. School desegregation had slowed from some 750 systems desegregated during **BROWN**'s first four years, to 49 for the following three.

> Freedom Riders relying on Supreme Court decisions for integrated facilities were brutally beaten.

JAMES FARMER,
civil rights activist:
*"In South Carolina . . .
there were several young
white hoodlums . . . and
they blcoked the door and
said, "Nigger, you can't
come in here."*
He said,
*"I have every right to
enter this waiting room
according to the Supreme
Court of the United States
in the Boynton case."*
They said,
"Shit on that."

He tried to walk past, and they clubbed him, beat him, and knocked him down."

Even in Montgomery, Alabama, site of the successful boycotts of 1955–56, segregated customs were returning to the buses.

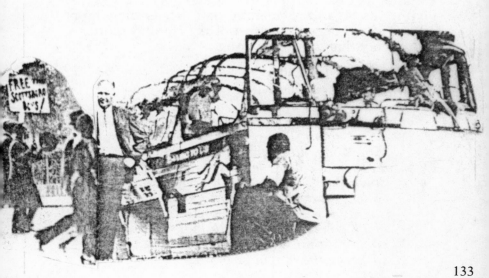

Black Mobilization

The broader implications of the BROWN decision finally became reality when blacks finally managed to mobilize (i) blacks; (ii) whites; (iii) and the executive branch of the federal government. The first happened when groups like **Student Non-Violent Co-ordinating Committee** abandoned the litigating strategies of the **National Association for the Advancement of Colored People,** and engaged in civil disobedience and community organizing. The second happened when civil rights organizers realized that racists shooting at whites would disgust the rest of the country more thoroughly than racist shooting at blacks.

> DAVE DENNIS,
> civil rights activitist:
> *They were not gonna respond to a thousand blacks working in that area [Mississippi]. They would respond to a thousand young white college students, and white college females who were down there. ... the death of a white college student would bring on more attention to what was going on than for a black college student getting it. That's cold, but that was also in another sense speaking the language of this country.*

The third happened when Kennedy realized (i) that his electoral victory depended upon blacks in the north and (ii) that America's position abroad depended upon people's perception of how the United States treated its black population, in part due to the international travels of then Black Muslim leader Malcolm X.

JFK carried Illinois by only 9000 votes where 250,000 blacks were estimated to have voted for him. Michigan was carried by 67,000 votes where another 250,000 blacks were estimated to have voted the Kennedy ticket. Some 40,000 blacks were key to JFK's 10,000 vote margin in South Carolina.

> JFK,
> message to Congress,
> 2/28/63:
> *"race discrimination hampers our world leadership by contradicting at home the message we preach abroad."*

ARTHUR SCHLESINGER,
Presidential aide:
*"Three weeks after Oxford [where Kennedy sent
troops to protect James Meredith, a black student
attempting to attend college in Mississippi], Sekou
Toure and Ben Bella [African leaders] were
prepared to deny refueling facilities to Soviet
planes bound for Cuba during the missile crisis."*

When these mobilizations occurred,
the Constitution was amended (with
Number 24, in 1964) to eliminate the poll
tax (which had been used to discourage
poor blacks (and whites) from voting. (In
1961 the District of Columbia had been
given electoral votes with the Twenty-
Third Amendment.)

POLL TAXES BECOME EXCESSIVE

Results

Additionally Congress passed a number of Civil Rights measures, particularly the **Civil Rights Act of 1964** which prohibited segregation in public accommodations. (Though the Supreme Court did not have the Fourteenth Amendment to uphold this law (recall the CIVIL RIGHTS CASES), it did have the commerce clause).

Finally, Congress' **1965 Voting Rights Act** insured that blacks had an enforceable right to a meaningful franchise.

KENNEDY'S DEFENSE OF BLACKS PLAYED WELL IN AFRICA!

HOW DO YOU SUPPOSE YOUR SOUTH AFRICA POLICY PLAYS?

In addition to the BROWN decision, the Warren Court instituted a number of other reforms in America's constitutional order:

More Judicial Progress

- Individuals held to have a right to form groups for political purposes. NAACP V. ALABAMA (1957).

- Police forced to gather evidence properly, prohibited from using materials obtained during unreasonable searches or seizures. MAPP V. OHIO (1961).

- Schools stopped from forcing students to pray. ENGELE V. VITALE (1962).

- States forced to apportion their legislative districts on a "one man one vote" basis. BAKER V. CARR (1962), REYNOLDS V. SIMS (1964).

...YOU HAVE THE RIGHT TO REMAIN SILENT... IF YOU GIVE UP THAT RIGHT, WHICH WOULD BE PRETTY DUMB, BUT I WOULDN'T PUT IT PAST YOU....

"After his retirement, Chief Justice Earl Warren was asked what he regarded to be the decision during his tenure that would have the greatest consequence for all Americans. His choice was BAKER V. CARR, because he believed that if each of us has an equal vote, we are equally armed with the indispensible means to make our views felt.—Justice William Brennan.

● States required to provide criminal defendants with counsel if they were unable to pay for one. In GIDEON V. WAINWRIGHT (1963).

● Right to privacy recognized (also allowing a couple to receive birth control information without governmental interference). GRISWOLD V. CONNECTICUT (1965).

● Police told to read suspects their rights. MIRANDA V. ARIZONA (1966).

The net result was a system more solicitous of the rights of individuals and minorities, and more open to democratic transformation.

7. REACTION REDUX

Richard Nixon thought very little of Earl Warren's conception of the Constitution, and he promised the American people he would work for his own constitutional order if they elected him president.

They did, and he did.

BUT I GAVE THE COUNTRY (EXPLETIVE DELETED) AND (OATHS OMITTED)!

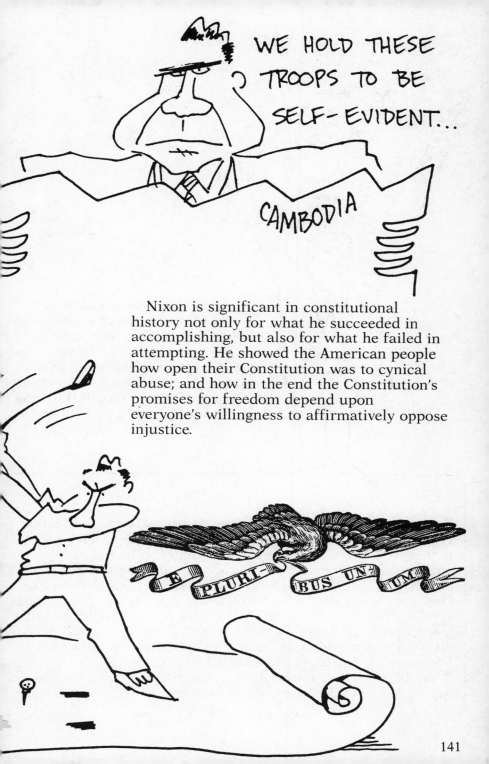

WE HOLD THESE TROOPS TO BE SELF- EVIDENT...

CAMBODIA

Nixon is significant in constitutional history not only for what he succeeded in accomplishing, but also for what he failed in attempting. He showed the American people how open their Constitution was to cynical abuse; and how in the end the Constitution's promises for freedom depend upon everyone's willingness to affirmatively oppose injustice.

E PLURI- BUS UN UM

Nixon began his attempts at constitutional counterrevolution by trying to bring unprecedented power to the executive branch. The trend had been developing in a number of forms for a number of years, but Nixon brought it to new levels of quantity and quality.

He increased the White House staff from 1700 to over 3500. He impounded moneys appropriated by Congress which meant that he refused to spend money for programs he did not approve. (Some presidents had done this sparingly in the past, but the enabling legislation gave some discretion.) Contrary to laws enacted by Congress, Nixon announced he would no longer enforce Title VI of the 1964 Civil Rights Act which directed that government funds could not go to institutions practicing discrimination; and he attempted to dismantle the Office of Economic Opportunity. He established a White House "Plumbers" unit to spy on Americans he did not like. Finally, he waged war in Cambodia without the sanction of Congress.

Vietnam

Nixon's freewheeling war-waging was the
consummation of a long process begun as
early as 1854 when President Franklin Pierce
sent troops to Nicaragua without
congressional authorization. Wilson sent
troops into Mexico, Eisenhower did it in
Lebanon, and Johnson did it in the
Dominican Republic. Kennedy began the
process for both Johnson and Nixon in
Vietnam.

One problem with Vietnam was that it lasted too long.
Another was that the carnage began to reach genocidal levels.
Eventually tens of thousands of Americans were killed or
wounded. The figures went into the hundreds of thousands for
the Vietnamese. Another problem with the Vietnam situation
was that no American President had the gall to formulate a
constitutional declaration of war. Young Americans got sick of
being drafted into a dubious cause that made them cannon
fodder, and they began to protest. One way the nation tried to
palliate them was by guaranteeing 18-year-olds the vote with the
Twenty-Sixth Amendment.

Draft-age people got to vote. Nixon continued to wage war.

Watergate

Nixon took his claims of executive power so seriously that he had his lawyers tell the courts that he could ignore the Fourth Amendment's search and seizure clauses in the interests of "national security." The Supreme Court rejected this position on June 19, 1972. An eighteen minute gap was later found on tapes made in the Nixon White House a day later. The Saturday before various burglars had been caught with wire tapping equipment in Democratic Party Headquarters in the Watergate Hotel.

Subsequent court hearings indicated that the White House had been involved in the break-in. The Senate created a Selected Committee and later an Office of Special Prosecutor (to be appointed by Nixon) to investigate. Various incidents of White House corruption and abuse of power came to light. The first Special Prosecutor (Archibald Cox) asked for Nixon's tapes to see how deeply Nixon had involved himself in obstruction of justice. Nixon went through two attorney generals before he could find Assistant Attorney General Robert Bork to fire Cox. After a grand jury named Nixon as an unindicted co-conspirator to obstruct justice in March of 1974, the next Special Prosecutor again asked for Nixon's tapes. He refused, and both of them went to the Supreme Court. On July 24, 1974 the Court put one halt to Nixon's inflated claims of executive power. In a unanimous vote the Court held that his claims of executive privilege concerning the tapes were bogus, and ordered him to release them forthwith.

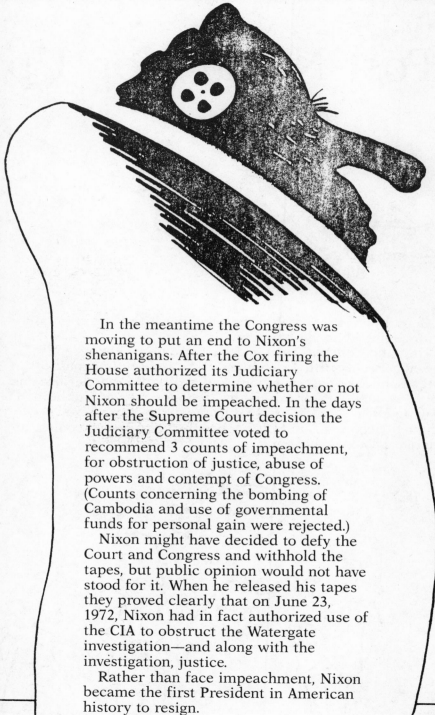

In the meantime the Congress was moving to put an end to Nixon's shenanigans. After the Cox firing the House authorized its Judiciary Committee to determine whether or not Nixon should be impeached. In the days after the Supreme Court decision the Judiciary Committee voted to recommend 3 counts of impeachment, for obstruction of justice, abuse of powers and contempt of Congress. (Counts concerning the bombing of Cambodia and use of governmental funds for personal gain were rejected.)

Nixon might have decided to defy the Court and Congress and withhold the tapes, but public opinion would not have stood for it. When he released his tapes they proved clearly that on June 23, 1972, Nixon had in fact authorized use of the CIA to obstruct the Watergate investigation—and along with the investigation, justice.

Rather than face impeachment, Nixon became the first President in American history to resign.

Post Nixon Mop Up

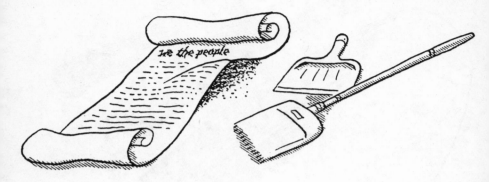

Gerald Ford became President and pardoned Nixon for any wrongdoing he might have done.

Ford and Congress then had a chance to use the recently enacted **Twenty-fifth Amendment** for a second time (passed after Kennedy's assassination), and Nelson Rockefeller became Vice President. (Prior to this the 25th Amendment had been used to make Gerald Ford Nixon's Vice President. Nixon's original vice president Spiro Agnew had pleaded no contest to charges of tax evasion, and he resigned his office.)

In addition to the investigations it sponsored to check Nixon's abuses of power, the Congress also passed a number of laws.

With them Congress hoped to bring the Executive branch's capacity for mischief under some control:

1972: **Case Act.** International agreements by the executive to be controlled by Congress. In theory the President can no longer wage foreign policy at whim.

1973: **War Powers Act.** Passed over Nixon's veto. Requires President to consult with Congress before committing American troops to combat situations. In theory the President can no longer wage war at whim.

1974: **Budget and Impoundment Control Act.** Designed to prevent president from refusing to spend moneys that Congress has appropriated.

1974: **Federal Election Campaign Act.** Designed to curtail the power of money to control American elections. (In the 1981–1982 election cycle, the Republicans raised $175,000,000 more than the Democrats.)

1976: **National Emergencies Act.** Congress sets controls on the President's power to declare national emergencies, and terminates emergencies declared during the 1933 depression, the 1950 Korean war, and the 1971 monetary crisis, none of which had been technically repealed. In theory the President can no longer assume emergency powers at whim.

LOTTA GOOD WHIM DOES IF YOU CAN'T WAGE ANYTHING WITH IT!

The Burger Court: The Good News

Nixon's attempts to change the Constitution in the short term failed miserably. He enjoyed greater success over the longer term through his four appointments to the Supreme court, one of whom, Warren Burger, replaced Earl Warren as Chief Justice.

The Burger Court did not prove to be as innovative as the Warren Court, either because it thought the court was getting out of touch with the country and losing its legitimacy, or because it was a more conservative court—depending upon your point of view.

In the end the Burger Court's impact on the constitution might be viewed as mixed.

On the one hand the court rejected "Nixonism" at a number of junctures: it repudiated impoundment, endorsed busing to achieve school desegregation, and invalidated Nixon's attempts to stifle publication of the Pentagon Papers. TRAIN V. CITY OF NEW YORK (1975), CHARLOTTE V. MECKLENBURG BOARD OF EDUCATION (1971), PENTAGON PAPERS (1971).

In addition, the Court decided that the constitutional right to privacy afforded women a limited constitutional right to abortion. ROE V. WADE (1973). Women's rights were additionally expanded in 1984 with the cases of HISHON V. KING & SPAULDING, and ROBERTS V. U.S. JAYCEES, which allowed women to sue private organizations for sexual discrimination. The Burger Court also sanctioned the power of the states to break up huge estates for distribution to tenants, thereby insuring that local governments had power to enforce a more equitable distribution of property. HAWAII V. MIDKIFF (1984).

The Burger Court: The Not So Good News

On the other hand, the Burger Court refused to limit Nixon's Southeast Asian adventures in HOLTZMAN V. SCHLESINGER (1973).

It made both the President and the CIA less accountable to the public, and has given additional power to the President to circumscribe the rights of Americans to travel to places like Cuba. NIXON V. FITZGERALD (1982), CIA V. SIMS (1985), REGAN V. WALD (1984).

It cut back on the rights of blacks to affirmative action, and cut back on the rights of citizens in general to vindicate their rights in court. FIREFIGHTERS LOCAL 1784 V. STOTTS (1984), LOS ANGELES V. LYONS (1983).

It made unions more open to defamation actions by lifting certain federal restrictions, and also stated they have no rights to negotiate over plant closings. BILL JOHNSON'S RESTAURANT V. NLRB (1983), FIRST NATIONAL MAINTENANCE CORP. V. NLRB (1981).

It helped Wall Street stock scammers in BLUE CHIP STAMPS V. MANOR DRUG STORES (1975) and ERNST AND ERNST V. HOCHFELDER (1976).

In INGRAHAM V. WRIGHT (1977), it sanctioned the use of beating as a punishment option for school officials.

In SAN ANTONIO INDEPENDENT SCHOOL DISTRICT V. RODRIGUEZ (1973), it refused to hold that states had to finance school districts equally.

It cut back on restrictions on police in terms of searches and interrogations. U.S. V. LEON (1984), N.Y. V. QUARLES, (1984).

Carter and Reagan

In 1976 the American people, disgusted with Republicans, tried giving power to the Democrats. While the Democrats, under Jimmy Carter, held the White House and Congress they did little to protect the interests of the constituencies that got them there in the first place (i.e., women, minorities and unions). After the Democrats abandoned their constituencies, their constituencies abandoned the Democrats. Not surprisingly, Ronald Reagan was elected President in 1980, but only 27% of the potential electorate voted for him.

FORTUNATELY, THEY'LL TOLERATE PLENTY!

When Reagan took office he continued the drive for Executive power, despite his rhetoric. He used the Justice Dept. to promote his brand of racism in actions against local affirmative action programs, and in BOB JONES V. U.S. (1983), where he argued that schools that espoused racism should be given tax exempt status. In 1983 Reagan unilaterally conquered Grenada. In 1985 he invented a new emergency, and called it Nicaragua.

While he waited for members of the Supreme Court to retire or die, he worked hard on the federal judiciary. His appointees tended to be both ideological and young. It has been estimated that he may appoint as much as 50% of the federal bench by the time he leaves office in 1989. In the meantime his Attorney General Ed Meese began hollering that federal judges should follow the "original intent" of the Founding Fathers when they framed the Constitution. This supposed "doctrine of judicial construction" was, of course, nothing but ideology dressed in high falutin words. We have seen how the Framers looked for the Constitution to change and to grow.

"Irangate" grew out of the brave efforts of Ronald Reagan to send weaponry to the Ayatolla Khomeni in exchange for American hostages during his second term. Somewhere along the line some of the profits from these transactions were skimmed and sent to Reagan's contras in Central America in violation of various congressional mandates. Reports began to surface that the contras were running drugs, and money from their supporters were being used to defeat candidates opposed to Reagan's aggressions against Nicaragua. The constitutional questions, of course, involved the extent to which the American people and their so-called representatives would call upon the President to obey the laws of the land, like any other citizen. Had Reagan been running any other organization he would have been summarily retired, fired or arrested. Perhaps the greatest scandal was the extent to which the establishment press dove into a continual grovel, begging the president to act like a leader and prove he was neither criminal nor senile. If you are not in some lieutenant colonel's concentration camp in 1992 for having a copy of this book, Irangate hopefully will have caused no more damage to the Republic than did a little episode called Watergate . . .

8. REVIEW AND PROGNOSIS

Other Developments

While Reagan and his followers were pushing their version of the Constitution from the White House, other groups left and right, have been pushing theirs.

Concerned over Reagan's effect on the federal judiciary, many observers (including Supreme Court Justice Brennan) have encouraged aggrieved persons to turn to state constitutions and state courts for vindication of civil liberties.

> BRENNAN
> "I suggest to the bar that, although in the past it might have been safe for counsel to raise only federal constitutional issues in state courts, plainly it would be most unwise these days not also to raise the state constitutional questions."

From the other side, right-wing legal figures have attempted to intimidate left legal theorists. In hopes of dry cleaning the legal doctrines that emanate from the law schools, Robert Bork (ex-Nixon Asistant Attorney General and hatchetman, now a federal judge) accused the faculties there of being too liberal. The dean of the Duke law school did his part and called for some left academics to resign their posts and get out. Such pronouncements, of course, have nothing to do with McCarthysim . . .

Some of the greatest struggles have occurred over women's issues. A concerted attempt to pass the Equal Rights Amendment failed during the 1970s. While progressive women regrouped, reactionary groups attempted to eliminate the right to abortion. Besides calling for an anti-choice amendment, some anti-choice groups resorted to bombings in hopes of · changing the constitution THEIR way.

Another front has been more quiet, but has held greater potential for substantial change. Article Five of the Constitution contains a clause which allows it to be changed if ⅔ of the states call for a special convention. Over the past few years the New Right types have used "balance the budget" and school prayer rhetoric to come within a few states of reaching the 34 required for calling such a convention. If such a convention were held, Lord only knows what might happen.

Evaluation

Whatever forms the Constitution may assume in the future, we can at least look at how it has done in the past. Over the past 200 years has the Constitution done as well as all those other books say it has?

Perhaps the best way to evaluate the Constitution would be to view it according to the criteria the Framers set out for themselves when they drafted the Constitution's Preamble:

WE THE PEOPLE OF THE UNITED STATES

The good news is that this "we the people" used to mean mainly propertied white males. Now people understand it to mean every adult citizen, regardless of sex, race, wealth or creed.

The less good news is that the United States could make participation in the electoral process easier for a lot of people.

a more, perfect union
OR LESS

IN ORDER TO FORM A MORE PERFECT UNION

Perfection is in the eyes of the beholder. For the Founders this included a polity where control of the money supply was beyond the will of the people. In this area the Framers generally succeeded, because the banking interests on the Federal Reserve Board control the nation's currencies. The reader may conclude how this contributes to the nation's perfection.

In other respects the union has been maintained, but not without help from a bloody civil war (1861–1865) and a scam compromise (1876). Additionally, at various junctures the "more perfect union" has been achieved by excluding those who were thought not to fit in very well, e.g., by killing American Indians, disenfranchising women, and suppressing minorities.

establish justice (OR REASONABLE FACSIMILE)

ESTABLISH JUSTICE

Justice too is in the eye of the beholder. It has been defined as the assignment of merited rewards and punishments. Presently the United States rewards the top 10% of its population with 57% of its net wealth, and punishes with imprisonment more people per capita than any industrialized nation in the world, except for the Soviet Union and South Africa. The reader may draw his or her own conclusions.

insure domestic ^SUBSERVIENCE AND tranquility

INSURE DOMESTIC TRANSQUILITY

How tranquil the nation has been is open to question. The country's social structure has remained generally stable: For the past 35 years the top 20% of the nation has taken some 41% of the gross national income, while the bottom 20% has gotten 5%. In 1972 the top ½% had 20% of the wealth, as they had since 1945. The "levelling laws" which the Founding Fathers feared have not come into being.

But stability is not necessarily the same as tranquility, and frequently stability is merely tranquility maintained at the point of a gun. U.S. labor history has been characterized as the "bloodiest and most violent" of any industrial nation in the world. The moderate historian Richard Hofstadter (who noted the preceding) has also observed that our civil strife "rather resembles some Latin American Republics or the volatile new states of Asia and Africa." (He also notes the biased ways it has been used to benefit the establishment, which explains why "in turn it has been so easily and indulgently forgotten.")

PROVIDE FOR THE COMMON DEFENSE

The nation has been defended. The United States has never lost a war where it was defending its own territories. But it has also expanded its concepts of "defense" to include the right to send troops into black ghettoes, college campuses, Vietnam, Korea, the Dominican Republic, Lebanon and Grenada; sponsor the overthrow of governments in Chile, Cuba, Guatemala and Angola; drop mines in the waters of Nicaragua; drop bombs on Libya; go to war over oil in the Persian Gulf; maintain military bases in Germany, Turkey an the Philippines; spend some 30% of the federal budget (over $300 BILLION) on military related expenditures; and stockpile enough nuclear weapons to exterminate civilization 10 to 20 times over (although once would presumably suffice). Such an expansive concept of defense probably does more to subvert "the common defense" than to enhance it.

𝔭𝔯𝔬𝔪𝔬𝔱𝔢 𝔱𝔥𝔢 𝔤𝔢𝔫𝔢𝔯𝔞𝔩 ^MOTORS 𝔴𝔢𝔩𝔣𝔞𝔯𝔢

PROMOTE THE GENERAL WELFARE

The United States is wealthy. It produced the most substantial GNP in the world. How generally this wealth is distributed is another matter, however. The United States' per capita gross domestic product is 11th among industrialized nations, it has over 30 million people in poverty, and its infant mortality rate is 22nd among nations.

𝔰𝔢𝔠𝔲𝔯𝔢 𝔱𝔥𝔢 ^MIXED 𝔟𝔩𝔢𝔰𝔰𝔦𝔫𝔤𝔰 𝔬𝔣 𝔩𝔦𝔟𝔢𝔯𝔱𝔶

SECURE THE BLESSINGS OF LIBERTY TO OURSELVES AND OUR POSTERITY

The United States does not have the liberties on paper that other documents grant. For example, the American Bill of Rights does NOT contain certain provisions set out in the U.N. Declaration of Rights (e.g., the right to a job, to form and to join trade unions, the right to rest, leisure, and a standard of living adequate for health, well-being, food, clothing, housing, medical care, and necessary social services).

But paper liberties are not the only issue, even though they are significant in educating and inspiring people to demand the dignity they deserve. What is probably more important is the question of whether the nation really practices the rights it acknowledges on paper.

The history of civil liberties across the world seems to indicate that the less threats a nation experiences, the better its record on civil liberties. Thus England, an island protected by water, has done relatively well. With its weak neighbors the United States too has done rather well. It rates highly on Amnesty International's list (except for capital punishment), and most Americans are rightly proud of the freedoms they enjoy from day to day.

Unfortunately, the record also shows that when our government feels threatened, it can flush civil liberties down the toilet at the drop of a hat (especially if it's a militant worker's hat). Like the rest of the Constitution's benefits, the extent of civil liberties depends on what the American people demand.

Future

Whether the constitution's report card at its 300th birthday will change in a better or worse direction is open to question. Some of the most pertinent observations concerning its prospective developments have come from one who ought to know, former General and President Dwight D. Eisenhower:

> *This conjunction of an immense military establishment and a large arms industry is new in the American experience. The total influence—economic, political, even spiritual—is felt in every city, every State House, every office of the Federal government . . .*
>
> *In the councils of government, we must guard against the acquisition of unwarranted influence, whether sought or unsought, by the military-industrial complex. The potential for the disastrous rise of misplaced power exists and will persit . . .*

In other words, Eisenhower feared the effects that new and growing military and economic interests might have on America's fragile Constitutional order. How might they insinuate themselves into various levels of government and so pervert its democratic components?

It seems safe to say that Eisenhower's fears were well founded. It is not hard to argue that private concentrations of power have joined with government in hopes of re-organizing the American system according to a particular line of production and consumption. In exchange for a few pleasures, ordinary people are expected to shut up and produce. Their labor is expended on military goods which (i) keep the rest of the world in line; and (ii) provide real people with nothing of what they really want or need, thus forcing them to go on working. (You can't eat guns.) The possibilities of a world based on sharing, equality, peace, and abundance is sacrificed to considerations of power and profit.

The various branches of constitutional government have not done much to arrest these trends.

Past presidents in general and Ronald Reagan in particular have not been reluctant to give the "defense industry" whatever it requests. Nor have they been circumspect in resorting to military force at any time and at any place. The Constitution still states that the executive must go to the legislature in order to declare war. Presumably this clause exists because the Constitution's Framers knew that in order for one man to put the lives and happiness of the rest of the members of the society into jeopardy, he ought to at least have the consent of their representatives. However, Congress has done little to assert such principles. It has acted as if the passing of a few post-Watergate laws was sufficient. It has ignored the fact that power must consistently and continually be called to account for itself. The net result is an American society slipping slowly into the perpetual war state envisioned by George Orwell—with all the waste, repression, and authoritarianism that this implies.

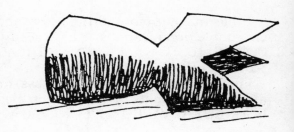

What About The Courts?

The judiciary has done little to slow these trends. Burger's Supreme Court worked hard to make it easier for the profiteers to control democratic discourse in this country, at the expense of the ordinary citizen. While it sustained the right to canvass, it also sustained the rights of newspaper owners, tv station owners, workplace owners, and shopping mall owners to keep proselytizers off their "private" property. SCHAUMBURG V. CBE (1980); MIAMI HERALD V. TORNILLO (1974); CBS V. DNC (1973); SEARS V. SAN DIEGO CARPENTERS (1978); HUDGENS V. NLRB (1976); PRUNEYARD SHOPPING CENTER V. ROBINS (1980).

On the one hand it has said that the government can restrict if not prohibit the exercise of speech in public places like phone polls and fairgrounds. COUNCIL V. VINCENT (1984); HEFRON V. ISKCON (1981). On the other hand it has said that government cannot control the speech of big corporations, even those which are publicly regulated utilities. FIRST NATIONAL BANK V. BELOTTI (1978), PACIFIC GAS & ELECTRIC V. PUC (1986).

It has made it more difficult for labor unions and progressive charitable organizations to have secure access to funding. CORNELIUS V. NAACP (1985); CHICAGO TEACHERS V. HUDSON (1986).

Finally, it has restricted Congress' means of controlling inordinate amounts of spending in election campaigns. BUCKLEY V. VALEO (1976), NCPAC V. FCC (1985).

The net result is that everybody has freedom of speech, but only the rich can use it. Therefore, whatever chance for democratic change we have under our constitutional order, the rich have the best chance of guiding it.

How the Supreme Court under the tutelage of William Rehnquist will affect the relationship of the people of the United States to their constitution is what the American people will feel about what his court does and what they will DO about their feelings. What the Court has done has always been subject to ratificiation or rejection by the American people, as evidenced, among other things, by the popular upsurges which followed after DRED SCOTT, the Depression, and BROWN.

> If in the end, we see problems in the constitutional roles played by an authoritarian executive, a lazy congress, or a dubious Rehnquist, the fault lies not only with those branches—it also lies with the American people.

What About The People? (What About You?)

Of course one other factor must be acknowledged when considering the future of our constitutional order and the role the American people play in it. If President Eisenhower missed anything when he described the new military industrial complex, it was the "mind industry." Some people have noted its existence:

The few cannot go on accumulating wealth unless they accumulate the power to manipulate the minds of the many. To expropriate manpower they have to expropriate the brain. What is being abolished in today's affluent societies, from Moscow to Los Angeles, is not exploitation, but our awareness of it...

The material pauperization of the last century is followed and replaced by the immaterial pauperization of today. Its most obvious manifestation is the decline in political options available to the citizen of the most advanced nations: a mass of political nobodies, over whose heads even collective suicide can be decreed, is opposed by an ever-decreasing number of political moguls. That this state of affairs is readily accepted and voluntarily endured is the greatest achievement of the mind industry.

—Hans Enzensberger, insightful contemporary dialectical thinker, even if he is a poet

In other words, along with the military industrial complex has grown a mind industry, to convince us that a state grounded in profits deriving from a war economy constitutes the best of all possible worlds. That the world might be better off with a little less authority and profiteering, and a little more sharing and tolerance are perspectives that seldom receive a serious hearing. The mind industry promotes militarized industrialism, and militarized industrialism pays for the mind industry's labors. The two feed on each other, and ultimately feed on the people of the world.

From the preceding it should be clear that the future prospects of the American constitutional order are not at all promising. Yet while it would be a lie to be overly optimistic, still it is wrong to be overly pessimistic. If we look at the history of constitutions (ours in particular, and constitutions in general) we will see that people have always struggled for humane systems as long as there has been oppression. They saw the power orders of their days, and had the courage to say "no" to them, and the tenacity to organize and do something to fight them. It is no accident that when history shows us constitutions changed for the better, we see behind those changes men and women who espoused certain values, and who organized and struggled to implement those values. These people included groups like the Levellers, the radical Pilgrims, the American revolutionaries, the Jeffersonian democrats, the abolitionists, the slaves who fought back, the Populists, the suffragettes, the workers who joined unions and took over factories, the civil rights activists and Vietnam protestors who took the streets. We need to remember these people and honor their memories by implementing their examples. We also need to acknowledge and support people involved in similar struggles outside the borders of the USA. If we forget any of these people, or their organizing efforts, or their struggles, we forget not only the best that is in our past and present. We also risk our future.

> *"The price of liberty is eternal vigilance."*
> —Thomas Jefferson

BIBLIOGRAPHY

For Further Reading

DOCUMENTARY ANTHOLOGIES

Hofstadter, R., ed. GREAT ISSUES IN AMERICAN HISTORY. Vols. i, ii, iii. N.Y., 1969. Documents from American history, 1584–1969.

Hofstadter, R., M. Wallace, ed. AMERICAN VIOLENCE. N.Y., 1970. Americans in their less legalistic moments.

Kenyon, C. THE ANTI-FEDERALISTS. N.Y., 1966. What Madison, Hamilton and Jay were writing against.

Kenyon, S. THE STUART CONSTITUTION. Cambridge, 1969. The legal struggles of England's 17th century.

Morison. S. THE AMERICAN REVOLUTION, 1764–1788. Oxford, 1923. Sources and documents from the revolutionary period.

ACCOUNTS FOCUSING ON LEGAL MATTERS

Abraham, H. JUSTICES & PRESIDENTS. N.Y., 1985. The politics behind the selection of every Supreme Court Justice through O'Connor.

Douglas, W. O. AUTOBIOGRAPHY. (2 vol.) N.Y., 1974, 1980. Memoirs of 36 years on the Supreme Court.

Ely, J. DEMOCRACY AND DISTRUST. Cambridge, MA, 1980. Law professor's justification of Warren Court jurisprudence.

Horwitz, M. THE TRANSFORMATION OF AMERICAN LAW, 1780–1860. Cambridge, MA, 1977. Early American law and early American capitalism.

Kairys, D., ed. THE POLITICS OF LAW. N.Y., 1982. Anthology of radical legal analyses, some less opaque than others.

Kelly, Harbison, and Belz. THE AMERICAN CONSTITUTION. N.Y., 1983. Scholarly review of the Constitution's development from its beginnings through the present.

Mason, A. THE SUPREME COURT FROM TAFT TO WARREN. Baton Rogue, LA, 1968. The Court from Reaction through innovation.

Murphy, B. THE BRANDEIS/FRANKFURTER CONNECTION. N.Y., 1982. Politics and Supreme Court Justices.

Schwartz, B. THE GREAT RIGHTS OF MANKIND. N.Y., 1977. Sources of U.S. Bill of Rights.

Tribe, L. AMERICAN CONSTITUTIONAL LAW. Mineola, N.Y., 1977. The definitive liberal treatise on Constitutional interpretation.

ACCOUNTS FOCUSING ON CONSTITUTIONAL HISTORY

Beard, C. AN ECONOMIC INTERPRETATION OF THE CONSTITUTION OF THE UNITED STATES. Beard's thesis has been qualified with years of further challenges and research, but his seminal study still defines the issues.

Friendly, F. and Elliott, M. THE CONSTITUTION: THAT DELICATE BALANCE. N.Y., 1984. The Constitution according to PBS, with all the good and bad that that entails.

Ellis, R. THE JEFFERSONIAN CRISIS. N.Y., 1971. The judiciary and the "Revolution of 1800."

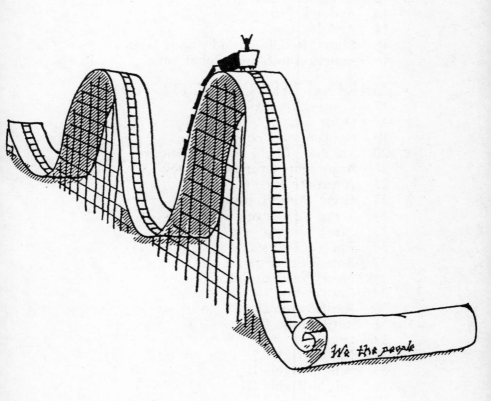

SUMMARY

ANTECEDENTS

MAKING THE CONSTITUTION

ARGUING OVER THE CONSTITUTION

WARRING OVER THE CONSTITUTION

YEARS OF REACTION

YEARS OF REFORM

REACTION REDUX

REVIEW AND PROGNOSIS

E PLURIBUS UNUM

A Calabash of Diamonds

A Calabash of Diamonds

by

MARGARET LANE
(The Countess of Huntingdon)

DUELL, SLOAN AND PEARCE

New York

To JACK

WITH LOVE

CONTENTS

ILLUSTRATIONS

following page 54

A Calabash of Diamonds

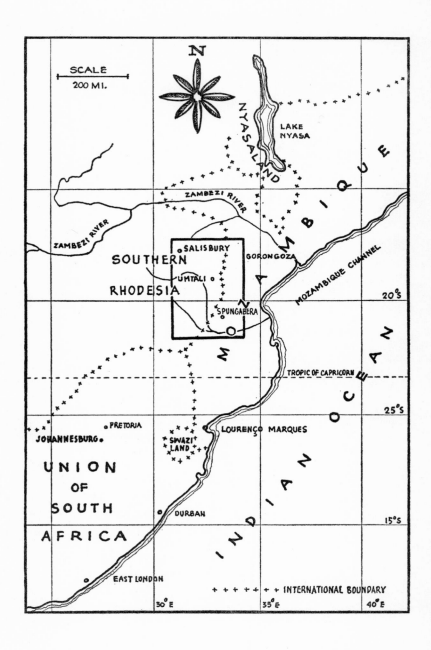

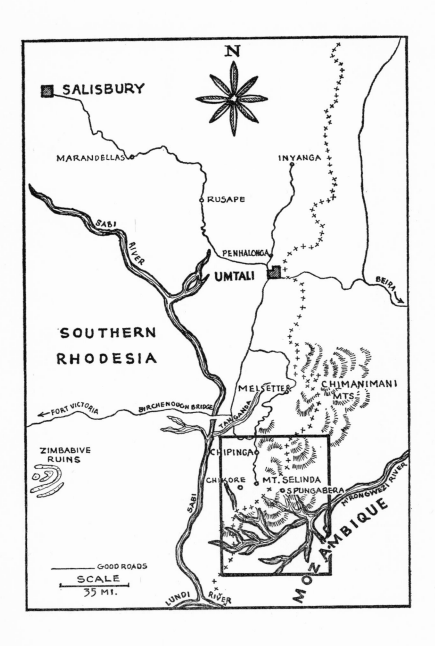

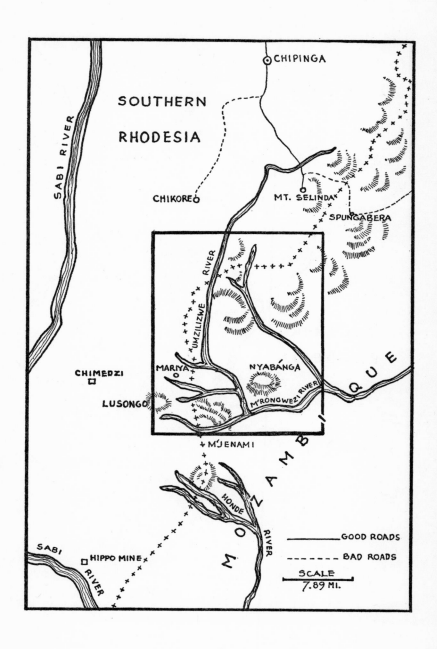

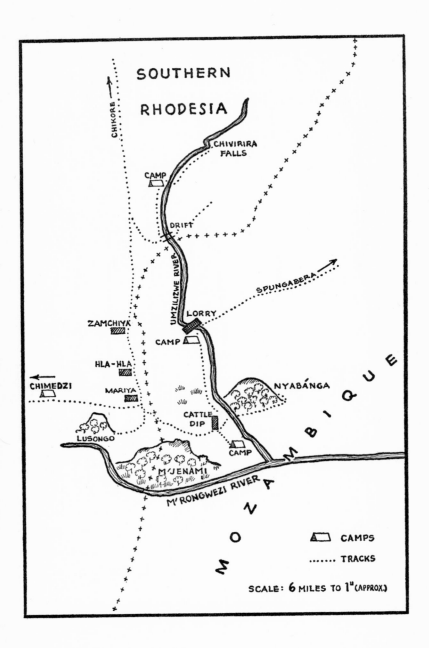

1

RUSSELL'S NARRATIVE

A GOOD many years ago, long before we had met one another, my husband was told the story of a buried treasure and given, by a man who believed he had not long to live, a written narrative and a map.

This man was a solitary hard-bitten sort of adventurer, of whose origins I know nothing. His name was Samuel Russell, and at the time I speak of he was living on the island of Moorea in the South Seas, married to a Polynesian wife, and making a modest living from vanilla and copra. Before the First World War he had been a prospector in various parts of Africa, travelling on foot and horseback in search of gold and other profitable minerals and penetrating far into undeveloped territories. He had worked up and down the eastern border of Southern Rhodesia and into the plains and hills of Mozambique, panning for gold in rivers and scratching up the earth, living off the country in the resourceful hand-to-mouth fashion at which he was adept. He had nearly died at one time of malaria and other diseases, and had left Africa, as he thought, for a while, intending to go back; but the war had intervened, and he had had other adventures, and was now too old and sick to believe he would ever return. He died, indeed, not long after.

Jack, whom I later married, had fallen in love with the

island of Moorea in the course of an erratic and leisurely voyage home from Australia, and had bought a house on the beach, built of white coral, and a small copra plantation, and was living happily in that gentle paradise with the sense of unplanned life stretching endlessly ahead, which sanguine temperaments enjoy in their early twenties. Russell, who at that time was getting on for sixty, was his neighbour, and they spent much time together. The friendship prospered, and some time before Jack gave up his life on the lagoon and came back to England, Russell, who had no son and knew that he was now too old to finish the adventure, wrote down for him all he remembered of the story and site of a buried treasure, one of the many under the soil of Africa, which he himself had failed to find, but which he firmly believed existed, guarded by powerful taboos and by the peculiar hazards of the country. He impressed on him the difficult nature of the search and the necessity of secrecy. "You're young," he said. "One day perhaps you will find yourself in Africa, and will be able to try your luck." It seemed unlikely, but possible; and what young man is indifferent to the sort of adventure Russell appeared to offer? Jack accepted the written narrative and a map roughly drawn on a scrap of paper. He put them away in a box and locked it, with the feeling that someday, somewhere, this esoteric knowledge might come in useful. He did not really believe he would ever search, but it was a satisfying thing to have under lock and key. The box eventually went back with him to England, where the papers lay undisturbed for thirty years.

Russell's narrative, which I have before me, soiled and frayed by much handling and by the red-brown dust of Mozambique which gets into everything, can be divided into three parts; and it will be easiest to consider these separately,

since the narrative itself follows no plan and moves backward and forward in time, confusingly enough. There is the story of how Russell first came to hear of the treasure; his account of its nature and history so far as he was able to discover them; and his own determined but frustrated attempt to find it, which seems to have taken place (he is bad at dates) about the year 1910.

At that time he was one of a trio of prospectors, working in partnership and living by what they found, like innumerable other forgotten pioneers. The names of the other two were Bullock and McAlly. Of Bullock we know nothing beyond the fact that his initials were E. S., that he was known as Ned, and that he had a brother Bob who for a time was associated with the venture. Of McAlly, Russell recorded nothing but that he was "a big New Zealander." They were in that eastern-most part of Southern Rhodesia where the Sabi, a huge river running almost directly north and south through sand dunes and swamp, is joined by the Lundi at a point that touches the frontier of Mozambique. They were working slowly north, sometimes on one side of the border, sometimes on the other. (There is nothing, even today, in that wilderness of bush and rock and scrub-covered hills to show where Rhodesia ends and Portuguese East Africa, or Mozambique, to give it its Portuguese name, begins.) They were travelling on horseback and on foot, with African bearers and a number of pack animals, making camp wherever the ground looked promising for their purpose, and then moving on.

At an unnamed native village they were asked for medicine for a sick woman, and were surprised to find, lying in one of the thatched huts, a handsome Zulu girl of proud appearance, who was alone there among a strange people, nearly a thousand miles from home. Now this is not Zulu country; the people are called Vandau and are an undistinguished branch of the

Mashona tribe. Nevertheless in this particular area there is a fairly strong admixture of Zulu blood, due to a small migration in the nineteenth century, as we shall see presently; and this girl had come from far-away Natal with her father, apparently on a search for lost relations. She was now stranded, her father having died in this strange country, and was being nursed kindly enough by the local people, who recognised her quality and told the travellers that she was of noble birth, related to a chief. As pioneers they had a rough knowledge of medicine, and while they carried out their prospecting in this area Ned Bullock treated the girl as best he could, not yet aware of the nature of her malady. After a time she seemed to recover, and eventually he persuaded her to go with him, as his mistress.

She seems to have been a remarkable creature, dignified, gentle, and handsome, as many Zulu women are; she remained devoted to Bullock until her death. None of the three men bothered with her real name. At the first encounter they had nicknamed her "the Countess" because of her air of breeding, and the Countess she remained, accepting the change of name with perfect dignity.

Some time after this (I do not know how long) the Countess confided to Bullock a Zulu secret, which she had learned before her father's death when they had been living together among the border tribes. Somewhere in the area, she did not know precisely where, a great treasure was buried, in a place known to the Zulu elders of the region. How it came to be there, and what it was, was an involved story. It was proper that her father, as a Zulu dignitary of high rank, should have been entrusted with this knowledge, but the Countess's information was fragmentary, picked up from scraps of the old man's conversation. Russell's narrative contains a rough account of this story as he and Bullock gradually pieced it to-

gether. He gives no details, but the main facts correspond to the little that is certainly known from Zulu history.

In 1837 a Zulu chief named Umgila, one of the many who flourished precariously under Dingaan (murderer and successor of the great Chaka), was engaged in a private war with his brother, who disputed his right to the chieftainship. After a long struggle Umgila was defeated and finally driven north out of Zulu territory. He led his followers by degrees for about six hundred miles, eventually settling among the Mashona people of Gazaland, on the Longwegi River. Some say that he conquered this peaceable branch of the Mashona, others that he came with only a small body of men and a great number of women, widows of his dead warriors. At all events he established himself there in authority, and his followers intermarried with the natives, producing a mixed race who called themselves Mashangana. These people were proud of their Zulu blood and aped Zulu customs, but were, according to Russell, far inferior to their warlike ancestors.

Umgila lived to a great age. The date of his death is not recorded, but Russell was certain it could not have been earlier than 1890. He died possessed of great riches, in cattle, gold, ivory, and diamonds. The diamonds came from the Kimberley mines in Griqualand, which were opened in 1870 and developed their fabulous wealth under Cecil Rhodes. Native labour was drawn from many parts of Africa, and Umgila annually sent his quota of men. For many years large gangs of Mashangana would travel on foot the hundreds of miles to Kimberley, work for a spell of six months or a year, and come back with their earnings and possessions packed in a small tin trunk, which was carried on the head. In those early days it was easy for a native digger to conceal an uncut stone and bring it away, and Umgila made it a rule that each of his men should bring him at least one diamond. In this way, at

some risk to his miners but no trouble to himself, he amassed a considerable treasure. He was already rich in ivory, and his wage-earning men brought him tribute in English gold; but the detail with which the Countess electrified her hearers was that he had died possessed of a fair-sized calabash of diamonds.

This, in accordance with Zulu custom, was buried with him, together with his weapons, his drinking vessels, and everything else of value that he owned. The site of the grave would be kept secret and would also be sacred, a place of reverence and fear for several generations. Nevertheless, at this time there must still have been many of the older men of Zulu blood who knew where it was, and it was possible that the grave might still be marked by some observance. There would probably be a mound, with a planted tree on top, and on ceremonial occasions a pot of native beer would be carried to the place and left beneath the tree to propitiate his spirit.

Russell does not say whether the Countess originally told them this story with the idea of helping them to find Umgila's treasure. Most probably she did not; she was a Zulu and, like most Africans to this day, would regard the opening of a grave as the most dangerous impiety possible to commit, a desecration inviting terrible revenge. But she had cast in her lot with Bullock and was dependent on her new life, different in thought and habit from all she had known, and so, one supposes, was open to persuasion. She agreed to help them, and for many months, Russell says, of secret and patient enquiry they worked their way up and down Umgila's territory, ostensibly busy with nothing but mineral prospecting, but in reality searching for clues and information.

Their plan, at first, was to prepare the Countess for an expedition without them, since it would have been natural for her as a Zulu to ask to be shown the chief's grave, to pray

to his spirit and scatter a handful of earth. Also they well
knew that she would have a better chance of gathering information if she were not accompanied by white men, always
objects of suspicion, to whom no sacred thing may ever, in
any circumstances, be shown. But by the time their plans
were ready the Countess's malady, which they now knew to
be consumption, took a turn for the worse, and she was too
ill to travel.

Russell is vague about dates, but it seems that the partners
set off on their search without her in 1910 or '11. Making their
way through Rhodesian territory, they crossed the Mozambique border at a point which Russell calls "Mandhlami's
kraal," struck south to the Longwegi River, and followed its
course until they found, without much difficulty, the site of
Umgila's deserted kraal, which was on the south bank and still
identifiable. This was in the dry season, between March and
October, when the rivers are low and for the most part
easily forded. The kraal had been abandoned after the Chief's
death, and was still not too thickly overgrown for them to be
able to distinguish the floor of the principal hut, made, according to custom, of beaten ant-heap smeared with bullock's
dung and blood, a mixture which dries almost to the hardness
of cement. The huts had been built in straight lines in a square
enclosure bordered with planted trees. The trees were now
old and of a good size, forming three sides of the square,
which was completed by the river. Even at this season the
water was deep here, forming a long, beautiful, and shady
pool where Umgila's wives, "the old queens," used to bathe.

Russell and Bullock had convinced themselves, from all
they had learned of Zulu custom, that the chief was probably
buried under the floor of his hut, or in the courtyard surrounding it. He would be lying not more than six feet down,
in a chamber roofed with wood and stones, perhaps lying

on the bodies of the slaves who had dug the grave. Russell could not remember why they had been so much obsessed with the certainty of this idea, for the burial of a chief under his own hut, though common, was by no means invariable. The Countess had said only that he *might* be there; she had no positive knowledge. They accordingly made their camp beside the river and criss-crossed the floor of the hut and courtyard with trenches to a depth of about six feet, without result. It was not an encouraging dig, for, as he wrote, "To us, accustomed to mining, it was quite obvious that the natural stratification of the alluvial pebble beds and formation beneath had never been interfered with."

Their next attempt was made at the foot of a large tree at some distance from the chief's hut, but still within the confines of the kraal. Here the grass had been carefully cleared, and in the roots of the tree stood a clay pot with the stale remains of sour-smelling native beer. These were promising signs, but when they had wasted a further day in digging the ground they learned from the local natives (who as always were never far away, uneasily watchful) that this had been a favourite sitting place of the old chief's, and was therefore a place for honouring his spirit. They next, rather desperately, dug up the whole kraal, which must have taken many days of hard labour, but found nothing for their pains but the grave of a woman, containing bones and some beads of an ancient pattern.

At this point, exasperated by the impossibility of getting the truth from any of the local natives, they inveigled the headman of a nearby village to the kraal and strung him up to a branch of Umgila's tree. This reckless action produced an important clue, which at the time, however, they failed to profit by. When the man had been hanging long enough to be near death, and in a suitable state of terror, they offered to

cut him down on condition that he would tell them where Umgila was buried. On being released, however, he was unable to tell them anything coherent. All he could do was to point away to the north and pour out a flood of choking speech in which one word was many times repeated, *kya-banga,* a word which made no sense to any of them. "Fearing," says Russell mildly, "that perhaps we had carried matters a bit too far, we let him go." Clearly they had not improved their chances with the natives.

A series of misfortunes now beset them which must have convinced the onlookers that Umgila's spirit was moving towards revenge. The three men sickened at the same time with malaria, and for a time could neither pursue their search nor move on. Their resistance was low, for at this latter end of the dry season the country was burned to a cinder and there were no pumpkins or other fresh vegetables to be had, with which they normally varied their meat diet. They were living wholly on such meat as they could shoot, and the remains of dried biltong that they carried with them. They were tormented by thirst, and made matters worse by drinking great quantities of the river water, which gave them dysentery and weakened them still further. (They later learned that the local natives did not drink this water but fetched every drop from a stream two miles further north; but by the time they discovered this the damage was done.) Their own natives, too, were suffering from the water and in a state of terror at being involved in the digging up of graves. The three men, sick as they were, had to take it in turn to watch them night and day, for it was only too evident that at the slightest relaxation of discipline they would down tools and disappear into the bush, leaving them with no choice but to abandon their gear. This decided them to pull out of the unwholesome area while they still had the strength, and to

return after the long rains, when conditions might be improved and their own health better.

Accordingly they set out, as soon as they could, in a northerly direction, to climb by degrees into wooded and hilly country, where the air is cool at night and the mosquitoes are fewer. No sooner did they leave Umgila's neighbourhood, however, than a new trouble broke out among their carriers. They complained that the trail was "heavy" and showed a great unwillingness to follow it, throwing down their packs, demanding rest, and proposing trails at random in other directions. The three pushed on, however, disregarding the protests of the natives as only men can who carry rifles; and before long were in the high veldt, making slow progress across a series of hills and valleys towards the Rhodesian border.

It was on this part of the trail, Russell says, that he overhead the word *kyabanga* in the conversation of two of his carriers, but being languid with malaria at the time, attached no great importance to it. They fell silent in any case as soon as they noticed he was near. He and the Bullock brothers were by this time so "saturated with malaria" that they had neither heart nor energy for anything new, and were concentrating on getting alive and without further mishap out of this part of the country. It was not until much later (he does not say when or where) that Russell fell in with an old Zulu bullock driver who had spent some time in Umgila's country, and who innocently told him, when asked, that the word *kyabanga* did not *mean* anything, so far as he knew, but was the name of a hill where a great chief was buried. From his description it seemed that the trail which Russell had taken into the high veldt must have passed very near this hill, which would therefore be only a few miles away from Umgila's old kraal, in a northeasterly direction. This was important news,

but it had come too late. The partners were in no condition to continue the search; their money had run out, and they would have to recover financially as well as physically before they could hope to return to Mozambique.

They decided to break up their partnership for a time, always intending, later, to renew the search; but this was not to be. Ned Bullock went off to Gadzema to the Grant mine, taking the Countess with him, and it was not long before she died of tuberculosis in Hartley Hospital, and so passes out of our story. McAlly had some time before this gone off to Nigeria to look for tin, and was never heard of again. Bob Bullock, being married, decided that he must have nothing more to do with risky adventures; he settled down in Penhalonga near Umtali.

Before anything further could be done, the 1914 war had broken out, and this made a gap of several years in which Ned Bullock and Russell were both away from Africa. Ned Bullock died of shell shock after the war, and it seems that Russell himself never found money or opportunity to return. How he came to end his days in the Pacific, living at ease with a handsome Tahitian wife, I do not know; but as a final scene it fits well enough with his tough and at the same time easy-going character.

2

THE COVER STORY

THIS, then, was the story that was first told to me ten years ago, as a curious footnote to one of Jack's occasional tales of the South Seas. He never dwells on personal reminiscence, and has an economical, half-diffident way of bringing out, when pressed, the most surprising and recondite information. It was so with this story of Russell and the African treasure. We had been married a number of years and it had never been mentioned—whole areas of chequered life lay between that period and this—and now the box was unearthed and Russell's map and narrative dropped in my lap by Jack, almost with an air of astonishment at my interest. We read it together, not stopping to disentangle the confused threads but swallowing it whole—the old chief in his grave, the Countess, the pioneers, the uneasy natives, and, at the heart of it, hidden in the dark of an airless cavity among ivory and bones, the calabash of diamonds. How big was a calabash, I wanted to know? They varied; they were commonly used for fetching and ladling water, and were carried on the head. As big as this? Or that? One couldn't tell. At all events a calabash was a notable thing to have filled with uncut stones.

We brooded luxuriously on the story, never for a moment seeing it as being in any way connected with ourselves but enjoying it for its own sake. It was simply a richly romantic

thing to possess and dwell upon. If only Jack could have gone in Russell's lifetime, we said, staring at one another. If only we knew some adventurous young man who had none of our ties and preoccupations and could embrace the adventure. We gazed at the map again—such a hopelessly scant little scrawl, yet, somehow, authentic—and turned once more to the closely written pages. "To sum the thing up," Russell had written, towards the end, "the evidence for the existence of the treasure is, for one who is as well acquainted with African customs and languages as I am, overwhelming. What then are the chances of successfully locating the francs? * In this connection it must be remembered that the natives of the locality, whilst by no means hostile, would not respond to direct enquiry even if they knew anything. . . . The plan of action must be decided on the spot. My opinion is that there is an even chance of success for a man of the right sort, who is out for an adventure anyhow, and is patient and observant. . . . Local information should be sought for the best route to take as the tracks may be improved since my time. Best to take out a mining licence in P.E.A.,† and then there is no kick coming and no suspicion. The real object should, it goes without saying, be kept dead secret. Beware especially of Native Commissioners and their spies."

It did not sound as though it had anything to do with us, but we spent some pleasant evenings wishing that it had. It seemed sad to let such a secret wither unused. Russell and Bullock were both dead; McAlly had disappeared years ago; it was unlikely that he could be still alive. Of Bob Bullock, the brother, Russell knew only that he had settled in Penhalonga, and if alive could "give some information that may help, as he has, I believe, my diary of the trip; anyhow he

* treasure, loot.
† Portuguese East Africa.

knows the country and can give valuable advice. So far as I am aware the rest of the world knows nothing."

I think our feeling at this time, apart from sheer pleasure in possessing such a story, was regret that there was no younger, more adventurous man to whom we could confide it. It was not a secret to be lightly given away, for, quite apart from the hazard of the thing and the complications that sprang up thick as briars as we discussed it, Russell had bequeathed this information with great seriousness, frankly weighing the chances, as one might bequeath an attractive but highly dubious investment. It was a nice present to give a younger brother, if we had had one; but we had not; and we finally concluded that the only person whom we could remotely imagine undertaking the search was Jack's only nephew, Peter Cameron.

Some time passed before we were able to tell him anything. I think at the time he was still in West Africa or the Solomon Islands, pursuing a modest but promising career in the Colonial Service. He had had an adventurous war, had made some enterprising journeys in different parts of the world, and was regarded by us as tough, intelligent, and in certain perfectly congenial and unimportant respects, slightly dotty. He was thirty years old and physically strong, and we could just imagine him setting off on his own one day to look for Umgila's treasure.

On one of his leaves we told him the story under promise of secrecy, and found that we had not been wrong in supposing that he would be stirred by it. He yearned over it, as we had done, and with the same regret. How could he raise the money for such a venture? Besides, he was newly married and had his career to consider. We observed with regret that Peter was settling down. Still, we spent an enjoyable evening with Russell's map and an atlas, in that intoxicating sort of discus-

sion which the very notion of difficult travel induces, and
parted for the night in an atmosphere of conspiracy and blood-
brotherhood, soothed by the reflection that if things were
different, and life more as it ought to be, we three would
have been off to Africa in the morning.

As it was, things being as they are and life what it is, the
map and the narrative were put away again and given no
further thought for another eight years.

How it came about that in the spring of 1958 we began
to think of the possibility of going to Africa ourselves, I am
no longer clear on. We had been unsettled and bemused by a
journey to the Far East the year before, and were thirsting
to try some new continent that neither of us had seen. Except
that Jack had spent some weeks with Alec Waugh in Tangier,
we had neither of us so much as set foot in Africa; and the
more we considered this, the more our thoughts turned to
Mozambique, and the unimaginable territory of which we
knew nothing beyond the spidery lines of Russell's map. The
thing, I believe, that most provoked and stimulated us was our
ignorance. For all we knew, the treasure might have been
discovered years ago; Jack remembered that Russell had
said, in discussing this possibility, that some time in the
nineteen-twenties a mysterious quantity of uncut diamonds
had appeared on the market, which nobody could account
for, and which had made him wonder. Then, supposing that
it was still there, how did one set about searching for such
a thing? We had no idea what the country was like, beyond
that, from Russell's description, we assumed that it was
difficult. We had only the haziest idea of where it was. We
did not know how to get there, or what would be the best
procedure when one arrived. What we should need, if ever
we decided to go, was good advice, and this, because of the

necessity of secrecy, was clearly the one essential we could not have.

The more we thought of it, the more tantalising the whole thing became, finally resolving itself into a single question: why should we not try? If we did not go, it was more than unlikely that anyone ever would, for so far as we knew there was no European alive who had heard of the treasure but Peter and ourselves. Perhaps it was already too late. It was more than forty years since Russell had made his attempt, and there was no knowing whether any of his clues were still valid or the places recognisable. If we did not go soon we should never go, for it was not the sort of adventure for late middle-age. In any case, was it the kind of enterprise in which we *ought* to be involved? I am afraid we brushed this consideration aside. The lure of treasure is too strong for any but characters more disciplined than ours.

We began to study atlases and bought a large-scale map of southern Africa. This, to our surprise, told us almost nothing. We could see the Sabi River running like a strong artery down Rhodesia, and the point at which, among fringes of swamp, the Lundi joined it; but as soon as the eye travelled further east into Mozambique, it lost itself in a desert of blank paper. We applied to several of those beautiful map shops whose windows, baited with terrestrial globes and ordnance survey maps in leather cases, delay one so pleasantly in walking about London; but none of them, it seemed, could furnish us with a map of Mozambique. Faintly exasperated by this apparent inefficiency, we went next to the library of the Royal Geographical Society, and here it was borne in upon us for the first time that details of this part of the Portuguese hinterland were perhaps not to be found on any map. Maps of Rhodesia turned blank and pale as soon as they came to the border; the Portuguese had mapped the developed coastal area with thor-

oughness, and had left the remote interior alone. In some maps a network of rivers appeared, unnamed. In others, a few names were to be found, but the rivers were unaccountably running in other directions. In no two maps did the names of the rivers agree. Gingerly, and assuming innocuous geographical expressions, we approached the Portuguese Embassy, and after parrying a great many courteously inquisitive questions were told that they had no maps of this area at present. The proper department would have them in Lisbon, no doubt. They could be sent for. We gratefully made arrangements for this to be done, but days and weeks passed and nothing came.

We now realised with some alarm that if we were to have any hope of keeping our motive secret we had got to invent a plausible cover story. People who contemplate making an African journey are invariably questioned, usually with goodwill, sometimes with a curiosity that is very like suspicion. Was there a political motive behind our idea? Why were we interested in this particular territory? We had been told that the Portuguese are inclined to be sensitive about their African colonies. They welcome tourists to Beira, to the Gorongoza Game Reserve, and to the Indian Ocean resorts along the coast; but they do not care to have foreigners poking about and going where they choose. We were several times asked at the Embassy, was it our intention to write articles? We gathered the impression that, if this had been our aim, it would have met with skilled discouragement.

Nor was it any use, we found, explaining ourselves by saying we were going on safari. A very few enquiries among people who had indulged in this costly pastime convinced us that, if this had been so, we should never have given a thought to this part of the map. We should be going, of course, to Kenya or Tanganyika, hiring American cars and camping

equipment and taking a White Hunter. That was what every-body did. That was the way to shoot game, with gun or camera. It cost a good deal, of course, but you had marvellous servants and finger bowls at dinner. It had been brought to a fine art and was very comfortable. Nobody, said the few who knew anything about it, went down to the area we were vaguely indicating on the map. Wasn't it a malarial and tsetse fly area? Hadn't the game been systematically shot out by the Rhodesian Government, and wasn't it in any case primi-tive and nasty? We found that the best reply was to ask for guidance, and to receive with patience a great deal of in-formation about parts of Africa we did not want to go to.

The need for a cover story became urgent, for without one we plainly saw we should get nowhere, or at least not to the places we wished to see. It could be eccentric, but it had got to be innocuous and sufficiently convincing to allay sus-picion. This was not easy, and when we had invented our tale we were tormented by the doubt that between us we ought to have been able to think of a better one. However, we could not. It had got to have some element of truth in it, to account for our searching, and we finally hit on the simple expedient of using the topographical part of Russell's story and chang-ing Russell himself into my uncle.

Now, my mother had had a strange and ne'er-do-well step-uncle, who had attracted her greatly as a child, and with whose shady adventures she had long ago regaled me. He had been in prison once, which was a great scandal, and had wandered about the world in an undesirable way, and had been eventu-ally killed, I believe, in the South African War. I remember little about him beyond the fact that, on the rare occasions when he came home to roost, he used to stand on his head to amuse my mother, and that when he did this, a gold sover-eign always rolled out of his pocket. This was attractive; also

the fact that he was much disapproved of in the family for his boon companions, with whom he used to sing in harmony when he came home late, taking off his shoes to cross the shadows in the street as though they had been streams. There was also a dark suggestion that there had been something irregular even about his death; that he had been shot for desertion or some other misdemeanour, instead of in the proper manner, facing the Boers. My mother had remembered him fondly, with indulgence for his faults, and it seemed quite fitting that we should change him into the brother she had never had, and give him the adventures that had befallen Russell.

This, then, was the story with which we armed ourselves. My mother had had a favourite brother who had been an adventurer. He had spent some years pioneering in southern Africa, and had written my mother a series of interesting letters. These letters, with some of his old diaries of travel, had come to me after her death; and since my uncle had been a character, and the letters had a period interest and were amusing, I had been taken with the notion of following up some of his travels and writing an account of him. It was, in short, a pious task that I had set myself; one which we hoped no one was likely to investigate too closely.

This step taken, and a copy of Russell's narrative made and his map traced, we turned our attention to other practical matters. It was hard to know where to begin. Our ignorance of Africa was so complete that merely to look at the map brought on a feeling of almost panic helplessness. We were beginning to see that the journey we had in mind was less likely to be a trip than an expedition, and we had no idea of equipping an expedition, nor of what we should need, nor how we should set about it. Advice was what we must

have, and fortified by my uncle and his imaginary letters we
cast about for the best way of obtaining it.

It happened that Jack had years ago known a handsome
and resourceful Austrian who at one period of his life had
earned his living in Africa as a White Hunter. A White
Hunter can be roughly defined as a man skilled in the ways
of game and methods of hunting it, who for a high fee professionally takes charge of safaris, organizes the camping arrangements, directs the native servants, and provides his
clients with sport and excitement in conditions of reasonable
safety. It would, of course, be invaluable for us to be accompanied by such a man, but then there was the difficult
question: what should we tell him? He would be professionally interested in big game, and there might be little or
none in our special area. He would be the greatest help in
finding our way about, for he would presumably have some
knowledge of native languages, but how could we take him
with us without telling him the whole story? We knew
enough of the law of treasure-trove to be pretty certain that
if ever we found the treasure, whatever we did with it was
bound to be illegal. The laws relating to buried treasure vary
slightly from country to country, but they have one attribute
in common: they are always unfavourable and discouraging
to the trover. In most countries you must declare your find-
ings immediately to the police and hand over the whole treasure to the government. This applies, with variations, even to
treasure found on land owned by yourself, and is unqualified
in respect of treasure in foreign territory. Any attempt to
remove and keep such treasure would be not only difficult
but a penal offence, and we had glanced obliquely at the possibility that if we should try to smuggle anything out of
Mozambique (let alone what we did with it afterwards) we
might well end up inside a Portuguese prison. In the Union

of South Africa the possession of an undeclared uncut diamond is in itself illegal; and indeed the laws relating to diamonds all over the world are uniformly punitive and disagreeable.

It could therefore be only with the greatest caution that we could think of taking a partner into our enterprise. It would be better to have none: but how far should we get without one, with our lack of native languages, our total ignorance? In the end we wrote guardedly to our Austrian, knowing him to have been an adventurous man in his youth, and asked him whether he would be interested in joining us on a little expedition, and, if so, what was likely to be the cost? He replied, amiably enough, that he probably could manage it, though he did not know the part of Africa we mentioned, nor its languages, and had never heard that it was remarkable for game. He strongly recommended Kenya or Tanganyika. He also added, considerately, that he supposed we knew that the fees of a White Hunter for two months (the period we had guessed at) would be extremely high, even if we enlisted one on the spot, and that in his case there would be an additional expense, two hundred pounds or more, of a first-class return air fare between Mozambique and Austria. He suggested as an economical alternative that we should apply to a cousin of his, who was a travel and safari agent in Salisbury, Southern Rhodesia, and who would, he was sure, be able to fit us out with all we needed and no doubt be able to provide us with native servants who would act as interpreters. In any case, he thought it a good idea that we should learn some Portuguese, and he sent us his blessing.

We were grateful for this advice though we found it discouraging, for the more we learned the more obvious it became that we could not undertake the expedition alone. I think my chief apprehension was that Jack, who has been

known to break a leg in the most improbable circumstances, would damage himself, or get ill, or be bitten by a snake; and how should I cope with this emergency, possibly miles out in the bush, with no one to turn to but strange and perhaps disgruntled African servants? We needed at least a second man, but a strange White Hunter was, for various reasons, out of the question. He would formidably send up the cost, and how could we know, starting blind, that we could trust him? Supposing he downed tools when the moment of truth arrived and refused to have anything further to do with it? Supposing we were successful in our search, and he judged it more prudent or profitable to report us to the authorities? Supposing he just went off with the swag, leaving us alone in the jungle, secure in the knowledge that there was nothing whatever that we could do about it? It did not bear thinking of.

Our thoughts at this point turned again to Peter Cameron. He had left the Colonial Service some years ago and was now settled with a growing family, farming in Gloucestershire. True he would not know any of the native languages of our part of Africa, but he was tough, resourceful, and, what was even more important, one of us. We made a pretext for fetching him up to London and rather timidly outlined our scatterbrained idea. To our pleased surprise (for by this time we were so conscious of the daydream nature of the enterprise that we expected him to laugh at it) he responded at once, and before we knew what had happened we were all three of us on the floor again with maps, all talking together, thumbing through Russell's narrative, calculating wet and dry seasons, and whether Peter could safely leave the hay to his foreman if he were not back for the harvest. I remember that Peter's farming experience, which was not yet very extensive, fortified us extremely. He was used to driving

a Land Rover, and would, he said, go to Solihull for the three days' engineering course, in which they taught one to drive down chasms and through rivers and mud and to take the engine to pieces efficiently afterwards. He gave us the idea, too, that we might be able to buy some sort of detector, which would give us a clue to gold hidden underground and so save a great deal of trouble. Mine-detectors had been used with success in the war and were easy to carry, and Peter himself had a similar appliance, which he used on his cows, that told him whenever they had swallowed nails or had fencing wire in their stomachs.

This seemed an idea worth following, and so, while Peter undertook to discover whether the War Office had detailed maps of our territory, and Jack investigated the laws of treasure-trove with a discreet legal acquaintance, I went off in simple hope to South Kensington, to the Geological Museum, to try and get information about gold-detectors. We were not so sanguine as to suppose that a machine existed for detecting buried diamonds, but there *had* been a paragraph in the *Times* about a man who claimed to have invented an electric divining-rod that detected practically all metals, to say nothing of rubber and other uninteresting substances; and Russell had said that Umgila's hoard had included a good deal of gold, which might give us the signal we needed. The only difficulty was: what reason could I give for desiring this information? The keepers of departments in museums are usually helpful and will take trouble to satisfy serious enquiries; but they like to know what the information is for and why you want it. On the way to the museum I made up another story.

My nephew, I told the presence behind the desk, had a small farm, on which ancient coins of no great value had been occasionally turned up by the plough. This had given him

the idea (we exchanged indulgent smiles) that he might one day with luck uncover a hoard, and it was my intention to give him a modest metal-detector as a birthday present. Did such things exist? It must of course be portable and, preferably, not expensive. I entertained, I said, no extravagant hopes that he would ever be successful, but it was an interesting hobby and I wished to contribute to it. The presence shook his head. He knew of no device, he said, that reacted electrically to nonferrous metals. Iron was easy, the army mine-detector was the thing for that; but copper and gold, that was a different matter. Archaeologists would all be glad of a treasure-detector, and the Americans were said to be doing research on these lines; but so far nothing had been produced, and he was of the opinion that if anything so specialised were ever perfected it would be proportionately expensive. He roamed about over his bookshelves and searched for information in several volumes. They were full of helpful advice about iron, but had nothing to say about searching for Roman coins. The only method, he said, was to remove the earth skin by skin as an archaeologist does, and this was clearly no pastime to suggest to a busy farmer.

What about dowsing, I asked? This was a practice I knew nothing about from experience, but had so often been told by believers that it worked, and was an unpredictable gift possessed by many, that I would like to know what geologists thought about it. Would it be worth trying our luck with a hazel twig, just in case? The expert shook his head again and smiled. Official science, he said, took no cognisance of dowsing. There was a society of dowsers in existence (he wrote down its address) and he would not be prepared to say that there was nothing in it; but his own view was that successful dowsers were also, whether they admitted it or not, good amateur geologists, who knew from the geological

formation where water was most likely to be found and therefore frequently found it. If the dowsers' society could supply a diviner who specialised in copper or gold, it would be interesting to let him walk over the fields in question. He himself, however, would be bound to regard the experiment as being roughly on the same level as fortunetelling. I left him with a private resolve that I would try out a hazel twig myself when I had the opportunity; but I could not see us taking a dowser to Africa.

3

WE SET OUT

THE expedition now began to take shape; we planned to leave England at the end of April. We had sought advice from one or two acquaintances who had had experience of Africa, and now had a fair idea of what we needed and what we could afford. Our preparations were still based on guesswork, for the curious anomaly persisted that nobody could tell us anything about the terrain. Nobody, it seemed, knew anything about the Mozambique side of the Southern Rhodesian border, and our Portuguese advice was to leave that part of the country alone as being of no interest. The official Rhodesian handbooks we consulted spoke always optimistically (and to us ominously) of "development." The country was being opened up; millions of pounds were to be spent on this or that; roads and schools and hospitals were mentioned; the climate was recommended. We began to fear that when we arrived, with all the impedimenta of an expedition, we should find ourselves perhaps in a garden suburb, with Umgila sealed off under an asphalt playground. This would be the worst blow of all and so disgusting a possibility that we refused to consider it. Besides, in spite of the handbooks, there was still the enigmatic blankness of the maps and the total absence of firsthand information. There was nothing to do but to prepare ourselves for the sort of country

Russell had described and to hope that the intervening years had not brought about some ludicrous transformation.

Hearing that we planned to go where there might be no roads to speak of and that the country was said to be swampy, the Land Rover Company recommended two long-wheelbase vehicles equipped with a powerful winch and hauling gear, so that whichever got into difficulties could be pulled out by the other. We three could travel in one and our native driver and African servants in the other; vehicles of this type would be long enough to sleep in. On the other hand, a distinguished and kindly explorer whom we questioned was of the opinion that we were never likely to be out of reach of an hotel, or at least a rest camp. We could go in hired American cars and do the thing comfortably. He added, however, that this was merely his view of the probability; he had never been in that part of Africa and did not know the country.

The agent at Salisbury, written to at length, was more practical. He had no information about the Portuguese territory but, judging by the Sabi River area on the Rhodesian side, advised us to take a short-base Land Rover and a four-ton diesel lorry; and he undertook to buy these secondhand to save expense. He would provide tents and camping equipment, including a refrigerator, and basic supplies sufficient for two months. As to African servants, the smallest number he thought we could manage with was three, and these he would have waiting for us in Salisbury. They would be of unimpeachable character and would speak English. He did not think we would need the picks and shovels we had disingenuously mentioned as an essential part of the Land Rover's equipment. He thought it more important to have a snake-bite outfit.

All this was beginning to sound luxurious, but he made it clear that, by safari standards, our ideas were humble. Did we

really not wish for a White Hunter? An extra bearer, perhaps, to carry the guns? An African driver? We replied that we would do the driving ourselves and that one of us at least would have some practical knowledge of the motors. Unlike most expeditions, ours was to be a self-supporting venture. We were not making a film, we were not backed by a petrol company or any other advertiser, and we were not rich. The correspondence made us vaguely uneasy.

As a concession to me, who longed for the new experience of a south-bound voyage, it was settled that Jack and I should travel to Cape Town by sea, and that Peter, leaving a fortnight later, would fly to Salisbury. There we would spend a few days fitting out, buying boots and bush shirts and anything else we needed. We would have time on the voyage to make lists of necessities, to master the contents of a Portuguese phrase book, and think of a great many answers to awkward questions.

These hypothetical questions, and indeed the whole idea of our undertaking, retreated at once into realms of the utmost absurdity from the moment we first set foot in the ship. In our neat cabin, surrounded by flowers and potted plants from indulgent friends, it became impossible to believe that we were other than we seemed—a staid couple setting off for a routine holiday in South Africa. As the ship moved at majestic speed through waters that we knew so well, the discouraging observations of the experienced rang in our ears and made the whole thing ridiculous. "Why on earth do you want to go to South Africa? Have you got relations there, or what? I suppose you know that you're going at the wrong time of year? It's the winter there, of course. Terribly boring country, from all accounts. And the people! You'll have to keep your mouths shut on the colour question. . . ." I went to bed before we

were out of the Solent, and for a day and a night, without
waking or eating, slept.

After that, though I was wide awake and tried to appre-
hend it, the life of the ship persisted as a dream. We were enclosed in a world of solid business, of sober, sensible citizens
borne about the world on expense accounts, pursuing their
prosperous affairs. We were beset by deck games and after-
dinner dances, by fancy dress and competitions, by weirdly
monotonous food and weak tea, by polite conversation and
cocktail parties. We lay fallow in deck chairs, eating sun and
wind, swam doggedly in the ship's indoor pool for hours,
laboured in the gymnasium, and walked barefoot many wind-
blown miles a day in an effort to lose our London softness
and harden our muscles.

The relief of solitude first returned when we docked at
Las Palmas. Most of the passengers left the ship here; they
were going for pleasure, for holidays and honeymoons, the
victims of shipping lines and travel agencies. We saw them
at the rail in the first light, carrying their coats and rugs,
looking dubiously at this shore of metallic barrenness, at the
dusty palms in the municipal gardens rattling their sabres in
the persistent wind. I had picked up a travel folder the day
before and had read that it was "not surprising that the
Canary Islands conjure up thoughts of Elysium." Las Palmas
is a stony, treeless island, rising abruptly to shaly-looking hills
and to mountains covered with artificial snow. There is something wrong about this snow; there is too much of it, and the
whiteness is unconvincing. It is in fact a disagreeable mineral
deposit. The Irish steward whom we questioned said it was
a sad place, overcast with clouds whenever he had seen it,
and always with this dusty wind blowing. Its real business,
he said, was bunkering ships, and for his own part he never
bothered to go ashore; there was more gaiety in Belfast.

With Las Palmas mercifully left behind, and before us long days of ocean, wind, and sun—for the sun appeared in splendour when the island was out of sight and flying-fish began to spray out of the bow wave like sequins—we brooded, with an ever-growing sense of unreality, on the adventure before us. Supposing we found the diamonds; what happened next? It might be possible to get them out of Africa without suspicion if we moved quickly, but once in Europe we might find we had made a noose for our own necks. Which of us would smuggle them, and how? How quickly would news of the dig follow us from Africa? What hope had we of keeping a search secret? We asked each other these questions between long intervals of silence, sitting with our Portuguese grammars in our laps and the empty southern ocean streaming by. It seemed at least prudent to have a series of signals which could be sent home in an emergency— we supposed that this amenity would be allowed even in a cell—and we worked out a sentence in Portuguese which we hoped would mean "I wish to send a telegram to my mother." We then devised a number of code messages, all apparently innocuous and filial, with corresponding meanings to cover the most disagreeable circumstances we could think of. "Please reassure Mother all well" meant "Make immediate enquiries through diplomatic channels," and so on. It seemed unlikely that we would not be allowed to make this simple communication even under arrest, and we learned the sentences by heart with some earnestness, and wrote out the code to be posted in Cape Town to a resourceful friend in London.

That done, the voyage became once more a trance of idleness through which we passed with empty minds, believing nothing. We became tourists, and innocent, murmuring with surprise at the cold and drizzle of Cape Town, at the primitive discomforts of the South African train, the empty lunar

landscape, the depressing towns, the bad food and the grit, which deepened the long monotony of the land journey. But we ran into Salisbury at last, in a sunlit air so clear that it seemed to belong to the beginning of the world, and were greeted by a handsome man of stupendous height who proved to be our Austrian's cousin and our agent.

Everything was briskly and competently done; we were shepherded into a brand-new station wagon and driven through shining streets to our hotel, where Peter was waiting for us, signalling with his eyebrows that something incalculable had happened. It had indeed. Our travel agent had become uneasy about the expedition; he did not like—he put it more politely—to send three innocents like ourselves alone into the bush. He had got us the three best Africans he could, but was not happy about their ability to get us out of any unforeseen trouble. We did not speak any native language, and the *munts*—this was the first time we heard the contemptuous Afrikaans word for any African—were only *munts* and therefore not intelligent. So he had decided, he said, to send his son along with us. He was used to the bush; he knew how to handle natives. He was a good shot and, being keen on game, would come for the fun of it, since he. was luckily due for a month's leave and had nothing to do. Leave? We exchanged apprehensive glances and held our breath. The next instant we were shaking hands with a young and handsome man, again of prodigious height, clad in the khaki uniform of a Rhodesian policeman.

Michael was six feet five, in military leggings, with cartridges round his waist and a broad-brimmed hat with a strip of leopard skin round it. He was so impressive in appearance as to be disconcerting; he looked like the handsome star of an early Western and seemed not wholly unconscious of this

impression. When we had met his two younger brothers, who were the same size as himself, and their father, we began to get used to it; but it was unnerving, even in the hotel bar, to find ourselves in such conspicuous company.

At the first possible moment we shut ourselves into Peter's bedroom and tried to think what in heaven's name we should do. We had expressed our gratitude for the new arrangement, which clearly offered practical advantages; but if we had re-jected the-idea of a White Hunter as too dangerous, what were we to do with a policeman? The uneasy thought even crossed our minds that he might have been wished on us by un-seen powers: our expedition was eccentric; it did not carry conviction; we were suspected of having a political motive and were to be kept under surveillance. If a watch were to be set on our proceedings, what more convenient device could authority employ than this young officer, sent in the harmless guise of helper and friend? We considered these ideas with strong misgiving: it might be so, but there was nothing we could do about it. Besides—though this was an impression, not an argument—Michael looked far too open and naïve to be a spy. If he were one, we could not believe that he would be much good at it.

Still, this left us with the problem almost as intractable; for if ever we succeeded in finding Umgila's grave, the moment would come when we should want to dig, and this was some-thing which we should have to explain. Such a proceeding could not be accounted for by my uncle nor by anything, in the last resort, but the truth; and how would this sort of truth appear to an officer of police, whose duty would be to pre-vent such illegal action, or, if he could not prevent it, to report it? We argued round and round this theme late into the night and arrived at several provisional conclusions. First, it would be impossible to reject Michael without giving of-

fence and laying ourselves open to suspicion. Secondly, since
he spoke Shona, the prevalent native language of those parts,
and presumably had experience of life in the bush, he would
be of infinite help to us in finding our way, and obtaining (if
we could disguise our reasons for wanting it) information.
Then, of the three African servants who were now under
contract, two were intimately known to him. John, a Zulu
(we pricked up our ears at this) was his own batman, and
Shorty, the camp boy, had been employed for several years
in his father's stables. Only the cook, a Portuguese, was an
unknown quantity, and we felt that in dealing with all of
them Michael's presence and authority would be invaluable.
Besides, it was only too possible that we would never find the
place we were looking for, and in that case there would be
no occasion for enlightening him. If we did find it, of course
he would have to be told, but we would not deal with that
difficulty before we came to it. These things decided, we all
felt a certain relief that he was going with us, though Peter's
expression, I think, was more speculative than ours. Admitting
every argument and seeing no alternative, he was yet privately
convinced from the beginning that we should do better alone.

We now had to face some discussions with Michael's
father, who naturally felt that the point had been reached
when he ought to have a clearer idea of where we were going
and what we were about, since we might easily, fools that
we were, get into some difficulty for which he, professionally
involved, would feel responsible. It became plain, as we talked,
that this was his basic reason for sending Michael, and we
gradually relaxed the suspicion that there was anything more
than that behind the arrangement. Still, it was hard to convince him that our plans were sensible, since we were vague
about our direction and vaguer still about the time we should
need. He accepted my pious concern with my uncle's journey

but thought it a pity, since it might easily take us, he said, into tedious country where there might be no roads and where petrol supplies would be difficult. Much better, he thought, to concentrate on those parts of Southern Rhodesia which were known to be beautiful, where camping was easy and small game still relatively plentiful; or to go straight down to the Sabi and look for crocodile; or, if we were really determined to go into Portuguese East, to go in on the excellent Beira road and visit Gorongoza. He was a hunter himself, full of alarming stories of bush and game, and it was obvious that he thought our ideas both hare-brained and puny. He turned with a sigh to the question of guns and permits—so many rounds of this, so many of that—and, as a tolerant afterthought, some medical equipment. The one item which brought his private amusement to the surface was the pick, shovel, and crowbar that we kept insisting on, and which he waved aside as quite superfluous. What were we afraid of, he wanted to know? If we kept to the good roads there would be nothing to worry us. If we went in the bush, the ground at this season was dry. Nevertheless, when Peter put on his obstinate expression and said that he never went out in a Land Rover without them, even in England, he shrugged his shoulders and said they could be provided. (What was, in fact, thrown in at the last moment was a square-ended shovel and a mattock, with neither pick nor crowbar; but this we did not discover until later, when we were in the process of learning how vital it is to make a personal check of all equipment.)

One prudent decision, at least, came out of these colloquies, which were chiefly concerned with blankets, paraffin, water bags, bully beef, corn flakes, tinned butter, and the like—that we would be wise to go into Mozambique at once, crossing the border at an official frontier post and having our pass-

ports stamped in the proper manner. This, we privately decided, was a sound precaution, even though we should have to come back into Rhodesia by the same road and proceed south later. At the point at which we guessed we should want to cross there was not a frontier post for many miles, and we thought it unwise to make our first entry in so ambiguous a manner, when we might be stopped and questioned and would not be able to show any Portuguese authority. If we went first to Gorongoza, which was a thing that tourists did and which everyone understood, this would give some colour, perhaps, to our presence later in other parts of the territory where tourists were never seen and had no reason to go. We might, judging from Russell's map, find it necessary to cross the border several times; and since there appeared to be no roads to speak of, no towns, and certainly no frontier posts in this area, such activity with unstamped papers might lead to trouble.

Accordingly, with the full approval of Michael's father, who had at last found something rational to deal with, we decided to go straight to Gorongoza, which could be reached in two days' driving on a good road from Salisbury. We three would go alone in the Land Rover, without either Michael or the lorry, since we should spend the first night in an hotel at Umtali and the following three in Gorongoza itself, where there was an up-to-date rest camp in the game reserve. Michael would meanwhile see the lorry packed and would meet us at the point, back in Rhodesia and some miles south of Umtali, where the road divided into two branches, one going up into the high veldt and the other down to Birchenough Bridge and the Sabi.

After the strains of our three days in Salisbury it was ecstasy at last to be on the road and on our own. The necessity of avoiding Michael and his family, who waylaid us every

time we went in or out of the hotel and plied us with perfectly
reasonable questions, had made us jumpy. We had developed
a strong reluctance for conversation and a tendency to whisper
and glance over our shoulders when speaking to one another in
public places. Our shopping had been partially paralysed by
a national holiday, which we had not expected, and we had
spent a good deal of time in one or other of our bedrooms,
receiving our last injections, talking incessantly, and occasionally being overcome by hysterical laughter. It was a wonderful
relief to be alone at last, packed into the front seat of the
Land Rover and driving at speed through a dazzle of sunlit
air, a hilly road before us and an empty horizon. Everything
in that sparkling light seemed new: rolling savannah, distant
farms, the dramatic outcrops of granite that broke the plain
and breasted the sky like medieval fortresses. Only the dust,
for which we had been prepared but which far outdid anything we had imagined, took the fine edge off our pleasure
and turned us quickly into mummies of dust with apricot-
coloured faces. The Rhodesian roads are made of dust, with
two parallel strips of tarmac laid like tramlines, on which
one travels. All is well if yours is the only vehicle; the strips are
good and the dust lies undisturbed; but as soon as another
vehicle comes in sight, both must relinquish the offside tram-
line in order to pass, and both are enveloped in a dust storm
through which nothing is visible. As all Rhodesians drive
extremely fast and when overtaking in dust cannot possibly
see if anything else is coming, there are frequent accidents;
and as we had been warned of this and were going at a
speed which everyone else regarded as contemptible, we travelled for many miles in impenetrable fog, enduring the heat
with windows closed and coughing plaintively. After a time
the traffic dwindled to nothing, and we enjoyed the intoxicating pleasure of running for hours in solitude in the middle of

the road, gazing to left and right over the sunburned landscape as though ours were the only vehicle in creation. How
long would the tarmac last, we began to wonder? It came to
an end in the moment of framing the question, and we shot
on to a plain dust road, ribbed from side to side with deep
and mysteriously uniform corrugations. We had been warned
about this as well and advised that the only way to take it
was at speed, but our Land Rover was not young, and she
rattled and shook with such agonising noises that we could
not bear her suffering and dropped down to a tender twenty
miles an hour, tasting each corrugation to the bottom and
riding our seats like one of those punitive appliances that had
rolled and bucked us in the ship's gymnasium.

We were in no condition when we reached Umtali to present ourselves with decency at the hotel, which was unexpectedly grandiose and disapproving, with too many African
servants in red tarbooshes and too many watchful men in
tropical suits drinking whisky among too many potted palms
on the verandah. Our arrival was not improved by the appearance of our luggage, which had been augmented by a number
of ill-packed cardboard boxes, all of which had to be carried
up to our rooms (since the Land Rover did not lock) and
which shed packets of corn flakes and lavatory paper when
handled. We summoned what dignity we could and spent
an unprofitable night there, to be shamed all over again by
the morning procession of luggage through the palm court.
Remembering the dust of the day before, we had changed into
bush shirts and khaki trousers, and these, deliciously light and
cool though they were in the early heat, added another faint
discomfort by making us conspicuous; for Umtali is a de luxe
and urban place, bent on appearing like a tropical Cheltenham,
and its women totter about the pavements in high-heeled
shoes, more or less looking as though they are going to the

races. Still, though we provoked some knowing smiles, "bush-bashing" is a sport well understood in Umtali, which is the centre of a romantic and mountainous district where sturdy Rhodesians go camping for weeks together; and we were able to repair a few of the omissions which we had already noted with dismay in our equipment. The most serious was that the Land Rover had been sent out without tools of any kind, without even a spanner, and Peter, who had already had difficulty in buying a pick and a crowbar, spent some further exasperated hours alternately fuming and telephoning in a garage. After some argument a full set of tools was promised to follow from Salisbury; for the rest we assumed, when any listed necessity was not to be found, that it was bound to be on the lorry. This comforting belief lost ground as time went on, but we were not yet aware of the full extent of our folly in not personally checking every item.

The road from Umtali to the Portuguese border now ran between hills and rocky heights through a landscape of considerable splendour; but as soon as the frontier was passed, with its wearisome official delays in the burning sun, it began to drop into lush and cultivated country, steamy and dense and green, with banana plantations and well-tended pineapple fields and roadside paths constantly in motion with groups of walking people. These Africans, so near in distance to the Rhodesian native, look quite different, and the change in the appearance of the women is very striking.

In Rhodesia, women's fashions are a product of the mission school; girls wear a rough approximation to a cotton uniform, and in later years, in and near the towns, cheap and ugly ready-made cotton dresses, with any piece of utility or finery added—a shrunken cardigan, a blanket, or a tablecloth—and, of course, the universal baby-sling, tied tightly across the breasts, flattening and dragging them down, and worn in-

cessantly with its sleeping weight from the moment when a little girl is old enough to carry a baby.

On the Portuguese side, though the disfiguring method of baby carrying was universal, an ease and native brilliance was immediately apparent in the dress, which was a cotton kilt swinging below the knees, with odds and ends of different cotton materials wound with considerable gaiety round the body. The Rhodesian women habitually cover their hair with a scarf or scrap of stuff, tightly tied, but the Portuguese women go bare-headed, with close-cropped skulls and many varieties of earrings, so that the general effect is freer, more graceful and natural, and infinitely more becoming. Their carriage, like that of African women everywhere, is remarkable for a leisurely, relaxed, and stately balance, the naked feet placed softly and steadily in line, the head erect and moving hardly at all (for there is usually something heavy balanced upon it, a water pot, a bunch of bananas, even a suitcase) while shoulders and arms maintain a sinuous rhythm which cradles the heavy baby on the back.

Some of the women sprang off the road as we passed, snatching the bundles and pots off their heads as they did so and waving and laughing at us out of the grass. They seemed delighted with this fleeting glimpse of strangers, and indeed the road from Umtali to Beira must be one of their chief sources of entertainment, running as it does for hundreds of miles without village or turning, a ribbon of communication across unmarked, ancestral and unchanging bush. They were not the only ones who frequented it either, for we would often see, far ahead in the shimmering mirage of some switchback rise, a group of dusky figures squatting in close conference on the road. These, when we approached, would get up with deliberate dignity and, moving off into the grass with

measured stride, would only at the last reveal themselves as baboons.

We were excited by this first glimpse of the true *indigènes*, and by everything else we saw, for there was a holiday feeling about this part of the journey that intoxicated us. We were on our way, with everything still untried, and these first three days were providing a delicious respite. Nothing could possibly worry us at Gorongoza; nobody would question us; nobody could doubt our reason for being there. We had nothing to do but sharpen our unaccustomed senses and enjoy them.

We had not been going for many hours before I bought, at the cost of an hour's excruciating discomfort, some useful experience. We had stopped to take a drink from our water bottles and Jack had wandered across the road to admire an unfamiliar and luxuriant creeper, which was hanging in bunches of velvet pods from a tree. These unknown beans were extraordinarily pretty; as green as moss and covered with delicate velvet. He picked me a spray, and I stroked the pods with my fingers and agreed that they were the prettiest I had seen. A few minutes later my fingers and the palms of my hands began to burn, and I found on examing them that they were covered thickly with almost invisible hairs. I tried to brush these away, but the burning increased, and had now spread to my face, my neck, my forearms, and my knees— everywhere, in fact, that my hands in the last few minutes had happened to touch. It was more than burning, it was burning and itching in one, and responded to scratching like a heath fire to the breeze. In no time at all I was in a desperate state, unable to sit still, trying not to scratch and failing, sighing like a furnace in my restlessness and indeed feeling horribly like one. I begged Peter to stop, so that I could wring out a cloth in cold water and try for some relief. He oblig-

ingly did so, but I could see that he thought I was making a great fuss. His expression of masculine patience deepened perceptibly when I asked again, and by the time I had occasioned a third and then a fourth delay he was sitting with eyes closed and eyebrows raised while I frantically tried every bottle in the medical bag, swabbing myself with cotton wool and hissing with self-pity. All was of no avail. The damnable itching subsided only with time, dying away without a trace after an hour of misery. We made a resolution that in future we would touch no more unknown plants than we could help, and as we jolted on towards Gorongoza I remembered an ominous remark of Michael's mother: "Everything in Africa has a snag. Bilharzia * in every pool, a crocodile in every river, a thorn in every bush, and snakes everywhere." I could have wished she had thought to mention the buffalo bean, which I had so innocently fondled, and which we all of us came to know more intimately later.

Gorongoza embraces two thousand square miles of varied country, forest, plain and swamp, all of it flat. It has no fence or boundary, and the animals wander out or in at will but show little inclination to stray, for inside the reserve they are wholly unmolested and food is plentiful. It is run with efficiency by the Portuguese Government, is expensive to stay

---

* Bilharzia is a microscopic parasite that spends one phase of its career under the shell of the tiny water snails infesting African rivers, especially in places where the flow is sluggish. If it invades the human body, by being drunk in unboiled water or by getting in under the nails or through a scratch in the skin, it causes a long-drawn wasting disease and, finally, death. No precaution is effective against it except thorough boiling of all drinking and washing water and not going into the rivers. It causes widespread ill health and early death among Africans and is difficult to treat because the symptoms often appear for the first time several years after infection, by which time it is too late.

at, and is heavily booked for the whole of the dry season. Chitengo, the rest camp, accommodates about fifty visitors at a time in *rondavels*, which are sophisticated adaptations of native huts, and in concrete bungalows with shower baths. The camp is surrounded by barbed-wire fencing and is closed at sundown: there has been no accident so far, and the Portuguese, their eyes on the tourist revenue, do not wish for any. For the rest, there is a fancy bar with an outside terrace which does its best, with coloured tables and sunshades, to look like a resort, and a restaurant in which one eats wholesome and uninteresting meals. There is also an office, presided over by a handsome young Portuguese in well-pressed shorts and handsewn moccasins, and an African clerk, who does a brisk trade in "native" souvenirs of a mass-produced and cynical description.

We three were allotted one of the bungalows of two bedrooms with a washroom and shower bath in between. The bedrooms were furnished with the most striking economy we had seen anywhere, each containing two beds, a small bedside table and mat, and nothing else. One sat and slept on the bed and kept one's clothes and possessions on the bed or on the floor, a choice which presented a certain difficulty, for it was too hot to bear anything on the bed beside oneself, and the floor was not conspicuously clean. Neither, however, by this time were we; so it did not greatly matter.

The routine of life in the reserve is simple and regular; there are two trips a day with a native guide, with an interval for food and sleep in the afternoon. It is wise to leave the camp at first light, for this is the time when diurnal creatures first come out to feed, and the lions, who have been out all night, are coming home. The animals keep fairly strictly to their areas—zebra and wildebeest on the open plain, where speed and distance are their safety; lions in the jungle grass

at the plain's edge, where they can lie unseen; elephants in the forest, where vegetation is thick and the light poor and they are almost invisible. The advantage of taking a guide, which you are not obliged to do, is that he not only knows the maze of vehicle tracks, in which it is easy to be lost, but knows also where the game is likely to be and has highly trained faculties for seeing, hearing, and smelling it. One goes everywhere by car and is not supposed to get out, though it is safe enough in areas where there is neither lion nor elephant.

The lion is the great, spoiled, blasé star of Gorongoza, following a way of life which suits him to perfection and tolerating sightseers because they are really a very minor inconvenience. The teeming herds of zebra are all his, the hartebeest, the waterbuck, the impala. Man does not compete with him as a hunter but comes and goes respectfully in a motorcar, a harmless phenomenon of which he takes no notice. At Gorongoza he still is, or has the illusion of being, a king. The lions have even taken over the old rest camp, abandoned when the present one was built, and several prides inhabit the empty cottages. They lie flattened on the cement floors in the heat of the day, gazing out through the broken doorways with an expression of languor; sometimes upside down with limp paws in the air, steadily regarding the intruder out of the tops of their eyes. They have everything there that a zoo can offer except bars, and not a cottage is vacant. The principal bungalow has an outside staircase and a flat roof, and as soon as the evening air is cool enough the pair of lionesses who inhabit the parlour go nimbly upstairs and sit on the roof, yawning from a heavy meal and a too-long siesta, tasting the first faint breeze and deducing from it, perhaps, the movements of the zebra. The herds of zebra are so large that the lion is assured a lifetime of good living. He has only to kill and eat them, and no one could doubt the success of his hunting who has seen family

after family sleeping off the effects of the night's kill. The lions we saw in the early morning were all prone and bulging; it was difficult, if one wanted to take photographs, to find one on its feet. They would lift a massive head out of the yellow grass if the Land Rover crept impertinently close, and as often as not would let it fall back again, as though drunk. Cubs were shyer than adults, and would quickly become uneasy and slink away, and this in turn would suggest to their sleep-sodden mothers that they ought to get up and follow, which they usually did, with a look of justifiable annoyance; but the male lions, once they had taken the weight off their feet, were impervious to sightseers and showed impatience only if one were ill-mannered enough to talk or make a noise with a camera.

On our second morning, when we had gone out before six o'clock and the sun was just risen, we saw a pride of lions coming home from the kill and stopping to drink at a pool on the open plain. We were sitting in the Land Rover, watching a distant herd of zebra through field glasses, when five shadows, very close to the ground, came into the field of vision and went down to the pool. It was a big lion, two young and handsome lionesses, and two half-grown cubs. Though cautious, and making themselves rather flat like stalking cats, the females and cubs took little notice of us. These lions have never seen a gun and do not associate motorcars with man. The male lion ignored us completely, striding deliberately past when he had drunk all he wanted and throwing himself down conspicuously in the shade of some palms. The sky was already busy with wheeling vultures, and some nervy and elegant jackals were trotting in long sweeps round the inner conclave of hunched forms who were finishing off the zebra with much ill-tempered spreading of wings, abusive squawks and ungainly predatory jumps at one another. When we

passed by on our way back to camp there was nothing left but some ribbons of satin-striped skin and a delicate skeleton.

On the last night before we left Salisbury we had dined with Michael's parents and an agreeable young man, son of an old friend, who was learning his Africa from the privileged viewpoint of aide-de-camp to a governor. It being established that we were going on safari, and for the first time, the talk had naturally turned on the hairbreadth escapes from death which the three of them had (it seemed, repeatedly) suffered, it being a natural human instinct to wish to alarm the beginner as much as possible. They had all been mauled by either leopard or lion, or had at least assisted at a mauling; deadly snakes had dropped on them from trees; their dogs had been devoured by crocodiles; their bearers had fled when they were cornered by wild pig, and they had been charged almost monotonously by elephant, buffalo, and rhino. We remembered all their stories now that we were wandering in a reserve more thickly populated with wild game than any area open to hunting safaris; but in spite of the great herds that we watched from under the palms and fever-trees, in spite of the smell of lion in the long grass and the neat, round, fibrous packages of elephant dung, twice as big as a cocoanut, that from time to time we found moist and fresh in our path, it was almost impossible to feel the stimulus of danger. African boys whose work is to clear the paths go far afield in the forest and sleep under shelters of branches and palm fronds. "There is no danger for them," said the young Portuguese in the office, "unless an elephant treads on them in the dark. That, of course, can happen." The lions are too preoccupied to be dangerous (though it is unwise to get out of one's car); the rhinos are few and so unreasonably nervous that they have been seen, even by the game warden, only twice in a number of years; and the elephants, which are numerous, are peaceable

on the whole and confine themselves to those parts of the forest where they are not easily seen. However, they can be irritable and are more sensitive about their privacy than lions. We had been told that they dislike the sound of a running engine, but our guide, who spoke a few words of English, told us that we must not stall or turn off our engine when we were near elephant, since it was sometimes important to get away very quickly.

We drove gingerly every afternoon through those parts of the forest that elephants were known to frequent, the three of us in front and Francisco, our guide, peering and occasionally pointing over our shoulders. We tried to ask him what we should do if, at a turning in the path, we should meet an elephant coming from the other direction; but his English was unequal to this, and my Portuguese phrase book offered nothing which had any bearing on this question. We met no elephants on the paths, though their balelike droppings punctuated our progress and showed that at least they used the paths at night: in the day they preferred to browse their way steadily through the intricate undergrowth; and it was here, rising like islands out of a sea of green, that we eventually found them, a herd of five, moving majestically through a screen of trees and leaving a trail of torn branches behind them. We stopped the Land Rover, keeping the engine running, and saw the elephants pause in their progress and lift up their trunks like croziers in our direction, delicately sifting the air. Unalarmed, they twined their trunks back into the branches and went on, and we edged ourselves quietly forward a yard at a time, keeping them well in sight. We could see them clearly now, a tall elephant with a calf moving at her heels, another of equal size, and several apparently half-grown ones behind. As they moved out of our range of vision, we followed them, Francisco urging us gently forward with

movements of his hand and Peter determined to leave the wheel and get out for just a moment with his box Brownie. We were now well into the trees, when the leading elephant suddenly got tired of us. She turned, flapping her ears and throwing her trunk dramatically into the air, making at the same time a hateful noise like badly changing gears. For a split second I thought that something hellish had gone wrong with the car, until I found that the noise was the elephant trumpeting and that she was advancing heavily towards us through the bushes. "Keep going, boss, keep going," said Francisco urgently, but the only way, unless we were to charge the elephant, was to go backwards, and this we did, in a series of eccentric leaps, mangling branches, glancing off trees, Peter straining to see out of the back window, Francisco shouting 'Keep going!' and all of us too suddenly thrown together to have much idea of the whereabouts of the elephant. Fortunately elephants are usually satisfied with a short display of temper (though we did not remember this at the time and discovered afterwards that we had all, in the moment of panic, been visited in a flash by one of the Salisbury stories, which ended with the words, "stamped the car flat into the ground, like an old tin can") and the massive creature, seeing us in full and horrified retreat, soon tired of the demonstration and went back with a justified air to her quiet browsing.

We sorted ourselves out as soon as this was feasible, all talking at once and laughing a little too shrilly, like people who by their own fault have just missed being run over, and found Francisco as ludicrously breathless as the rest of us. "They are dangerous," he said at last, laughing and wiping his eyes, and this really seemed to sum up the impressions of all of us. We had been lucky to get so easily out of a tight corner, and our feelings of awe were increased when Peter

pointed out that we had been charged by elephant. We considered this unexpected aspect and were impressed.

"Are you really sure that that would count as a charge?"

"Certainly. What else do you suppose the brute was doing?"

"I imagined a charge as being more determined, somehow. Involving trampling."

"You will have to be satisfied with this. It could have trampled if it had wanted."

"So you really think we can say we have been charged by elephant? Like everybody at dinner?"

"Of course we can. I mean we have. And if you hear me saying so, I'll thank you not to throw any doubts on the story."

In a sense this little episode gave us the feeling that we had earned a sort of passport that we needed. The visit to Gorongoza had been a feint, though an enjoyable one, and now, as well as establishing that we had gone into Portuguese territory for a conventional purpose, it had furnished us besides with several little histories of our own, which we sensed would be useful when we rejoined Michael. So far, in Africa, we had had very little to talk about besides the things that could be spoken of only alone, and now we felt we were equipped with conversation, which could be spun into a firm fabric of protection.

We needed it after leaving Gorongoza, for our last precautionary operation before joining Michael was to make a short stay near Penhalonga in the hope (or perhaps the fear) of learning what had happened to Bob Bullock. We knew from Russell's narrative that his principal partner, Ned Bullock, was dead; but Bob Bullock, the brother, had married and settled down before the First World War; and though it was unlikely that he was still alive, he might have left a family,

In Mozambique, African women go bareheaded, with close-cropped skulls and many varieties of earrings.

At Gorongoza, the lions have taken over the old rest camp. They lie flattened on the cement floor in the heat of the day.

In our first camp, by seven o'clock we were sitting down to breakfast under the trees.

Shorty, our African camp boy, was unmarried, cheerful, and a known menace to women.

At Chimedzi camp.

Michael had given up the use of bed, preferring to scoop out a hollow in the ground.

Both by training and temperament Shadow, our Alsatian dog, was an uncompromising Rhodesian.

Peter took sights and calculated distances, and decided that the meandering line was the M'rongwezi.

From the summit of M'jenami we could see for many miles into Mozambique.

The elder of our two guides to M'jenami regaled us with a farewell tattoo on his large drum.

Mr. Hla-Hla, one of the big men of Mariya, introduced us to Chief Zamchiya.

Chief Zamchiya, beautifully dressed in starched and well-pressed khaki jacket and shorts, his brass badge of office gleaming at his breast.

He shifted his ground and pointed to the northeast. "I go to that hill."

As if to set a seal on a wonderful day, a girl arrived in the camp, bearing on her head a great pot of wild honey.

After watching us for a while in silence, the boy struck a tentative note and then another on his home-made zither.

After the climb up M'jenami, it was wonderful to spend the next day doing nothing.

Chief Chiquoqueti was not pleased to see us.

From here the grass and the trees were too much for the Land Rover and we set on foot, searching for the trail to the summit of Nyabánga.

The men dug like demons, believing that each next blow would reveal
Umzila's grave. The blows of the pick could have been heard a mile off.

who in turn might know something about the old adventure, or who might even have (it was possible) Russell's diary. We had taken the precaution, in Salisbury, of going through the appropriate section of the telephone directory, and were relieved, I think, rather than otherwise to find that there was no such subscriber in Penhalonga. I think we rather hoped that we should find nothing, for if Bob Bullock were still alive or his children there, Russell's name would have been difficult to mention. They might guess at once what had brought us to Africa or, worse still, tell us that the treasure was no longer there and had been long ago discovered. Or they might only exchange significant glances and say nothing. We built up a morbid picture of them as secretive and rich, uneasy when the name of Russell was mentioned, and not at all pleased to see us. Would we be able to ask about the diary after all this time, on the specious grounds that Russell was my uncle? I would have had to attempt it, of course, if we had come on its tracks—such a detailed check on the later narrative would have been invaluable—but I was thankful when we drew a blank in the telephone directory. Still, we knew that we must enquire more thoroughly than that, and planned to spend two nights in the near neighbourhood of Penhalonga, staying with someone to whom Peter had a rather roundabout introduction. This lady was a tobacco farmer, an English widow who managed her own estate; and when we learned that she also made room for a few paying guests, we proposed ourselves for a visit after Gorongoza, asking her also to find out for us if there were any people called Bullock living in the neighbourhood.

It was with some anxiety that we took the long, hot, dusty road back into Rhodesia, for our carefree diversion was now over and everything from now on would be part of a progress towards an incalculable end. We were thirsty,

dusty, and tired long before we had reached the road for
Penhalonga, and had not improved our condition by drinking
cold beer in a dirty bar *en route* and recklessly eating the
fierily peppered shrimps that the Portuguese proprietor had
pressed on us. We looked, and felt, unpresentable and became conscious of this when our dusty vehicle ran into the
courtyard of a long, low farmhouse with a pillared portico
where elderly ladies and dogs were sitting in the shade. One
saw right through the house to a brilliant garden with a view
of fields and hills and romantic highlands, and before we had
had time to taste the full contrast between ourselves and this,
we had been shepherded into familiar country-house bedrooms, all chintz and jugs of flowers and little pictures, and
were refreshing ourselves with a trolley of tea in private—
lace-edged cloth, walnut cake, excellent dropscones and
butter and blackcurrant jam. It was like one of those trick
pictures that used to appear long ago in children's annuals:
one way up we were in Africa, every nerve of our bodies
alive to the surrounding strangeness; the other way up we
were having tea in Gloucestershire.

All this in itself was a sort of bizarre pleasure, which we
were able to enjoy once it was established that our hostess
had not been able to hear of any Bullocks in the neighbourhood—"except some people who used to be here, I believe,
but they went away years ago." She knew nothing of them,
and accepted the enquiry as springing from natural interest
in some long-ago wartime acquaintance of Peter's father. We
turned with relief to our Gorongoza episodes, which proved
to be splendid fuel for conversation.

There was a retired tobacco planter staying among the
several ladies in the house, a seasoned sportsman and expert on
all the sights we ought to see in Africa; he responded to fresh
blood as though our presence had given him a magical trans-

fusion. He put us through a course of questions, too eager
to advise to be able to wait for the answers. The direction we
thought of taking was not the smallest use. We must go somewhere else. We must go to Victoria Falls. We must see
Rhodes's tomb. We must follow the Garden Route. Mozambique was a dead loss; we mustn't think of it. Zimbabwe,
which I had cautiously mentioned, was "a bore—just like an
old brick-works." He droned happily on, fountaining advice.
How many servants were we taking? Were they any good?
He was disappointed to learn there were only three. "Some
of them are all right," he said, "but one has to know how to
handle them. One must remember these Africans have only
just dropped from the trees." On the second evening a dread
of his questions and advice began to oppress me, but Gorongoza came once more to our rescue, and we were soon listening in silence to sagas of lion and crocodile, of elephant and
buffalo and pig—to our relief and the sportsman's satisfaction.

4

RUSSELL'S COUNTRY

WE had arranged to meet Michael at a road junction some forty or fifty miles south of Umtali, and here indeed we found him, rather to our surprise, for we had received several garbled and mysterious telephone messages to the effect that he was delayed, or the cook was delayed, or that there was something wrong with the lorry. The lorry was impressive, looking as though it were on its way to relieve a garrison, piled to a great height with boxes and gear and things which lurched and bulged under a green tarpaulin. In the crevices of this travelling storeroom, in the utmost discomfort but glad at least to be out of the blazing sun, were our three Africans, clutching little cardboard suitcases and fending off the wooden boxes which incessantly and painfully fell down on them. Michael was driving, looking more splendid than ever now that we saw him in the open, with his cartridgebelt and boots and leather leggings, his broad-brimmed hat tilted rakishly over the eyes and a scarlet handkerchief negligently knotted at the throat. Beside him in the cab, occupying the passenger seat with an air of authority, was a large Alsatian dog whose name was Shadow and who also, we learned, was a member of the police. That is to say, he belonged to Michael and went with him almost everywhere. Never was a dog, it seemed, more dedicated to his profession. If he were not a full

and official member of the British South African Police, he did not know it.

We set off now in convoy, but with a sufficient distance between the vehicles to keep the Land Rover out of range of the lorry's dust. We were heading for the hill country, the high veldt through which Russell had travelled when leaving Portuguese territory. These were the foothills that, further east, ran up to about six thousand feet and became the Chimanimani Mountains; the invisible frontier ran diagonally through them. Mount Selinda, the missionary station that Russell had mentioned in his narrative, was in the midst of these, at the three thousand level, in a tract of tropical rain forest. We had thought a great deal about Mount Selinda and its missionaries. All that we knew of them was that they were American and Protestant. We did not suppose that they would help us if they knew what we were looking for; on the contrary, it was more probable that they would put unthought-of ethical difficulties in our way; but we did imagine that they would have a sound working knowledge of the country and might indirectly be able to help us a great deal. It would be foolish to neglect any local information that might be picked up at the mission.

Since leaving Salisbury, however, Peter had spent some time brooding over the War Office map of the area and had come to the conclusion, from his general feeling for the direction in which Umgila's country probably lay, that we would do better to address ourselves to another mission, Chikore, which we could see at a point perhaps fifteen miles southwest of Mount Selinda, in the unforested foothills to the east of the Sabi. Russell had never mentioned Chikore, and this seemed strange, for it was nearer than Mount Selinda to the area that we privately thought of as his country; but we had already learned that Peter had an eye for terrain and that his brain

received messages from even the most inadequate map, which ours did not; so we bowed to his instinctive feeling that Chikore and not Mount Selinda was the place to make for. As it turned out he was perfectly right, and the reason that Russell had never mentioned it was probably, as we learned later, that it was a very much smaller and younger mission than the other, and may even not have been there at the time of Russell's journey through the territory.

The country through which we followed the lorry changed its character dramatically every few miles, as though bent on showing us every bizarre variety. At first the road, a passably good one, ran like a new-made gash through a forest of scrub, endlessly up and down over switchback hills, with a perilously narrow cement bridge over a dried-up rocky stream-bed in each of the bottoms. Then for an hour or so the soil was a uniform light grey, smooth and hard, as though it were made of asbestos, pricked out with a few parched bushes and scattered with stones; then it was suddenly bright red clay, ridged and veined with erosion, piling up in steep banks on either side of the road, overhung with lush and extravagant vegetation. Native huts here, when one caught a glimpse of thatch among the green, were set about with banana and papaya, the huge leaves bright as banners in the heat. Then, without warning of change, it was open country again, with splendid rocky kopjes on either side, some thickly forested and some clothed in scrub, and all of them crowned with rosy heights and crags.

Michael had been down here before, while we were at Penhalonga, and had already chosen the site for our first camp. This was on a bank of the Tanganda River, and to reach it we left the road, bumped through a dusty native kraal, which seemed to have no one in it but chickens and children, crossed a harvested mealie patch still bearing the tattered

remnants of stalks and foliage, and came to rest on a level grassy bank, set about with bare and monstrous baobab trees. A person who has never come face to face with a baobab can have no idea of the strangeness of the spectacle. They are grey in colour, of immense girth, and so gross in shape as to be rather shocking. The higher they grow, the bigger they seem to get, in grotestque defiance of the usual habit of trees; and their bare swollen branches (for this season of dry heat was their winter, and they were leafless) writhe off from the summit in all directions, looking for all the world like upturned roots. There is an African legend to explain the baobab, which certainly looks as though it needed explaining. God was so angry with the sins of the people that he took all the trees away as a punishment so that they should have no shade. He was softened eventually by their prayers and repentance and agreed to put the trees back, but in doing so, as a warning and a reminder, planted all the baobabs upside down. Seen naked, with their rootlike branches gnarling against the sky, one would say that that is exactly what has happened. I delighted in their appearance but never became entirely reconciled to their strangeness, which has a sinister quality, like the threatening trees in a *Red Riding Hood* pantomime: it would not be out of character if a baobab were to lower a distorted arm and claw up a victim.

Though surrounded by these leafless monsters, the place was fresh with shade, for there were several fine specimens of a noble-looking tree as well, about the size and shape of an English chestnut, covered with dark foliage and vermilion flowers not unlike rhododendrons, with heavy pods the size of rolling pins hung freakishly here and there; and it was in the shade of these that our tents were commodiously set. There were two tents a good distance apart, each under its particular tree; Peter and Michael were to occupy one and

Jack and I the other. Our three boys, it appeared, would sleep in the lorry, where they had some odds and ends of bundles and blankets, which did not look at all comfortable, but which Michael assured us they preferred to the bother of erecting a third tent. Ours already had a pair of camp beds inside made up with blankets and sheets in the proper fashion, and the cook had set out a metal-topped table with a cloth and four canvas chairs, so that it all began to look luxurious and safari-like. The cook himself was very magnificent, disguised from head to foot in a chef's white outfit in which he moved with slow dignity through the long grass, bringing tea on a tin tray with an organdie tray-cloth and a plate of biscuits artistically arranged. He did everything slowly and with an air of melancholy, watched in every movement by a group of baboons on a sandy cliff on the other side of the river, sitting close together in a row, as though at the circus. It seemed rather ridiculous in these surroundings to be sitting round a plastic tablecloth drinking tea; but there was no doubt, from the gravity of his deportment, that the cook felt that the correct thing was being done, that we were behaving as people did who went on safari, and that his dignity was sustained by the repeated slow traverses that he made, bringing a little hot water or an extra teaspoon.

Presently the sun set, and there was a moment of delusive dusk, and then it was dark. Shorty had dug a trench and built a fire in it, and his muscular figure, with shirt-tails hanging out of his shorts at the back, was seen in silhouette against the blaze, dragging up lengths of tree trunk and rolling and kicking them into the right position. A cloud of bats came out of the trees and flickered and swooped about in the light of the fire, flying high up on the edge of the rosy smoke. The river kept up a continuous murmur and the baboons barked with surprise from time to time; we could no longer

see them in the surrounding dark but we could tell that they
were there. Presently the cook brought across a fine bright
gas lamp from his kitchen quarters, and its brilliant moon,
phosphorescent and greenish, isolated us still more from the
surrounding darkness. I had the feeling that we were being
watched by more than baboons, and no doubt we were, for
occasionally we would hear a murmur or a smothered laugh,
and a twig would crack that had not been cracked by the fire.

Michael, who was too young and too energetic to sit still
for long, and who had been stumbling about in the darkness
ever since he had finished his tea, now reappeared in the
circle of lamplight, his thumbs in his cartridge belt, and announced that he had been bargaining for a goat. It was, he
said, a good idea to have fresh meat whenever the opportunity
offered and so save our stores. He had bought a nice little
goat for fifteen shillings, and we would have part of it for
supper. Even before he had finished speaking, the goat,
which was indeed small and very young, was led bleating
into the camp where it was received with delighted laughter
by our three boys, who began arguing excitedly and lugging
it about with vigour in the shadows. I retired into my tent
and lit a candle. I did not know how they would kill the
goat, but I imagined they would cut its throat and I did not
wish to be present. It had a very childish voice and its cries
were unnerving. I put my trust in Michael, whom I could
see from where I sat on the edge of the bed, standing hugely
in the firelight, hands on hips, watching whatever it was that
the boys were doing. It would soon be over, I thought; but the
laughter and the bleating dreadfully continued, and presently
Michael came over, a little abashed, and asked whether any
of us knew any method of killing a goat. The boys, it seemed,
had never done it before; and although they were willing to
try were already so far gone in giggles that he doubted

whether they would make a job of it. He himself, he said, had never killed anything at close quarters like that, and he didn't fancy blowing it to pieces with his rifle. So in the end it was Peter with one of our revolvers who put an end to the goat's anguish, and it was slung up at once to the branch of a tree in the beam of the Land Rover's searchlight and skinned in a dancing cloud of flying insects.

Early next morning, in the brief half-light before sunrise, the deputy headman of the village presented himself as guide and took Jack off into the hills to shoot guinea-fowl. He proved to be a charming and courteous character, in freshly washed green shirt and khaki shorts, and, like every African villager that we met, he was frankly delighted to see that we had rifles. Firearms are forbidden to the ordinary African, only a chief being allowed to possess a shotgun; and even they are kept deliberately short of ammunition. This means that the small wild game that they long for must either be trapped or shot with a bow and arrow, and consequently meat is the greatest of all luxuries. A stranger with a shotgun or a rifle is a man to cherish, for it is etiquette that he should ask permission to shoot, should accept a guide, and share whatever he kills with the headman of the village. His camping nearby may mean that by evening there will be fresh meat for everyone.

In this area, however, game is scarce, as we had been warned it would be. The government had cleared it of tsetse fly only by taking the drastic course of shooting or driving out all the wild game and temporarily forbidding the keeping of domestic cattle. This had robbed the lion and the leopard of their living; they had followed the wild buck over the border into Portuguese territory, where there was no tsetse-fly control and predators could do pretty much as they liked. They were only just, said the headman, beginning to come

back. There were buck now in the hills above the river, and the leopards were helping themselves to goats in the night. He hoped very much for meat from one of our guns, but the only game that Jack saw in the course of two long early-morning forays was eland—a noble bull and two cows pacing majestically along the brow of a hill, upwind of the hunters and so unconscious of them. Jack had no intention of killing anything like this and watched them go with pleasure, admiring their beauty. The headman was disappointed but too polite to say more than that it was a pity. He led him a long way above the valley to a place he knew as a favourite roost of guinea-fowl; they exploded out of the grass and trees as he predicted, heavy as pheasants but clumsier, flying stupidly after the long and chilly night. They were shot with ease and brought back to camp in limp handfuls, warm bunches of grey and miraculously spotted plumage, and the headman carried his share back to the village.

By seven o'clock we were sitting down to breakfast under the trees, glad to be out of our tents, which caught the early sun and were like ovens. It was an interminable meal: the cook wished us to begin with corn flakes and tinned peaches, then to proceed to goat's liver, bacon and fried tomatoes, which were certainly delicious but took an unconscionable time to produce. Each article—bread, butter, weak tea, salt, marmalade—was brought separately on a tray, the cook dressed as before and stepping with slow care through the long grass between his kitchen and our table, which were a considerable distance apart. We were hungry and ate everything, Michael yelling from time to time, boss fashion, for more butter, more hot water, or more milk, and the cook, answering the summons with deliberation, staring morosely at Michael whose ringing voice and lordly ways he appeared to resent. By the time we had finished it was nine o'clock and

our shirts were patched with sweat. If meals were to be conducted at this pace and in this manner, it seemed that the days would have to be given up to consuming them, and that nothing else would be possible. Already the cook was gravely bargaining with a beautiful young woman who had appeared shyly behind a tree with a couple of fowls, and was now kneeling respectfully at his feet, her baby on her back, offering the birds in both hands and answering him in a soft voice and with the most ravishing of smiles. I never saw another such beauty in all the time we were in Africa, so slender-necked, so patrician in feature, with such enormous eyes; and it crossed my mind that perhaps she was more Zulu than Mashona, and that Umgila's warriors might have been her ancestors. It was tempting to imagine the Countess looking like this, and perhaps the cook was not wholly unmoved by her appearance, for after prolonged discussion he bought the fowls, which when dinner came proved to have been very old ones.

We were by this time anxious to move on, for however pleasant our camp, with running water and shade, it was nowhere near the area where we wanted to be, and the three of us were secretly getting restless. Breaking camp so soon, however, was out of the question, and Michael seemed surprised that we should want it. The *munts* had by now totally unpacked the lorry and strewn everything in inconceivable confusion in the grass. Nothing seemed to have been packed with any system; everything was mixed together in a score of tea-chests, so that when anything was wanted they had emptied half-a-dozen boxes before they found it, and the stuff was thrown back higgledy-piggledy, without the least attempt at method or order. In the midst of this rich wreckage the cook kept his state, with a large meat safe full of bananas (I never discovered why he found it necessary

to keep bananas in the meat safe; the meat was invariably hung from the branch of a tree), a small refrigerator which ran on paraffin, a Calor gas stove, and a few rather thin and inadequate-looking saucepans. There was also a large dog kennel, which was supposed to be for Shadow, but which the cook used for keeping sacks of sugar in and any dead guinea fowl or live chickens that were waiting for the pot. Sacks of potatoes, bags of flour, and mealie meal lay round him as he worked, and were kicked, sat on, or walked over as occasion demanded. He had a fire continuously burning in a trench but scorned to cook on this; it was used for boiling kettles and heating washing water. One had to agree, after taking a quick look at these essential arrangements, that packing up would be a long day's work, and that to move after only one night's camp was impossible. It was not wholly easy, either, to convince Michael, for, seen simply from the point of view of safari, the site was good, and he knew better than we did that in the dry season this was sufficiently rare. Besides, he was excited by the eland that Jack had seen and was sure that we should find duiker buck in the hills. We would eat well there, he said, and he would even show us the proper way of making biltong. Rhodesians have an almost mystical reverence for biltong, which they carry in the pocket and chew like tobacco, but even this enticement was abandoned at last, and it was agreed that we should leave for Chikore the next morning.

There was a town, Chipinga, to be passed on the way; the last we should see, for all beyond was bush. We approached it with some misgiving, for in one of the official pamphlets we had studied in London it had been fulsomely described and in such a way as to make us fear that this outpost might be the death of all our hopes. It was the centre, said the pamphlet, of a vast development scheme, a sort of

settlers' paradise spreading its civilising influence across the hills. Schools, hospitals, hotels, modern housing, new roads, and residential areas were mentioned; and the crowning glory, which made us even more uneasy, was a nine-hole golf course. If such an urban development had taken place, within forty or fifty miles of Umgila's village, what hope had we of finding the old sites, which perhaps by now lay beneath metalled roads and petrol stations? What hope would we have of pursuing our search unseen, on the cement pavements of a settlers' suburbia, between the all-night café and the cinema? We need not have worried. Chipinga, like Martin Chuzzlewit's Eden, was not all built and fell quite touchingly short of its Utopian description. It was, in fact, a short, straight, wide and dusty street, bordered by a few one-storey buildings of impermanent appearance and by two garages, one on either side, littered with the rusting skeletons of cars. The only live and prosperous-looking things about the town were its motorcars, which were mostly large, shining, and American, the property of farmers who had come in to collect their mail, pick up a spare part, do a little shopping at Meikles' store, or go to the bank. If, instead of these, there had been a few dejected-looking horses hitched to posts, the main street might have served as a set for an early silent Western; and there were moments, as we improved acquaintance with the place, when we felt that to shoot it out with the inhabitants from the top of the Land Rover was the only means of breaking its stifling calm. Instead, on this first occasion, we went innocently into Meikles' store to buy cartridges, and our own calm was shattered soon enough.

We had left Salisbury in the happy belief, fostered by Michael's father, that, as we intended to shoot only small game for the pot, no permits were needed. To shoot an elephant, or a rhino, or a crocodile, or indeed anything that

people on hunting safaris wish to shoot (with one exception, the lion, which is classed as vermin) one must first buy a permit, varying in price according to the kind of animal one hopes to kill. A twenty-five-pound permit entitles one to buffalo or zebra or the like, fifty pounds covers "royal game" —elephants, rhino, leopard, eland, waterbuck, crocodile and so on—the numbers being determined by the game department locally, according to the supply of game in a given area and taking into consideration the value of the animal. In "native districts," those usually not conspicuously fertile areas of Rhodesia, which are given over solely to African farming and habitation, the shooting of game is generally prohibited, and hunting safaris give them a wide berth. Part of the disgust with our expedition which Michael's father had so civilly tried to conceal had been due to the fact that we had disclaimed any desire to shoot big game, royal or otherwise, and were moreover planning to spend most of our time in native territory. Obviously, he said, we would not need permits; nobody was going to waste time worrying about the kind of small vermin we were likely to shoot. Nevertheless, when we took stock of our ammunition at Chipinga, having expended only a few rounds on the Tanganda guinea-fowl, we were surprised to find that there was very little left and that the heavy boxes on which we were comfortably depending contained shot of formidable size (suitable perhaps for ostrich?) and enormous rifle bullets, both hard and soft-nosed, of the sort that are recommended for elephant and rhino. This was the sort of thing that was always happening to us. To expect to find any given part of our equipment simply because it was down on the typewritten list soon became for us one of those superstitions that nobody in his right mind subscribes to, and we never unpacked a box or delved into a tea-chest without the most cynical misgivings;

but the almost complete absence of the kind of shot we had specified was a disagreeable surprise, and we were thankful that we had found out the discrepancy while we were still at Chipinga. Accordingly, we applied to the general store for reinforcements, and were further taken aback when we were refused further cartridges without permission from the Commissioner for Native Affairs.

This important personage turned out to be a small, dark, unsmiling, unfriendly official, dressed like a town clerk and housed in a bare bungalow in the police compound. One look at his stony expression, which deepened in displeasure as we introduced ourselves, was enough to bring rushing to our minds the ominous words at the end of Russell's narrative: "Beware especially of Native Commissioners and their spies." We had never meant to go near one or foreseen the necessity to do so, and here we were standing helplessly in the creature's office; and he was not at all pleased to see us. He asked at once for the registration numbers of our vehicles, and when he had carefully written these down, asked us coldly why we had not informed him of our presence in his area. He studied the point of his pencil while we explained that we were making a purely private journey and had not known that this was necessary, and then wrote for some minutes under cover of his blotting paper. It was essential, he said at last, that he should know where every car was in his area and why. We should have reported to him on arriving at Chipinga and must keep him informed of our movements so long as we remained in the district. We had no business whatever to have shot anything, not even guinea-fowl, and we must certainly, he said, looking hard at Michael, have been aware of this. We explained, with many civil apologies, that we had really not understood this, and that all we had shot were a few birds for the pot. We were now asking for his permis-

sion to buy a little more ammunition for the same purpose, as we were going to be a long time out in the bush and might sometimes need to supplement our rations. He looked for a long time at Michael's cartridge belt before replying, and something like a suggestion of pleasure came into his face. Permission was refused. He sprang to his feet and went to the map on the wall. Here, he said pointing to two remote areas a long way to the north, he was prepared to allow us to shoot an occasional bird, nothing more. The fact that we were not going to be anywhere near these areas seemed to gratify him. Where *were* we going, then? We said we were undecided. He came back to the table to make a note of this, and the interview was over.

We trailed back up the dusty street with mixed feelings. It was an abominable piece of luck that the mistakes made in Salisbury over our ammunition should have landed us in the arms of the one man in the region whom we most wanted to avoid. He had not liked the look of us, that was evident, and was annoyed that he had not been officially consulted. Now he would believe that, having failed to obtain permission to shoot for food, we would be tempted to do a little discreet poaching, and we had an uneasy feeling that the "spies" whom Russell had mentioned (whoever they might be) were probably already receiving their instructions.

However, there was nothing to be done about it, except perhaps to leave Chipinga as quickly as possible, before he should have time for further obstructive thoughts. This we did, pausing only to do a little unofficial ammunition deal with a Greek storekeeper in a back street and to fortify ourselves with lunch in Chipinga's solitary hotel. Unpromising though it looked, this one-storey dump proved unexpectedly sympathetic, for it was clean and not uncomfortable, and the catering was tackled by the Italian proprietor and his wife in a

spirited attempt to provide something resembling Italian food
and at the same time satisfy the Rhodesian appetite. The two
do not, of course, go together, but the good couple were trying; and our first experience of a meal in this frontier town
gave us an insight into the magnitude of the problem. The
luncheon menu, which offered no alternatives and was an
arbitrary succession of courses, was as follows:

AVOCADO PEAR

TOMATO SOUP

BAKED FISH IN TOMATO

KIDNEYS ON TOAST

CURRIED MEAT AND RICE

PORK CHOPS, VEGETABLES AND SALAD

CHOCOLATE PUDDING

CHEESE AND BISCUITS

POT OF TEA

We tried to refuse a number of the courses, but this caused
disastrous confusion among the African waiters, who thought
that we were finding fault with the food and appealed to
the proprietor. If one of us did succeed in rejecting a dish,
we were not brought the next course, which we had asked for,
but were kept waiting until it fell due in its proper time. One
of us could not, for instance, choose curry and cancel the
chops while the other decided on pork chops and did not
want curry. If we insisted, the inexorable order of the menu
was still maintained, the pork-chop customer having to sit
and wait while the other ate his way through a mound of
curry, and the curry fancier having to take his turn at waiting while the other fought his way through two pork chops
of enormous size, three vegetables, and a salad. This is not
a happy social arrangement, but we could see that it was our
fault; all round us in the dining room dusty-haired men in
shorts with weathered faces were eating steadily through

the luncheon from beginning to end without argument or fuss and drinking tall bottles of beer into the bargain. We wondered how such lavish catering could pay, for this meal was by no means expensive. Fortunately the proprietor did not notice our puny behaviour and embraced the chance of conversation when we went out to settle the bill.

He and his wife had come from Como about fifteen years ago. The country, he said, was fine, but business was poor; there were "no plenty people." His solution was for the government to allow lots and lots of industrious Italians in, though he admitted that jobs for Europeans were hard to get since people could employ Africans for less money. He was immensely proud of being a naturalised Rhodesian. "My children no speaka English like I do. They speaka like you. They Rhodesians, justa like you." We felt obscurely proud of this ourselves, the more so as we were momentarily on our own, without Michael, who was paying a social call at the police barracks; but on second thought credit was more probably due to our authentic-looking khaki shirts and dusty Land Rover. He took it for granted, like the district commissioner, that we were on a hunting expedition, and saw us off with cheery admonishments to "shoota plenty lion."

As soon as we left Chipinga the road began to climb, drawing itself steadily upwards into thick woods where the soil was red and moist. The air became cooler; one could taste that it was no longer sterile with heat but had the memory of last night's dew on it, the promise of dews to come. After about three hours we passed a number of native stores at the roadside, cubes of whitewashed brick about the size of cowsheds, just big enough to hold a counter and open shelves, and judged that we must be approaching Chikore Mission. Other evidences soon appeared; groups of girls in cotton gym-tunics stirring up the dust of the road with bare

feet; young men on bicycles who dismounted as we approached and raised a disciplined hand; scores of native huts in groups by the roadside and a general purposeful movement of coming and going. We slowed the vehicles down by tacit consent and the lorry, which had been leading, fell to the rear. Michael had all along been dubious of the mission; like Russell, but for different reasons, he was accustomed to giving such places a wide berth and did not relish the idea of spending even a night in a mission compound. Missionaries are by no means universally admired in Africa, nor their activities approved of. From the point of view of the average Rhodesian, who is sensitive to any threat to white supremacy, they stir up a lot of trouble by giving the black man ideas above his station. They offer him education, which is a mistake; they teach him a few of the white man's habits, which is impertinent; and worst of all they treat him almost as an equal, calling him "mister" on occasion and even shaking hands. To go into an area where such perversions were practised was enough to make Michael's hackles rise, and since we wished to make a friendly approach to the Chikore missionaries we hoped to keep him in the background as much as possible.

We drove gingerly along the paths of the mission, past open one-storey brick buildings which were evidently classrooms, past nondescript huts and bungalows and tennis courts, wondering whom we should find to speak to and whom we should ask for advice and permission to camp. We drew up indecisively outside a small suburban-looking house with children's toys and tricycles in the garden, and almost at once fell over a pleasant, harassed, and wispy young American woman with a baby. She directed us, without unseemly surprise, to the secondary school at the bottom of the hill. The superintendent of the mission was away that day, but we would find Mr. Abbott, the headmaster, and he would take care of us.

It was necessary to move quickly now, for it was nearly five o'clock and in an hour it would be dark. We sought out Mr. Abbott in his classroom, explained our needs, and asked permission to camp, and after the briefest possible delay were setting up our tents on a cheerless and uncomfortable piece of ground, which was the only one available. Short of accommodating us on the football ground or in one of the classrooms I do not know where else he could have put us, for the whole place was tidily laid out in approximate imitation of a campus; whereas here, on a sort of vacant lot among weeds and rubble, we had at least the vestiges of privacy, a sappy undergrowth screening us on one side, so that we could set up our transient arrangements without giving free entertainment to the populace. But it was not a nice camp, and the cook and Shorty sulked immediately. In the first place, there was no stream, so it was triumphantly announced that we could have no tea, and there could be no washing or cooking. Mr. Abbott had said that we could take all the water we wanted from his outside tap, and we were only a few hundred yards away from his bungalow; but there were three dogs sitting on the Abbott's back porch who barked very angrily indeed when they saw Shadow, and none of our boys would go near them. It was dark by the time the tents were up, and the cook was wandering about very slowly with his little gas stove, complaining that there was no level ground where he could set it up, and that consequently there was no way of cooking dinner. Shorty had difficulty in finding wood for the fires, and when he did find some it was wet and would not burn. Everybody was tired and out of temper. Even Michael, whose good nature was unshakable and whose first thought was always to make an efficient camp, however difficult our eccentricities made it, leaned moodily smoking against the

bonnet of the lorry, and we could see that for once he was on the Africans' side.

We did what we could, building up and fanning the reluctant fire against the night which already promised to be cold. We put on sweaters and drank some whisky, staring at the hissing logs and marvelling that one could so abruptly begin to shiver after the heat of the day. We were hungry now, and in sudden impatience with the cook's lamentations, we cut up a brace of guinea-fowl, already plucked and cleaned at the last camp, for Peter to roast over the heart of the fire on a piece of iron netting, heavy as a gridiron, which he had stumbled over in the hardware store in Chipinga and thought might come in useful. He is one of those men who pride themselves on their cooking, and if one is not too nice about his methods the results are often successful. It was so tonight. By the time he had seasoned and oiled the pieces of flesh the centre of the trench was glowing with red-hot ash, and they went on the hot gridiron with an audible sizzle. While we sat watching them change in colour and form, dropping their succulent juices on to the embers, the cook appeared out of the velvety dark and with silent disapproval laid a table. He set out knives and forks, bread, salt and pepper and butter, and a dish of cold baked beans in tomato as a neat but eloquent comment on the situation. He had from the first maintained that it was not correct to cook on an open fire, and that he would have nothing to do with it. When Peter had hopefully bought a round iron cooking pot in Chipinga, the sort that is in universal use on African fires, he had grandly pretended not to know what it was, and had told us through John, the Zulu, who spoke some English, that he had always cooked in a hotel and was not accustomed to such things. But now the guinea-fowl were ready and we were ravenous, and cheerfully risked his silent disapproval.

We ate with our fingers, sometimes holding the lightly charred bone in the corner of a handkerchief to avoid burning, and using the rest to mop the delicious juice which ran down our chins. We ate no bread and there was plenty of meat for the four of us, and I never remember a more satisfying meal. I do not know what the Africans ate: their staple diet was boiled mealie meal, which they squeezed into firm grey lumps the size of tennis balls and dipped in gravy; but on this occasion, with no piece of ground level enough to suit the fanatical requirements of the gas stove and the cook in a crisis of dignity, I suspect they dined poorly.

The night was unbelievably cold. We had discovered at Tanganda that we had been equipped with only a single blanket apiece, and Jack and I had bought a couple of gaudy African ones at Chipinga, for which we were now thankful. Peter was impervious to the cold, having sensibly brought a down-quilted sleeping-bag into which he retired each night like a wasp into its hole, and Michael slept on the ground in the open, so near the fire that he charred his blankets and clothes on several occasions, and in any case slept too soundly to feel anything; but Jack and I were pierced through and through with the cold, and my hipbones ached and locked in a wrong position, as though a suicide's stake had been driven through my body.

At six o'clock, however, the African sun rose blazing out of the darkness, and in the same moment we heard the voices of children singing hymns. We got up without regret and thawed our bones. One could see by daylight, even more clearly than before, how comfortless was the spot that we were in, and we were glad to find that the boys were packing to leave. We had been offered baths at half-past six and breakfast at seven by the hospitable Abbotts, so leaving Michael to break camp and go on ahead (he had himself, to our

relief, declined any closer acquaintance with the missionaries)
we three went up to the Abbotts' comfortable bungalow, and
for half an hour forgot the very reason for our expedition
in the sensual pleasures of thick towels and unlimited hot
water.

After breakfast (a delicious reminder of how wonderful
fresh orange juice, fried eggs, and American coffee can be)
we were taken off to another bungalow to meet Chikore's
missionary superintendent. He turned out, rather unexpectedly, to be young, good-looking, and athletic, with crew-cut
hair and an enthusiasm for Africa and its people which threw
up a fountain of facts at the first approach; exactly, as Peter
said afterwards, like striking a gusher. He was in love with
his job, and with his marvellous luck in being here in Africa,
and was saddened only by the fact that the gospel he had
come to preach left singularly little mark on the African
people. About ten per cent of the boys and girls, he said,
adopted a nominal Christianity while they were in school;
after that one could not count on more than two per cent.
Belief in magic and the fear of evil spirits went far deeper
than any temporary love of God. They were avid for education, but did not want the pill inside the sugar; if they accepted it at first out of politeness, they spat it out again as
soon as they got home.

Both "Chuck" Blakney, as he apparently was called, and
Mr. Abbott had been at pains to learn Chindau, the local
language, and Mr. Abbott in particular had a good, detailed
knowledge of the surrounding country, since there were a
number of native village schools in the area, taught by
Chikore-trained teachers under the guidance of the mission,
and these had periodically to be visited. The missionaries had
good maps and spread them out eagerly on the floor for our
inspection, but, as we expected, they all went blank at the

Rhodesian border, and beyond it could tell us nothing. Still, it was probable that the missionaries themselves could tell us much, and I cautiously began to ask them relevant questions.

It had already been explained at breakfast that our choice of this part of the country for our trip was due to our interest in the early adventures of my uncle and our desire to identify the places where he had been. They had eagerly asked for his name and further details, and I told them as much as I dared, not without a tremor of discomfort. I had the feeling that if they had known the truth they would have disapproved of it, and would have disapproved still more of our not telling it. Still, I was determined to try them with a few place names from Russell's narrative, and with studied carelessness asked them if they had ever heard of the Longwegi River. After a considering pause they shook their heads; then, pushing his forefinger doubtfully about the map, Chuck Blakney asked if the name might not be a version of M'rongwezi. There was, he said, a considerable strain of Zulu blood in these people, and on either side of the Portuguese border many rivers and natural features had two names, one Chindau, one Zulu. A Chindau name beginning with *l* would in Zulu as likely as not begin with *r*, and the apostrophised *M* in M'rongwezi was so universal a characteristic that, in trying to identify a name, we could safely discount it. We examined the map with bated breath and exchanged glances. The M'rongwezi River was indeed where we had supposed, from Russell's description, the Longwegi would be. The letters *g* and *z*, Blakney added, were also interchangeable between the two languages, so that it seemed pretty certain that this was the river my uncle had mentioned in his letters. In any case, he said, if we were going that way he could give us an introduction to a local chief, Zamchiya, who knew much more about the native names than he did. If his guess about the river were

right, the area we wanted to explore would be in Zamchiya's territory, and he might be able to give us a guide, for it was tricky country.

This seemed a marvellous step forward, and by tacit consent we mentioned no more names. We did not wish to pinpoint our objective, for if Umgila's kraal and possibly Kyabanga were in this chief's territory, it was more than likely that he would know about the treasure and would suspect us as soon as we mentioned these vital places. Our best plan would be to meet Zamchiya and proceed cautiously on any information which he was able to give us; we said we should be grateful for an introduction.

Mr. Abbott now sat down to write a letter and to type out instructions for finding the chief's village, which was called by his name according to African custom, while Mr. Blakney described the man on whom so much would depend. He was, he said, a remarkably fine person, a Christian, mission-educated, speaking quite good English, and was, so far as he knew, the only African chief to become a schoolmaster. He taught in the village school in Zamchiya, and administered territory on both sides of the Portuguese border. It was a long way off, and the roads—the two young men looked at each other and laughed. Well, at least we couldn't say that we hadn't been warned. We could find Zamchiya all right if the vehicles held out. If one of them broke up, they said, we could always pile into the other and come back to Chikore.

In the moment of parting Mr. Blakney showed us a further kindness which was to be more fruitful than he knew. Since I seemed interested in native history, he said, he would lend me a book which would tell me something about the people of Gazaland, the old name for the territory into which we were going. I could return it when we came back through Chikore, which we were almost bound to do. It was a pity

we had not been able to stay longer, for there were some mysterious African ruins within reach of the mission which we might have cared to see. Most people, he said, had heard of Zimbabwe but had no idea that the country was dotted with remains of the same culture, which few white men had seen. They were hard to find and difficult to see, and we must not expect the natives to be eager to show them, since anything unknown was regarded with fear and they believed these places to be inhabited by powerful spirits. Right here, he said, returning to the map, right in the part where we were going, was a big hill, almost a mountain, called M'jenami, which certainly had some traces of African ruins, though nobody from Chikore had ever seen them. They had heard from other missionaries that they were there, and that except for these missionaries they were unknown to Europeans. If we found them, he said, he would like to hear about it, for one day he might be able to go into that country and see them for himself.

We promised we would do our best, and parted from our kind Americans with more gratitude than we could well convey. They had given us our first clue to Umgila's territory.

5

A LITTLE MUTINY

AS soon as we were out of sight of the mission we stopped the
Land Rover and eagerly unfolded our maps. If Mr. Blakney
were right, and the M'rongwezi were the river we were looking for, we surely had only to follow its course eastward into
Portuguese territory to find the site of Umgila's old village
(if this were still visible), and from there strike a trail into
the high veldt which might, or might not, bring us within
range of Kyabanga. Russell's map had not been drawn to
scale and was no more than a scrawled memorandum; still, it
was clear enough; the Longwegi, flowing from west to east,
crossed the Rhodesian-Portuguese border an unspecified number of miles north of the point where the Lundi and the Sabi
became one and turned their course eastward for the Indian
Ocean. In some of our maps no river at all was shown that
crossed the border; in one, such a river was clearly marked,
but without a name. In our three War Office maps a river
appeared in the right place but so variously drawn as to look
like three different rivers, and named Murongwezi, Morun-
guese and Mossurize—variants, one would say, of the M'rongwezi which had been carefully spelled out for me at the
mission. It seemed to us then, as it seemed even more positively
later, when we had learned more of the variations between
Chindau and Zulu names and the fanciful divergences of maps,

that the M'rongwezi was indeed Umgila's river, and that we were on Russell's trail and solid ground at last.

We were elated by this confirmation of our hopes, which had been based on Peter's obsessional study of the dreadful maps (no two of which agreed, and which were becoming frayed as we snatched them fiercely from hand to hand), and calculated that, if we followed the missionaries' advice about our next camp, we should that very night be within reasonable distance of M'jenami, which seemed to lie slap across the international boundary and to command a view of the M'rongwezi River. M'jenami was suddenly of the greatest importance to us. From its summit we should get an open view of the surrounding country and would be able to take bearings on any other hill that was to be seen. Once there, with Umgila's river in sight, we could not be many miles from Kyabanga.

There was another point about M'jenami which we saw at once could be turned to our advantage. The missionaries had said that there were mysterious Bantu ruins on the mountain, and these, surely, would give us the perfect excuse for camping in the vicinity and doing some otherwise inexplicable prowling. We were all the time nervously conscious of the necessity of convincing Michael that we were behaving normally; our Africans too, as we had learned from him, were asking questions, and it was desirable that they should be satisfied about our motives, or they would talk; and we were also aware, as Russell had been before us, that we were never free from native observation. Four Europeans on safari, moving through country to which white men on safari never came, was altogether too rare and sensational an entertainment to be missed, and we quickly got used to the circumstance that as soon as we stopped anywhere, however briefly, an audience, usually children with goats and women with water-

pots, would silently appear out of the bush. From every point of view this theory of Bantu ruins was a godsend, and we worked up a by no means altogether false enthusiasm for them as we bumped and lurched over the execrable road which would bring us to Mariya.

This was the spot at which we had agreed to meet Michael, having sent him ahead with the lorry to look for a suitable camping place in the vicinity while we stayed to collect information from the missionaries. They had told us that there was a village school at Mariya, which we could hardly miss, and also a bore-hole with good water. We had arranged to meet there, at the school, at noon, and followed the atrocious road with rising spirits, buoyed up by the belief that if we made a convenient camp near Mariya we should be within a few miles of our objective. Alas for our hopes, we had not allowed for the unpredictability of Michael, and were about to run into a series of maddening difficulties.

At first the road wound through steep and rocky woodlands, and we crossed the River Nyangadza, which had plenty of water in it, three times, always at shallow fords which were easily negotiable. The road was punitively bad, but we had seen nothing yet. Presently it dropped down out of the hills into flat bush and native farming country and became ridged and hard-baked track, which had never been made for vehicles at all but had been worn through the bush by the feet of men and animals. It was a featureless landscape now, and all the streams were dry. We came to Mariya about noon and found it to be a collection of shedlike brick buildings, evidently classrooms, circled about with a number of native huts. The bore-hole, a deep well worked by a primitive handpump, was under a shelter of thatch a little distance from the road, and there was a busy traffic of women, children, and goats threading their way through the grass in every direction. The

air was full of dust and the sun fierce, and to find a margin of shade we had to run the Land Rover under the open front of one of the classrooms. There was no question of finding a more comfortable spot if we were not to run the risk of missing Michael, and since school seemed to be over for the day we took our books into the empty shelter and settled down to wait.

It was a fairly dirty place, open down the whole length of one side like a cart shed and furnished with a few rough tables and benches which had been made by fixing legs here and there to the split trunks of trees. It contained nothing else whatever except excrement in the corners and a universal covering of dust. We sat on the benches and read for four hours, denied even the comfort of the Land Rover since the sun had found it at last and the only shade was under the classroom roof.

The nonappearance of Michael was certainly worrying, but we comforted ourselves with the news, politely offered in English by the African schoolteacher, that a big blue lorry driven by a European had gone through Mariya that morning without stopping. At least we were all headed in the same direction, and we supposed that he would be back in his own good time if nothing had gone wrong with the lorry. The hours of waiting, too, were not wholly wasted, for I had time to look through the book Mr. Blakney had lent me, and in it found information which seemed unexpectedly to confirm Russell's story.

At the beginning of his narrative Russell had given the name of the buried chief as "Umgila" or "Langilibilele" and had said that his son Gungunyana had had trouble with the Portuguese, and that as a result of this trouble the old kraal had been deserted and the people scattered. I had pricked up my ears at Chikore when Mrs. Abbott, over breakfast, speak-

ing of Mount Selinda, had said that an important chief called Gungunyana was said to be buried in the precincts, though nobody knew where, for this suggested that there was still some living memory of Umgila's son, and not so very far from his father's country. Now, turning the leaves of this excellent book, *The Life of a South African Tribe* by Henri A. Junod, in one of the historical chapters I came across a paragraph about a Zulu chief, Muzila, who had been defeated in a war of succession with his brother, had moved with his followers to Gazaland, and been eventually succeeded by his son, Gungunyana. There was very little about him, but the paragraph stood up suddenly from the page as though it were magnified. Surely, surely, this was our very man? The names Muzila and Umgila were clearly variants of one name, *Mu*, *Um*, or *M* being the prefix, and the *z* and *g* interchangeable according to whether it were spoken in Zulu or Chindau.

There was one other detail, which might or might not be relevant. The paragraph mentioned "his capital, Mandla-kasi," and we wondered whether this might refer to the abandoned village where Russell had first dug or perhaps to the one he passed on the border as he crossed into Portuguese territory, mentioned by him in the narrative as "Mandhalami's kraal." It would be unwise to lay too much stress on this last similarity, since we were ignorant of the language, but we felt sure that the book's Muzila was our Umgila, and we set great store by this casual historical reference, for it convinced us that Russell's chief had really existed, and in that part of the country where we had hoped to find him.

By four o'clock it seemed depressingly likely that something had happened to Michael, and that since it would be totally dark by six we had better make preparations for spending the night. We asked permission of the schoolteacher, whose name was Abel and who seemed glad of an opportunity

of practising his English. He offered us the classroom to sleep in, and threw some sticks on the fire outside his hut so that we could boil our kettle. We had nothing with us but some tea, a tin of milk, and some Ryvita, and were getting hungry, so it seemed sensible that Peter and I should go back to the last native store we had passed to buy some bully-beef and bananas, two staples which, together with Coca-Cola, can be found in the meanest native store in Africa. This store had been mentioned to us by the missionaries since, though a poor little store in itself and not very clean, it was owned by a successful African farmer called Hla-Hla, one of the big men of the neighbourhood, whom we came to know and appreciate some time later. We did not see him on this occasion but got what we wanted from the storekeeper and crashed our way back over the trail in a hurry, not liking the idea of finding our way in the dark.

When we got back to Mariya the big blue lorry was breathing its Diesel rhythm in the middle of the road and Michael and Jack were examining a map by the light of an electric torch. Even as we came up to them, probing with our headlights across the ruts and stones, the sunless twilight faded like a theatrical effect and darkness took its place, broken only by our headlamps and the red glow of the schoolteacher's cooking fire. The bad news was broken without delay. Michael was so late because he had gone another twenty miles further south, and had made camp on the first river he had found with water in it. This was the Honde, a long way from where we wanted to be, and at the sight of our blank faces he said he could see no good reason for our wanting to be nearer to Mariya. It was no use arguing; the camp was made, and for tonight at least there was nothing to do but go to it. Not for one night but two, Michael insisted; the *munts* were acting sullen at having to break camp so often, and we had

better stay put for a while if we wanted to avoid trouble. He had gone so far because all the rivers were dry, and he had had to go all that distance for a running river. We wanted water in our camp, didn't we? He seemed surprised that we received all his reasonable arguments so dejectedly.

We decided to split up two and two, as the road was going to be difficult in the dark. Michael and Jack went ahead in the lorry and Peter and I followed in the Land Rover in a cloud of choking, reddish, impenetrable dust. There seemed to be no way of avoiding this; if we dropped behind to let it subside we immediately lost the lights of the lorry and found ourselves crashing and lurching through the long grass among the scrub and without any clue to our direction. Even attempting to keep up, and staying within the dust storm that was our guide, we missed the lorry's lights on several occasions, and each time lost all sense of being on a road. Head thrust out of the side window as we pitched shatteringly from hole to hole, Peter would shout furiously "I don't believe this is a road we're on at all!" I would open my window for a moment for a better view, holding my breath against the dust. "I believe you're right. It does seem much more like a ditch." More crashing and lurching and crawling over boulders. "Good God, I know what it is, it's a dried-up water-course!" He stopped at this and got out to have a look, and after a moment's hesitation I got out too, jumping down in the dark into an invisible bush which clasped me in a barbed-wire embrace and ran delicate three-inch thorns into my flesh. We had lost the lorry's lights by this time, but there was nothing to do but go on. Even on foot the twenty miles could scarcely have seemed longer, and the groan of the Land Rover's four-wheel drive made a bassoon accompaniment to the rattles and crashes of our belongings as we bounced in the air and were hurled at the metal sides. After

a time Peter shouted above the din with regained confidence, "I believe it's a road after all! I saw the lorry's lights," and there they were, sending a faint glimmer through the dust and trees a hundred yards ahead. Encouraged, he trod cautiously on the accelerator, and we struck a rock with such force that we came to a shocked standstill, straining and shuddering like a ship aground. We were properly stuck this time; the rock was under the body of the Land Rover, supporting it like a pedestal while the wheels spun and made grooves in the hard soil. I scarcely know how we got off again: I took the wheel and roared the engine while Peter pushed, and after some agonizing minutes their combined strength succeeded in slipping her sideways. Speechless with temper Peter climbed in again, his clothes filthy and his face unrecognisable under a coating of cinnamon-coloured dust.

It seemed a high price to pay for getting to a place where we had no wish to be, and when we arrived at the camp we saw nothing to make us like it any better. The Honde River, for which we had made this lengthy and damaging detour, proved to be a miserable trickle among stones with stagnant, unwholesome-looking pools here and there; the perfect breeding-ground, one would say, for Bilharzia. The patch of open ground where our tents were already set was bald and uninviting, littered with the blackened relics of old fires, with rusty wire and pieces of dirty newspaper. The tsetse-fly control, it appeared, had camped here the year before and had left these souvenirs of their occupation. There were no trees of any size, so that we could see at a glance that there would be no shade, and the camp was surrounded by long rustling grass which Michael had already found to be full of snakes. He had shot a fine black mamba while the tents were going up, and had seen another which had eluded him;

he showed us the tattered trophy of his kill and flung it into the bushes.

We shuffled about in the darkness, dragging our immediate needs out of the Land Rover, depressed by the wretched change in our situation. The mantle of the gas lamp had naturally shattered on the journey and no spare had been provided. There was only one battered storm lantern, which the cook needed. He had used up all the Calor gas already and the refrigerator had gone wrong. We gloomily thanked Heaven we had thought to bring a private packet of candles, which at least would give us light for going to bed; for the rest we must make do with firelight.

After all the optimism of the morning our prospects had maddeningly deteriorated. We were now a good twenty miles from our objective and almost as far from the long southernmost spur of M'jenami, which we had fixed on as our next centre of operations. We were cut off from the area of search by hours of slow going over an execrable trail and were uneasy about the damage done to the Land Rover. Worst of all, we were condemned to this hateful place for two nights, for Michael was firm that the boys must have a rest from moving camp, or we should run into trouble.

All this was discouraging enough, but when the night was over and the hot sun was stinging our arms as we surveyed the sordid confusion of our camp, we were visited by new and irritable energy and determined to get back where we wanted to be, no matter how unpopular it made us. It was no good staying here, we told Michael. We were too far south for the country connected with my uncle, and had heard, besides, some interesting news of ruins from the missionaries, which made us anxious to explore M'jenami. We had not thought, we said, to mention before that my uncle had been particularly interested in Bantu ruins and had de-

scribed them in his letters to my mother. We could not let
this opportunity pass, and therefore proposed to spend the
day in looking for a good base-camp farther north, where
we could stay for several days while we explored the mountain. Michael, on the other hand, was all for pressing further
south to Hippo Mine where he had heard the game was plentiful and thought he knew the tsetse-fly officer. This chap
would be shooting out the game and it would be fun to help
him; it could not, he thought, be more than a day's journey.

The argument was developed during breakfast, interrupted
only by the sudden appearance of a long and extremely beautiful green mamba pouring smoothly out of the grass at the
side of the meat-safe. The boys scattered shrieking and
climbed into the lorry, while Michael, never so happy as
with his finger on a trigger, pursued it keenly but fruitlessly
into the grass. We took advantage of his momentary absence
to think of a few more reasons why we could not do as he
suggested, and when he returned we were civilly but reso-
lutely firm. We three would go off for the day and look
around and find a better camp site if possible.

Retraced by daylight, the trail was less alarming than it
had been in the dark, but it was bad enough, and we were
horrified to see the rock on which we had foundered. It was
a sort of flat-headed crag jutting out of the ground, cracked
and scored in evidence of our passage. So far as Peter had
been able to discover, the Land Rover had not been dan-
gerously damaged, but one of the track-rods was buckled
and the steering was heavy. He began to wonder lugubriously
where was the nearest point where repairs were possible.
It was just conceivable that Mr. Hla-Hla, the great man
who had a grinding-mill, a tractor and a lorry, might also
have a repair workshop; if he had not, it might mean going
all the way back to Chikore, for we could not risk a break-

down later on, when much might depend on our mobility, in conditions still unknown across the border.

It was, as usual, a morning so marvellous that it might have been the beginning of the world. Now that we could see where we were going, we found the endless sameness of the bush confusing; long grass and low trees, dappled with sun and shade, shut in the trail on every side so that one could not see more than a score of yards in any direction. The trail meandered where it pleased, sometimes dividing for no apparent reason and coming together again after a quarter of a mile, sometimes forking off in divergent directions, with small possibility of our knowing which was right. Left to myself I should have been soon lost, having a poor sense of direction and an incomplete grasp of the proper use of the compass; but we did not lose our way; Jack and Peter read their inadequate maps, paid attention to the position of the sun, and sometimes climbed on to the roof of the Land Rover to look for natural features predicted by the maps which were occasionally, but by no means always, there. We were beset by a thirst so fierce that there was no accounting for it by anything we had eaten and stopped every few miles to drink greedily from our tepid water bottles. We came to the conclusion after several hours that this was due simply to the stinging heat, to which we were not yet accustomed, and which made the roof of the Land Rover too hot to touch; even with the windows and the draught-vent open it was rather like travelling in a portable oven.

We reached Mariya before noon, and finding the school in session, with scores of little black heads in the classrooms and a loud chanting of multiplication tables going on, took the only alternative trail which branched to the west, hoping to find the second bore-hole of which the missionaries had

spoken. These bore-holes* were a government enterprise, designed to make country habitable which could not otherwise support life in the dry season, and they had told us that the one at Chimedzi was even better than the busy one at Mariya, since the water came up from the greensand and could be drunk without boiling. Chimedzi lay five miles to the west of Mariya, and though there was no village or visible habitation, we found the bore-hole easily, its wooden pumphandle protected from the sun by a thatched shelter and the surrounding dust churned into chocolate-coloured mud by the feet of men and cattle. We were now in gentle wooded country where the trees grew almost to forest size and there were dramatic rocks. Some miles away on our left we had seen a tremendous escarpment, its flanks clothed with some sort of scrub and its edge crowned with serrated rock, which in the distance and the dazzling light look extraordinarily like architecture. At each point where the ground rose sufficiently to give us another view of it the illusion became stronger, until we were impelled to stop and get out the field glasses. To the naked eye it looked now like a little town, and the glasses encouraged the *trompe-l'oeil*, for the rocks were regular and cubiform with slate-coloured tops, arranged like a seaside crescent and looking like nothing so much as Victorian boarding houses. All that was wanting was the flash of windows.

About six miles from this extraordinary feature and less than two from the Chimedzi bore-hole we found what seemed

* The two we saw were simple pipes sunk to the permanent water table and operated by a primitive hand pump. There had been great resistance on the part of the natives to using them, but gradually the dwellers in these seasonally dry areas had become reconciled, though many of the women habitually walked as many as fourteen miles a day for a running stream, fetching the day's supply in waterpots.

to us a perfect camping place, on gently sloping ground splendidly shaded by trees and under the lee of some small wooded crags; these too would give us shade in the afternoon. There seemed to be no native village anywhere near and it was very peaceful. We lit a fire and made coffee under the trees and ate our lunch of bully-beef and Ryvita, which experience had now reduced to a ritual of the utmost simplicity. The Ryvita would be dealt in rotation like cards, then the tin would be opened and passed from hand to hand and the meat dug out with clasp-knives and laid on the biscuits. There was not much washing-up after such a meal; the knives could be cleaned by plunging them into the ground and our enamel mugs rinsed at the bore-hole later. It was delicious to lie back afterwards in the shade and sleep, lulled by the crooning of the small doves which seem to inhabit every grove in Africa, undisturbed by the quiet rustling which by this time we knew to be made by little black boys appearing as usual like spirits out of the bush.

We returned to the Honde camp in high feather, delighted with our success, for our new place, as near as we could calculate, was only twelve or fifteen miles from the M'rongwezi and within easy reach of M'jenami, while the splendid trees and the bore-hole would give us both shade and water. We were dismayed, however, to meet a blandly discouraging response from Michael. It was all very well for us, he said, but the *munts* would not go to another camp where there was no river. They did not count wells and bore-holes and would not use them; there must be a river into which they could plunge to wash themselves and their clothes, and where John could do the laundry. It was their invariable custom; they thought it unspeakably dirty to wash in bowls, and it was no good expecting them to change their habits. He saw the point, he said; a river was essential. The obvious thing was to

move twenty miles further west and camp on the Sabi. The M'rongwezi, being in this area, was probably dry, but the Sabi was immense and never failed. There would be plenty to shoot there, he added wistfully. We should all enjoy it.

Always a weakling in argument, and now feeling the additional discomfort of a bad conscience, since Michael's transparent friendliness had made me fond of him and I felt uneasy not to be telling him the truth, I withdrew into my stifling tent and lay on the bed, leaving it to the others to convince him. They succeeded soon enough by their own methods, Peter being a forceful exponent of his own opinions and Jack persuasive, and it was settled at last that we should move in the morning. The boys had been soothed by the promise that we should settle for several days in the new camp and that Michael, to whom continuous restless exertion was a necessity, would take them every second day to the Sabi River. This had disposed, we thought, of all their grievances, but it now transpired that the cook had developed another. On a proper safari, he said, the minimum provision was one African servant to one European; there were four of us and only three of them, and therefore (he did not put it in quite these words but this was the gist of his thesis) the balance of nature was disturbed. Moreover, he himself could not properly be counted as one of the three, since his sole province was the kitchen, and he should not be asked to help in moving camp. And one final point: he should correctly be addressed as "Chef," and not as "Cook."

Michael strode away from him without answering, his face pink and his Rhodesian hackles rising. His own solution, he told us, would be to give him a hiding; but in deference to our feelings, and at some sacrifice of bossmanship, he would overlook the bastard's cheek this once and try to think of some workable arrangement. The cook was a city *munt*, a

soft *munt*; he had never been on safari in his life; it had been a great mistake to bring him. The trouble was, the only other applicant for the job, though a better cook and used to the bush, had been a known thief, and Michael's father had been reluctant to employ him. With John, the Zulu, there was never any trouble; he and Michael respected one another. John was twenty-four, a married man, and a Christian; he had sent his second wife back to her father after his conversion. He was gentle in manner and speech and never out of temper; he rarely took part in the others' quarrels, but was usually to be seen smiling at a little distance, hanging out clothes or ironing Michael's shirts on top of the meat-safe.

Shorty was a different character altogether. Thirty-two and coal-black, he was unmarried, cheerful, and a known menace to women. His legs were abnormally short but he was very powerful and could drag whole tree trunks up to the fire, which even Peter or Michael would have despaired of lifting. He was vain of his appearance and was always avid for pieces of cast-off clothing. His chief pride was a chauffeur's cap, ornamented in the front with a free-advertisement badge saying "O.K. Cigarettes"; with this he wore broken sand-shoes, khaki shorts, and a series of vests and sleeveless shirts in every conceivable stage of dissolution. He was hard on his clothes, and Michael had some difficulty in keeping him provided. We all of us in time contributed to his wardrobe, and he rang the changes on a bizarre collection of garments, usually split like a grin after a few days' wear, exposing his shoulder-blades and jaunty buttocks. I never saw anyone else who could so freely express his feelings by his walk. He set off on his forays after the girls strutting like a cockerel, and after a hearty swearing-at by Michael would move away from the scene of the scolding slowly, moving his buttocks with a provocative jerk which was the very epitome of dumb

insolence. But he was a friendly character and bore no grudges, and often gave Michael as good as he got, dodging his hand or boot with a flashing grin and enjoying the ready wit of his own impudence. We became rather fond of Shorty, who was one of nature's clowns and a cheerful sinner. He knew what sin was and greatly enjoyed it, being a member —who could have guessed it?—of the Dutch Reformed Church.

The cook was like neither of these, being a morose character with a sense of his own importance and a permanent grievance due to the fact that he genuinely felt he had been cheated. He had never been on a safari before but had heard great things about it, and I suspect he had calculated that it would enhance his prestige to have been on an expedition with Europeans. He had dressed for the part, and the part had folded under him. There were no elaborate camps and no finger bowls; no big game had been shot; he had not been addressed as "Chef"; and he had done a lot of hard travelling. Now he found himself many miles from home, in a harsh and burnt-up country where the rivers were dry, at the mercy of people who had insulted him twice by cooking their food themselves, and who had known no better than to buy him a kaffir pot. It was too much. He ceased to wear his chef's outfit as a protest, and though he took some part in the work of moving camp, he made it clear that he lowered himself unwillingly.

The crisis came at Chimedzi, as soon as the camp was made, when John had carried the luggage and made the beds and Shorty had dug two trenches and got two fires blazing, and the two of them with Michael in the lorry had taken empty paraffin drums to the bore-hole and fetched water. As darkness fell we had heard some unpleasant snickering laughter in the rocks above us and had thought that as usual we had

attracted an audience, as indeed we had; but it was not boys this time, it was hyenas; and this was the straw which broke the cook's resistance. He downed tools in tears, vowing that he was going home in the morning unless he were promised four pounds above his contract and a present at the end of it, and retired to sulk under a piece of tarpaulin.

We received this ultimatum with some callousness, not seeing how he was to carry out his threat without walking alone for several days through the bush; besides, we were tired of his tantrums and felt it was preferable to live on bully beef for ever rather than endure them. So we ate out of tins and ignored him, and John washed up in water that stank of paraffin. (Our camping in a place where water was fifteen minutes by lorry had revealed yet another gap in our equipment: the canvas water bags on our list proved to be only one, and that a small one, so that every journey yielded only half a gallon.)

It was a warm and marvellously beautiful night, quite dark except for the stars, which streamed like phosphorescence in a deep sea and, as the fire dwindled, shed a ghostly brilliance. I decided to sleep out. Even on cold nights I had found the tent oppressive, and now Jack, who had a sore throat and was feeling vaguely unwell, had taken to snoring on a scale that made sleep within a couple of feet of him impossible. I dragged my bed out, and Michael helped me to carry it to the fire. He had given up the use of a bed himself, preferring to scoop out a hollow in the ground and get into it with blankets. Certainly our camp beds were particularly torturous, and mine, as well as having a wooden crossbar at the exact point where a bed is bound to receive the human hip, had a habit of kneeling down in the night like a camel. Still, the pleasure of lying out under those stars, with the fire's glowing trench warming the blankets and the leaves

curling with heat a great distance above, was so exquisite that discomfort soon faded and one sank into sleep on waves of dreamlike contentment.

I was wakened suddenly, after a long time it seemed, by a stealthy rustling in the bushes behind my bed. I lifted my head and listened, a tremor of shock rippling over my skin. It was very dark, for the fire had died down and was no more than a trough of faintly glowing ash. I could just make out Michael, prone as a log on the other side, his head under the blankets, obviously fast asleep. From the two tents, a good way off, came rising and falling cadences of snoring. Nobody else had stirred. After a brief silence it came again, and my tingling senses told me it was nearer. Something was moving cautiously in the thicket, in the thorny tangle that lay between my bed and the foot of the rocks. I called to Michael. There was no response. After a shiver of indecision I got out of bed and shook him vigorously by the feet, which were sticking up oddly under his grey blanket. Still he did not stir. I grasped his shoulder, shouting in his ear; but all he did was to make some childish sounds and turn over in his sleep, for all the world like the Flopsy Bunnies when Mr. McGregor was putting them into his sack. I had never known anybody to sleep like this except a child, and I stood still with dismay at the realization that, short of pouring a bucket of water over him or pulling off the bedclothes, Michael was unawakable.

There was no question of crossing the open ground to either of the tents, so I got hurriedly back into bed, visited momentarily by that old panic of childhood in which one's legs feel morbidly vulnerable in the dark. No sooner had I I done so than a figure came silently padding out of the blackness, ears pricked, muzzle seriously intent. It was Shadow doing his nightlong round of the camp and pausing to investigate my disturbance. He stared into the bushes for a

moment, then turned away with an eloquent lack of interest that told me plainly enough I need not have bothered. Some small nocturnal animal, some hungry kaffir dog scavenging for food was all it was, and Shadow's expression, as he laid his muzzle momentarily on my pillow, was tolerant. He did not stay, but went off again on his silent reconnaissance.

I saw now that he was an invaluable member of our company, and that we need have no fear of night alarms while he was with us. He slept little during the hours of darkness: he always lay down with Michael at bedtime but was rarely there if one woke during the night, being seen only at intervals, making his stealthy rounds on the outskirts of the camp or sitting alert and aloof at a little distance. Michael assured us that no animal would approach the camp while Shadow was there, and he operated the same system against Africans during the day. It was his delight to go bounding through the bush after little boys, sending them mad with terror and stopping only reluctantly and at the last moment when Michael yelled at him. When we asked if he always gave up at the word of command Michael said, "Well...usually," leaving us with the feeling that there had been a few enjoyable sporting incidents. Both by training and temperament Shadow was an uncompromising Rhodesian.

6

M'JENAMI

BEFORE sunrise the little doves inhabiting all the trees and rocks of Chimedzi would begin their rhythmic daylong conversations, and I would get stiffly out of bed and mend the fire, dragging together the heavy logs that had burned through in the night and blowing the ash until I could boil the kettle. While the water heated I crouched beside the blaze, shivering in spite of my flannel pyjamas, warming the teapot and trying to distinguish between the musical phrases. The Chimedzi doves had three, and I was never able to discover whether these were different sentences, so to speak, or the characteristic calls of separate species. The opening statement, sleepily murmured at the first hint of light, was in three syllables, with a soft stress in the middle. It sounded as though they were calling "m'*faz*-i, m'*faz*-i, m'*faz*-i" over and over again, a word I heard often in jesting conversations between Michael and Shorty and which was Shona for "woman." Michael was particularly fond of a story about one of the African boys on his father's farm, who had asked for an advance of a pound above his wages because he wanted an *m'fazi*. The average bride price being anything up to thirty pounds, Michael's father had suggested that he wouldn't get much of a bride for only one, to which the reply had been, "That's all right, boss, she very second-hand."

Now it seemed that the doves were all calling for their brides, and the bush was alive with the gentle amorous rhythm. Presently another statement would be made, still in three syllables but with the stress shifted. "Kroo-kroo-*kroo* . . . kroo-kroo-*kroo*" they were saying now, as though developing the theme, or perhaps starting a different one, a second movement. Before that was quite finished a third would begin, this time in four syllables and very emphatic; I could find no words to fit it except the prosaic injunction "Take the *Ro*-ver," to which the lovely call had a ludicrous resemblance; and by the time I had made the tea and carried cups to Michael and the two tents this insistent invitation would be sounding from massed choirs all over the woods. I have since heard it reproduced in speech as "Kroo, who *are* you? Kroo, who *are* you?" and have been told that this is the call of the mourning dove, found all over Africa; but it never struck me at the time as at all sad, only infinitely gentle and affectionate. There were other birds at Chimedzi, in particular a long, ungainly hornbill, which sailed about the crags like a glider but always landed in an unbalanced fashion, as though performing this operation for the first time; but we knew none of them by name, and Michael when asked could only say that they were crows. He would have made a fine gamekeeper, having the instinct to shoot at anything that moved; when his gun was not to hand, which was seldom, he would throw up his arm at any bird and take a sight along a finger.

Our first necessity, now that we were settled within reach of Umgila's territory, was to make certain of our position on the map and to take bearings. The map showed a hill called Lusongo about six miles away, which we hoped would be the rocky escarpment we had examined through the glasses; but of this we could not be certain, for natives questioned at the bore-hole said it was Chitopa, and shook their heads when

we mentioned the other name. If it *were* Lusongo, it was nearly two thousand feet above sea level, and according to the map had a survey beacon on top. Since we were already at an altitude of about fifteen hundred this would make the height of the feature about four or five hundred feet, which seemed right; but there was no way of being certain except to climb it. We had had a good look at it from the top of our own crags, and had again marvelled at the architectural illusion of its summit, which varied according to the light between a uniform row of houses and a noble ruin.

After one or two false starts, following promising-looking trails through the high grass which ended at a mealie patch, we brought the Land Rover to the foot of the ascent and left it under the shade of a giant boulder. The hill was almost as steep as a cliff, and the grassy gullies by which we climbed were full of thorn bushes, the now familiar "wait-a-bit thorn" which is such an excruciating expert in delay, but we scrambled up slowly, Peter leading, clapping his hands smartly to discourage snakes. When we reached the top and came out on the very crags we had seen from Chimedzi, the sweat was running into my eyes so that I could scarcely see; but as our breathing quieted and we sat on the warm rocks in a welcome breeze, we slowly took in a view of some magnificence.

Lusongo—for so it proved to be, having a miniature cement obelisk stuck on its summit, marked with its name and altitude—was a huge rocky pile shaped on one face like a fortress and commanding a sweep of country that stretched in monotonous levels to the horizon. Only to the northeast, perhaps five miles away, was there a break in the monotony, a wooded hill shaped like a stranded mastodon, not high enough to be called a mountain but craggy and steep and about seven miles long, which map and compass confirmed as M'jenami.

Beyond it was the first faint outline of what might have been further hills, too far off in the heat-hazed distance to be more than a supposition. This was the direction, according to Russell's map, in which Kyabanga and the high veldt lay, and we guessed that from M'jenami we should be able to get a clear idea of this further country. To climb M'jenami, then, was our next target, and we gazed at it through the glasses with an illogical prophetic feeling that it was bound to yield us some essential clue. We would make an immediate attempt to search for ruins, and under cover of the search see if we could not discover something to our purpose. The missionaries had told us we should need a guide, and this we saw was essential; for apart from the fact that we might as well see the ruins while we were about it, we had learned enough to know that on a bush-covered seven-mile hill it would be only too easy to be lost.

We put our plans to Michael when we returned to camp and found that he had spent the morning bargaining for another goat, this being his sovereign device for keeping the *munts* happy; a scraggy animal had already been shot and skinned and partially committed to the pot. The cook, with an air of melancholy grandeur, had announced that he would stay, and was already peeling onions and preparing to astonish us with a curry. Michael obligingly went off to Mariya to ask the schoolteacher for a guide and for an extra campboy if one were available. The grievances of the last few days seemed all to have evaporated, and with the smell of cooking and with John and Shorty full of smiles the camp had quite an atmosphere of festivity. There was, indeed, to be a beer-drinking that night in the nearby village, to which they were all invited, and the promise of a party had cheered them up like magic. We had seen no sign of a village when we came to Chimedzi but had nevertheless discovered that the woods

were thickly populated, and from the top of our own crags, with the field glasses, had been able to distinguish a score of native huts, their thatch the same dry colour as the trees and to the naked eye quite invisible.

That night we sat round a fire of huge dimensions and ate a curry which really earned the repentant cook his title. We sent appreciative compliments to the chef, who came into the circle of firelight and bowed gravely. All was well. Already the drums were warming up for the beer-drinking, and Michael had returned with the promise of a guide for the morning. No difficulty had been made; the guide had said he knew the ruins well and would come at first light and take us to them. We could hear little snatches of singing coming from a distance, and as the night wore on the drums became louder and gayer, rumbling and thumping in a variety of rhythms, with bursts of sociable shouting and women's laughter. Our boys had been given a shilling or two apiece as a contribution to the beer-making, and the cook had unbent so far as to brew a little himself in the kaffir pot, maturing it by some private process during the afternoon. They returned in the small hours, falling over the washing-up bowl in the dark and giggling like children. The drums were still going, thumping and vibrating contrapuntally; each time a blessed silence fell another would begin; they did not die away until nearly six o'clock, when it was broad day.

At seven we were ready for our guide, but he did not come. The dawn chorus of the doves was over, and a brooding quiet had settled over the bush. Shorty was half-awake but unable to stand, so John was sent off to the bore-hole to make enquiries. He came back with the polite message that the guide was very sorry, he had broken his leg. This, Michael said, could mean anything. It could probably be interpreted as a hangover; or it could equally well be that he was

afraid of the ruins and had no intention of showing them to Europeans. Michael sent a sharp message to the local head-man; and this in time produced two old men with sacks over their shoulders, recommended by the headman as reliable and said to be conversant with the ruins. Hands on hips, with Shadow in attendance, he questioned them in Shona.

"Do you know any ruins on M'jenami?"

"Yes, boss."

"If we take you to the foot of the mountain in the lorry, can you find the trail?"

"Yes, boss."

"Will you take us there today?"

"No, boss."

"Why not?"

The old men grinned and looked at one another.

"The wind blew them away."

It was hopeless. Michael by this time had become infected with our determination and went off in the lorry to see the headman himself. He came back looking triumphant, with a sober-looking elderly man with pierced ear-lobes who said he would willingly act as guide for a few shillings. He knew the ruins well; there was no difficulty.

We provisioned ourselves with bully beef and coffee-making equipment, taking Michael as interpreter and Shorty with mattock and *panga*, the long-bladed African knife essential for slashing a way through dense growth, and set off in the Land Rover for M'jenami. We followed the old, dread-ful trail to the south, which had given us so much trouble in the dark, but only for several miles, stopping at a point which, in our need to refer to places which had no names, we privately thought of as "the baboon village." There was no village there, only a few tattered mealie patches which were already harvested, but it must have been much frequented by

baboons, for it was dotted about with those small thatched shelters in which boys are set on guard in the growing season to scare the baboons away with stones and shouting. We were now in a shallow valley, with gently rising ground on either side. To our right, less than a mile away, was one of the rocky faces of Lusongo. On our left, not yet steep but with the promise of heights to come, was what we knew must be the base of M'jenami. The grass was head high and very thick; there was no sign of a trail.

Our guide now surprised us by strongly urging that we should climb not M'jenami but Lusongo, where, he said, the ruins were much larger and had, moreover, been built by Europeans. This was suspicious. We had already climbed Lusongo and were pretty certain they were only illusory ruins on that extraordinary rock. This was carefully translated to our guide, who shook his head. Not only were there ruins, he said seriously, but also a cave furnished for habitation, with chairs and tables and even cooking pots. We exchanged glances. We had indeed seen a cave on the day we climbed Lusongo, containing the ashes of an old fire and an empty cigarette packet, and had supposed that they were the spoor of the survey department when they had been erecting the survey mark a few years before. The men had undoubtedly camped in the cave and must at some time have used cooking equipment. Was it possible he thought we wished to see such a place or that it held any interest?

We explained, through Michael, that we did not care for European remains but only for those on M'jenami, which were said to be African. If he did not know those ruins he must say so, and we would look for ourselves. Oh, he knew them well, he said. They were much inferior to the ruins on Lusongo, but if that was what we wished to see he would take

us to it. There was no path; if we had made up our minds, this was the point from which we should have to walk.

He turned resignedly into the long grass and we followed him, parting the feathery fronds with our hands and leaving behind a crushed and narrow trail. The sun was very hot, and we were glad when we came into the chequered shade of trees, for here the grass was mysteriously cool and we could feel the dew. We walked for several miles in this way, always on gently rising ground, skirting patches of mealie and millet here and there and occasionally passing small impermanent-looking huts, each one the nucleus of a primitive small-holding. At each hut we came to our guide paused and, if anyone were within, held a lengthy conference. From one of them eventually he recruited two more men who regarded us unsmilingly but seemed to come willingly enough, nodding their heads and pointing purposefully upwards.

From this point the going was steep and rocky and we began to climb, strung out in a long Indian file of which I was the last and slowest member. The grass was still so high that I often lost sight of the others, and would scramble out of the holes into which I fell with the anxious feeling that if I paused my absence would not be noticed until they reached the summit. Breathing heavily, we came at last to the top of a ridge and stopped to look about us. There was nothing to be seen yet but grass and trees, both just high enough to prevent our getting a view of anything else, and we stood round our guide enquiringly. Questioned by Michael, he now said he did not *precisely* know where the ruins were, but if we fanned out across the top we should surely find them. This we did, glad of the relief of having no further to climb, and shouting from time to time to keep in touch. Presently the word came down the line that our guide remembered now; the ruins were not on this first crest at all but on top of the

next hill, which had just come into sight through a gap in the trees, separated from where we stood by a deep col. It now became apparent that the mountain was not the simple feature it had appeared to be but a complex of successive ridges each higher than the last, culminating in a formidable cluster of naked crags. Like the summit of Lusongo, these crags had an architectural quality, as though they had been partially cut and shaped by man or been fortified by primitive stonework here and there; it seemed probable that the ruins we were seeking would be found somewhere in the body of this splendid bastion.

We descended the col, making our way painfully through intricate barriers of thorns, which the natives living on the lower slopes had apparently constructed as baboon traps. Why the baboons should go into them, as we did, instead of confining themselves to other parts of the hill, was not at first clear; but it transpired that the baboons lived chiefly in the higher rocks, and that the thorny maze was designed to discourage them from crossing the col and coming down to the mealie fields that we had seen earlier. We certainly found, when we had crossed the valley and were climbing the steeper face, that we had come into baboon territory, for we surprised two troops of them within half a mile; they sprang away downhill to the ledges of a cliff and followed our progress from a distance, barking indignantly.

The sun was now unbearably hot, filtering down in a chequered dazzle through the trees, which were too small to afford more than a momentary shade. The grass was less high, but the ground was strewn with boulders and dead thorns, and the grass itself concealed numerous ant-bear holes and fallen branches. The gradient had become increasingly steep; one had often to haul oneself up by handfuls of grass and we no longer spoke, having no breath to spare. I several times

stumbled and fell, and could hear nothing but the noise of my own panting, which was too urgent to disguise. When we came to the crags at last and dragged ourselves up them there was nothing to do but sink on the warm rock, the blood roaring in our ears and all of us speechless.

When he had regained his breath, which he did with enviable ease, our elderly guide courteously beckoned us across the promontory on which we found ourselves and pointed to some clumps of grass and flowering aloe growing in fissures of the rock. We gazed at them blankly, and then saw, as he continued to beckon and point, that in the midst of this tangle of growth and partly concealed was another concrete survey mark, rather bigger than Lusongo's, with a capital 'M' on one side of it and a capital 'R' on the other. This, then, was the official summit of M'jenami and marked the exact boundary between Mozambique and Rhodesia. We nodded and were turning away, more interested in our first view of the seemingly empty plains of Mozambique, when our guide electrified us by saying to Michael that this was the ruin we had wished to see, and that he was happy to have been able to bring us to it.

He seemed sad but not surprised when told that it was nothing of the sort and that he must take Shorty and the two recruits and search the summit until they found some traces of ancient stonework. He withdrew meekly with the others behind a rock, where they held a whispered conference and then squatted on their heels at a little distance and did nothing. It was very puzzling, but we did not greatly care; for though Michael was concerned for our disappointment and eager to resume the search as soon as we were rested, we had in fact found what we had come for, which was a view of the flat country of the M'rongwezi and a glimpse of further hills as yet unnamed. The crag on which we stood jutted sharply out into

the empty air over a dizzy drop. Below that again the skirts of M'jenami spread steeply down and away to an endless plain, dotted with trees and clothed in yellow grass. We could see for many miles into Mozambique, but though we raked the plain with field glasses there was no sign of any trail or habitation. Only, at about five or seven miles' distance, there was a serpentine line of denser vegetation that could have been larger trees and that suggested the presence of a river. Peter and Jack took sights and calculated distances and decided that this meandering line was the M'rongwezi. Its course was discernible for a considerable distance, being lost at length in a shimmer of light and heat that veiled it like a haze. In rainy weather visibility would have been greater, but there had not been a wisp of cloud for many days, and even the outlines of M'jenami quivered. We could not tell whether it would be possible to reach the river by Land Rover or to follow its course when we got there. We had reached a country in which the only sure way of travelling was on foot.

To the northeast, where Russell's map had led us to expect it, we could see the bluish outline of rising hills. How far they extended, or what their height might be, there was no telling; but there was one neatly rounded summit, almost the shape of an ant hill, which caught our attention. It was not marked on our maps and our guide and his aides could not identify it, never having been over the border into "Portuguese." Peter took careful sights and made a tentative pencil mark on the map. If we could postively identify any of these features we would be able to calculate our next move, and with luck might strike Umgila's kraal, where we hoped it would not be remembered how recklessly Russell and his friends had hanged the headman.

We reckoned that from the western foot of M'jenami, where we had started, to this eastern summit was roughly

seven miles. There was nothing to be done now but go down again, for the descent could hardly take less than a couple of hours, and there would be only a narrow margin of daylight left. There was no time to look further for ruins even if we wished to; in any case it had become obvious that so long as we stayed with our present guide we should find nothing. From his general demeanour and that of his supporters, as well as from various grins and winks from Shorty, we suspected that he had never had the smallest knowledge of any ruins, while the other two might possibly know the place but were not going to show it. The trip had been worth their while for the few shillings, and the Europeans had been gulled into the bargain. Our best plan, after all, would be to waste no more time on local talent but to go straight to the chief, Zamchiya, who was a mission-educated man and therefore, one would guess, less likely to be ruled by superstition. We did not know how far his territory extended but we knew it went some way into Mozambique and so must certainly include M'jenami. If he himself would give us a guide we should have an excuse for trying the mountain again, and might even (this was the point) gain information about the river and some of the hills beyond it.

We made our way down in a thoughtful silence broken only by occasional rifle-shots from Michael, who was relieving his feelings by shooting at several baboons. When the time came for our extra guides to leave us, they cheered up noticeably, and the elder of the two, who kept a large drum hanging from one of the posts of his hut, regaled us with a farewell tattoo. We were gravely joined during this performance by the headman of the place, a frail-looking ancient with the pierced ears of a Zulu, dressed in a straight cotton skirt and a very old, shrunken and dust-coloured cardigan. He courteously insisted on walking back with us to the Land

Rover, but when we apologised for having no present to
offer him (a customary gesture of politeness from passing
strangers) he accepted a two-shilling piece with dignity and
went his way.

The only other being whom we saw as we came down
the lower slopes was a nearly naked white boy herding goats,
from whom our guide and Shorty averted their eyes as from
an evil omen. He did not see us at first, being absorbed in
urinating among his flock, his back towards us and his head
bent; but so startling an apparition brought us to a standstill.
His skin was as light as ours and his close-cropped cap of hair
perfectly white; as he peered from side to side we saw that
his eyes were screwed up and his face distorted with the
effort of contending against the light. He was, in fact, an
albino. These freaks, Michael told us, were not uncommon,
for he had seen a good many in his lifetime here and there.
They were tolerated, though regarded as a misfortune. This
tolerance struck us as strange in people who regard any ab-
normality as evil, who smother first-born twins as the work
of devils and meet a difficult labour with punishment as proof
of adultery; the missionaries were finding it uphill work to
discourage such practices. Yet the albino was reluctantly accepted, though no one cared to encounter one. For Shorty and
our guide the poor white boy was a dubious portent for the
day of our first attempt on M'jenami.

Before having another try at the mountain there was much
to be done if we did not wish to repeat the first day's failure.
We must ask help from Zamchiya, for our experience with
guides so far had convinced us that any we were likely to find
for ourselves would be useless. Either they would know nothing and would not say so, or they would go to elaborate
lengths to confuse and mislead us. Anything not understood

must be kept hidden; a curse might fall on the man who showed the haunts of the dead to curious strangers. Russell, we remembered, had thought it possible that a mission-convert —"one of these educated gentlemen" as he slightingly put it— might be willing to reveal Umgila's grave for money. We had not got so far as that yet, and were not going to mention Umgila until we had to, since the name itself was dangerous; but we felt that Zamchiya, being a man of some education and used to the eccentricities of Europeans, might be willing to give us a guide and some sensible information about the country.

Before we could approach him, however, the Land Rover needed skilled attention. The steering was growing worse and Peter spent his spare time under the chassis, tinkering crossly with wholly inadequate tools and thinking of all the things that could happen as a result of the damage. I think it was at this point that Michael began to get seriously on his nerves, and a tension built up which was nourished by trivial incidents. Michael was optimistic and happy-go-lucky; according to him, one bashed through problems somehow; it would be all right in the night. Peter was cautious and exact; he saw no reason to suppose that a damaged mechanism would not give way when it was least convenient, and was irritated by cheerful assertions that we could fake up a spare somehow when we had neither the skill nor the equipment. He became acidly polite to Michael over the tools, which Michael constantly borrowed for the lorry and lost in the grass; and after a time the politeness wore thin and did not cover the acidity. Peter and Michael were both great borrowers, and soon we were all (with the exception of Michael, who had nothing to lend) involved in a crafty game of concealing essential equipment from one another. Electric torches, soap, lavatory paper, matches, the kettle were always disappearing

out of one's tent, and if we made a truce on these things with one another we lost them to the cook, who had always mislaid everything belonging to the kitchen and came prowling round after sunset like a jackal. This is one of the phases, I believe, through which all expeditions pass and which old campaigners learn to survive with good temper. We, being novices, were in the learning stage and had often cause to be thankful that Jack was born to be a peacemaker. The *munts*, incidentally, saw more of this than we supposed, for being unable to grasp our real names they referred to us always by native ones descriptive of behaviour. Michael, whom they knew, was of course "Boss Michael," but I was "the-woman-who-loves-the-fire," and Jack (apt description) "he-who-desires-peace." Peter I am sorry to say, being named in a difficult period, was "he-who-is-often-in-a-rage"; but this we thought it politic not to communicate.

Rightly obsessed by the Land Rover's symptoms and alarmed to find that the drums of petrol and diesel oil that we carried in the lorry were unaccountably low, Peter decided that there was nothing to do but return to Chipinga for repairs and supplies before we went further. He cringed with apprehension whenever Michael went off for wood or water in the Land Rover, driving with fearless dash as though on an assault course; sooner or later, he knew, something would give and land us in some unspeakable predicament. Michael was also fretting to move camp for all the old reasons which had to do with rivers, and accordingly once more we planned to separate. After much studying of maps and some mutually irritating argument, a meeting place was fixed at a drift across the Umzilizwe River, which we privately reckoned would bring us within reasonable distance of Zamchiya's village, also at a point at which we might cross the border into

Mozambique. We would meet there in three days' time and look for a new camp.

When we passed through Chikore we paused only long enough to confirm our guess that the mission had no repair shop and to accept with gratitude the offer of a night's stay on our return. It was extraordinary to discover what a changed aspect Chipinga now wore when we came into it after ten days in the bush. Before, it had seemed the final depressing remnant of everything most distasteful in "civilization." Now it was a metropolis, and we found ourselves gazing at its dead-end street and shoddy buildings with something like excitement. It was like home to join the queue in the one-room bank, open for its weekly three-hour session, and see the teller at work with a half-eaten apple and a revolver beside the till. The Italian hotel proprietor was an old friend, glad to see us in the bar since business was poor owing to the influence of the Dutch Reformed Church—"but they drink plenty brandy at home, is bad for business." Meikles' store and the Greek bazaar in the back street were dazzling in the variety of their goods, and we spent a happy hour shopping for water bags and torch batteries. Best of all was to soak in a hot bath at the hotel and have our clothes washed, for the soil of the Chimedzi camp had been composed of a reddish dust so fine that it rose in a cloud whenever one moved, sifting into hair, clothes, everything. Nor was this all, for it was the evening of the "Free Bioscope Show," which is the peak of Chipinga's social entertainment, and we gaped through several hours of motor-oil and farming documentaries, sitting on hard chairs with our mouths open.

After twenty-four hours of these pleasures the Land Rover was ready, the fuel drums loaded, and luxuries like fresh bread and vegetables packed around our feet. The steering felt healthy again, and we reached Chikore without mishap

in the evening, rehearsing a number of questions to which we hoped to get answers from the missionaries. These were chiefly to do with place names, for the time had come when we felt we must get some clue to Russell's likeliest route from the M'rongwezi and to the identity of the hill called Kyabanga. Unfortunately Mr. Blakney was away for that night, and no one felt able to advise on points which depended on differences between Chindau and Zulu. He was expected back some time the following day, and in the meantime they would give us guides to some known Bantu ruins which could be seen about seven miles away from the mission.

This was a loss of time, but it could not be helped. Once we had left Chikore we might never be able openly to ask such questions, and trivial though they might seem to the uninitiated, to us they were important. The nearer we came to it, the more dangerous it might be to mention Kyabanga; the ideal would be to gather some private knowledge from Chikore and arrive at the vital place apparently by chance. So we displayed a proper enthusiasm for the ruins, since we were determined if possible to wait for Mr. Blakney, and were sent off with two youths from the secondary school called Robert and Adonis. Robert, the younger, had been chosen because he positively knew the ruins; Adonis because he spoke English and had brains. It is difficult to judge the age of Africans, but I imagine they were about fifteen and seventeen. The missionaries had been amused and sympathetic over our failure on M'jenami, and assured us that these boys, being Christians, would be unlikely to mislead us through superstition. And so indeed it proved. After some miles of the usual intolerable trail, winding always steeply uphill into a cooler air and an almost English type of vegetation, they led us through a rank-smelling thicket and parted the leaves to show us the crumbling remains of stone walls.

Nothing was left of them now but their foundations, about four feet thick and two or three feet high. They were dry-stone walls, carefully built of uncut slabs, such as one sees in Gloucestershire, and so hidden and overgrown with trees and brambles that it was impossible to form any accurate idea of the shape of the original structure, though we guessed it to be roughly in the form of a ring, and the diameter, which we paced, was over three hundred feet. It had been built on the very crown of the hill and ran right to the edge of an escarpment, looking over a splendid gorge and endless empty miles of forest and bush. Robert, the younger boy, had become uneasy as soon as we came into this place, but Adonis was more sophisticated and scrambled about with us, peering under the leaves. When I asked him, however, to cut away a stout ivy with his *panga* so that I could take a photograph, the amiable smile faded from his face and he said in a shocked voice, "The trees must not be cut."

When we got back to Chikore Mr. Blakney had not returned. We lingered uneasily, afraid of outstaying our welcome in this busy place, where everyone, husbands and wives alike, seemed to rush from classroom to classroom all day long and there was no end to the orderly bell-ringing and chanting; but we wished, we said, to say good-bye to him, and packed our things in the Land Rover very slowly. And at last, just as we were shaking hands with our kind hosts, another Land Rover bumped across the campus and an energetic figure dived towards the whitewashed bungalow that served as an office. We caught him on the steps, and in the midst of much jovial hand-shaking I drew him aside and showed him a paper on which I had written some names, asking for help on spelling and pronunciation. Yes, he said after a moment, Umgila and Umzila were the same. He had

heard of him; he had been a chief, he thought, some place or other; since it was a Zulu name Umzila would certainly be the correct version. He had never heard of Mandhlami or his kraal, and shook his head dubiously over Kyabanga. Was it the name of a person or a place? What had my uncle said about it? There was a word in Chindau, *kabanga*, which meant "perhaps": could this have any bearing on the matter? I did not like the sound of this at all, for it seemed suddenly and dreadfully possible that this might have been, indeed, what Russell had heard; though on second thought his fair knowledge of the language made it improbable. "See here, though," said Mr. Blakney, frowning at the paper, "come and see Fred Sigauke in the office. He's our primary out-schools clerk and language expert; he taught us all what little Chindau we know."

He took us into a bare room where Mrs. Abbott and one or two young serious-looking Africans were unpacking crates of school books and stacking them on shelves. With them was a middle-aged, stout, extremely black man whose face creased into a smile at the sight of strangers and who was introduced to us as Mr. Sigauke. Yes, he knew the border country all right. Yes, yes, there was a kraal called Mandhla-ame; he pronounced it Mandla-āme, and corrected the spelling on my paper, holding it against a textbook close to his face. Peter and Jack affected to examine bookshelves, unable to bear the suspense of the next question. Did he happen to know a hill called Kyabanga? The office was suddenly quiet; I held my breath. Mr. Sigauke burst into a jolly laugh. Well, yes, he knew the hill, but I pronounced it wrong. It was *Nyabánga*, and it meant something, yes, yes, let him think, it meant "he who flourishes the big knife." Did he know by any chance where the hill was? We had heard the name, and

thought we would like to see it. Oh yes, he knew very well.
He had never been there. But he knew it was over the border
in Mozambique. As casually as I could, I unfolded our best,
but now tattered and dust-stained, map. Could he show us the
place perhaps? There was always a chance that we might be
going that way. He put on his spectacles and moved his finger
doubtfully over the map. Well, here perhaps, or here; he
could not say exactly. I saw that his finger was wandering
lost in the middle of Southern Rhodesia, and that the map
meant nothing to him, and was a mystery. It was all bush,
he said. Very sorry. He could not precisely tell.

This was enough, however, to send us off from Chikore
privately rejoicing. There could be no doubt now about the
name of the hill. Or could there? We made valiant attempts
to distrust our swelling optimism, to maintain that the difference of a letter must not be ignored, that the hill was not
necessarily our hill because all the other details fell into
place. It was no use. The river was similar in name and
identical in position with the one on Russell's map. Mandhlami's kraal was certainly Mandhla-āme, since it was customary
for a kraal to bear the name of its chief, as Zamchiya stood
both for the place and the man. The hills we had seen were
where Russell had marked the fringe of the high veldt; and
now the word that we had carried from the beginning as a
talisman had been recognised and confirmed as the name of
a hill some miles into Mozambique, in the direction in which
we had always believed we should find it. If only the hill
could be identified from a distance we should be spared the
doubtful search for Umzila's kraal, which now, more than
forty years since Russell had dug his trenches, might well be
unidentifiable. If Zamchiya could give us a guide who could
do this for us we should go straight to the spot on which our

search depended, without losing time in a hunt for obliter-
ated villages.

Michael was found at the drift according to plan, not at
all discomposed by the long hours of waiting and passing
the time with Shorty in washing the lorry. This river was
a tributary of the Umzilizwe and still had water in it, which
encouraged us to follow a trail to the northeast, where we
expected to strike the Umzilizwe proper.

This trail was by far the worst we had yet struck; the
vehicles groaned and crashed from rock to rock, and as mile
succeeded mile we were dismayed to think how often they
would have to tackle it, since there would be no other way of
leaving or returning to camp. But the Umzilizwe itself seemed
almost worth it. It was a real river even at this season, running
through a succession of wooded gorges above the spot we
finally decided on, where it spread itself into shallows that
could be crossed on foot. Here the ground was level and the
air sweet. Wooded hills rose up on either side and there was
ample shade. The tents were pitched within a few yards of the
river and our chairs set out in a little bower of trees which the
sun could not penetrate even at midday. As usual we were
further off than we wished to be, in the cul-de-sac of a
rough and destructive trail, but we had learned to be thankful for peace and running water, and in this bosky place even
the *munts* seemed happy. In no time at all John had got the
bushes full of washing, the cook was squatting in the shallows
scouring saucepans, and Shorty, watched by some giggling
girls on the further bank, was taking a modest bath in the
river with his clothes on.

We decided to rest for at least a day in camp, since Jack
was still troubled with sore throat and a general feeling of las-
situde and malaise, and was trying all the pills in the medical

bag with discouraging results. The river itself was tempting
to explore, and after a peaceful night we made our way on
foot through the gorges to some hidden falls, and passed the
day in the roar and spray of their waters. After so many days
in the burnt-up bush this green and virgin place was an oasis.
It was so hidden under rose-red cliffs and hanging forest that
one could easily believe no human being had ever been there
before, and indeed during the whole of that halcyon day we
saw no one. The invisible deity of the pool was presumably a
crocodile, whose basking place Michael found on a well-worn
ledge where the grass was littered with stinking fish-bone
fragments and there was a convenient muddy slide into the
river. This made Michael, for one, deeply happy, for he
was ashamed of having never shot a crocodile and carried a
paper-back treatise on the subject wherever he went. He was
intent all day on luring the creature into view, but it knew a
trick worth two of that and remained submerged, while
Michael fretted along the bank with his gun, eyeing every
floating twig and fragment of bark in the hope that they
might turn out to be crocodiles' nostrils. Shadow was eventually sent into the pool, being an old campaigner who had
done battle with a crocodile in his time; and when even this
living bait failed, Michael himself went in, looking deliciously
edible and gingerly swimming about with a hunting knife.
He took the precaution of getting Jack to stand on the bank
with a rifle, but how this would help, if the crocodile should
decide to engage, was never made clear. I think Jack was
relieved at not having to distinguish between them in a hurry.

The next morning, while Peter and Michael explored some
internal disorder of the lorry, which was refusing to start
unless towed for a short distance by the Land Rover, Jack
and I set out to find Zamchiya. Our best approach to the Chief
was through Mr. Hla-Hla, whose farm and store we knew,

and who was reputed to be an enterprising character. We found him to be both intelligent and charming, with a fair command of English, and eager to talk. He was so civil and communicative indeed, and so evidently flattered at being consulted about anything so educational as ruins, that we were devoutly thankful not to have Michael with us. One curt demand, one thoughtless touch of lordly Rhodesian manner, and Mr. Hla-Hla, we guessed, would have been lost to us. He had been schooled himself at Mount Selinda and was clearly one of those forward-looking Africans who are more than half in love with the white man's world. He asked at once if we came from a university, concealing his disappointment when he heard that we had only an amateur's interest in archaeology. Were there really ruins on M'jenami, he asked? He had never heard of them, but then Africa was littered with ancient ruins that white Rhodesians insisted were not Bantu. They had to be the work of the Portuguese or of Arab traders—anything rather than admit that the African might have been clever enough to build them. Chief Zamchiya might know something, certainly; he, Joel Hla-Hla, would take us at once to the school and introduce us.

Zamchiya school was larger and tidier than Mariya; it even had flower beds of a sort, which we pretended to study while Hla-Hla, hat in hand, went the round of the classrooms looking for the Chief. When Zamchiya at last emerged, he looked so genuine that our hearts failed us. He was a tall, powerful-looking man of perhaps fifty-five, dressed as we were in crumpled khaki cotton, but with a dignity of demeanour that was impressive; there was no mistaking that air of ancient authority. We exchanged courtesies, everything having become suddenly formal. We could not tell from his face, which was impassive, nor from Hla-Hla's, which was anxious, whether or not the Chief was pleased to see us. Our

intrusion in the middle of school was perhaps an impertinence, for all that he said when he had read the letter was, "I see." His reserved manner, however, meant nothing unfavourable and was more probably due to the surprise of the occasion. M'jenami, he said, was in his territory, and when we made our request for a guide he considered a little, and eventually said he would take us there himself.

This was better than we had hoped for, and we went back to camp in a state of nervous elation. Zamchiya, being Chief of the district, would know the country; as an educated man and a Christian he would probably have no objection to showing us anything; but he might also—and this was a thought which gave us pause—know all about Umzila and his treasure and be suspicious of Europeans in his territory. Was it this, perhaps, that had made him decide to accompany us himself? Or was his offer simply a gentlemanly gesture? One thing was certain: we must keep Michael as much as possible out of his company, since any brusqueness or ordering about would be fatal, and our hopes would depend entirely on good relations.

We held a furtive conference with Peter and decided that the best thing would be to persuade Michael to go off by himself for a couple of days to shoot, while we concentrated on the Chief and M'jenami. Fortunately he needed no persuading; he had been disgusted all along by the scarcity of game, and the thought of the tsetse-fly man at Hippo Mine, happily shooting everything in sight, continually fretted him. He jumped at the idea, eagerly agreeing that ruins were not in his line and that it would be better for him to bring back some buck for the larder. He would go off in the morning in the lorry, taking John; the cook and Shorty would feed us and look after the camp, and Shadow would stay and afford us his protection. It wouldn't do, he said as a simple pleasantry, to come back and find we had all been eaten by leopards.

"Though as a matter of fact," he added reassuringly, "a leopard rarely attacks a human being. They'll always take a *munt* by preference, if there's a choice."

Next morning we rose in the dark and breakfasted at sunrise, while Michael prepared the lorry for Hippo Mine. Jack was feeling worse; he complained of headache and was quite voiceless, and had also a slight temperature, so it seemed sensible that he should stay in camp. Shadow, too, had plans of his own, for when he had received his orders and the lorry started he shot like a missile after it and was not seen again. Listening, we heard the lorry stop and start again, and guessed that Shadow had gained his point and would now be sitting erect in the passenger seat, willingly enduring Michael's half-hearted scolding.

Peter and I set off in the Land Rover, bracing ourselves for the first five miles of the trail, which we had named Dead Man's Gulch and which was as murderous as ever. It seemed only a matter of time before the Land Rover would be literally shaken to pieces. By contrast the trails on the other side of the drift seemed almost like roads, and we sighed with relief as we rattled and bumped along them to Zamchiya.

The Chief emerged from the school as soon as we arrived, beautifully dressed for the expedition in starched and well-pressed khaki jacket and shorts, dazzlingly polished boots, a felt hat with a leopard-skin hatband, and his brass badge of chiefly office gleaming on a chain at his breast. He seemed pleased at the prospect of a day off, and carried a basket of oranges.

We left the Land Rover at the "baboon village" as before, and here the Chief surprised us by recommending, as our first guide had done, that we should climb Lusongo instead. This shook our confidence for the moment, for we thought we had already passed that tiresome phase; but he agreed amiably

enough to M'jenami and led us briskly into the high grass, forging uphill at a good four miles an hour. The route he chose was more circuitous than our first, and led steadily round to the other side of the mountain. Our hopes began to revive, for he walked with the purposeful speed of a man who knows where he is going and is oblivious of lesser beings panting behind him. We did not pant so much in the first two hours while he kept to the lower slopes, passing through a number of scattered small-holdings, but when once he began to climb it was cruel work, and no matter how harsh the ascent, through rocks and thorns and tangled nets of creeper, it seemed to me that his speed never slackened. I struggled a long way below the others, with crazed thoughts of burst lungs and heart failure, and not enough breath to shout after them for a halt. My boots were beginning to give trouble, for having been bought in Salisbury, where apparently boots for women are unknown, they were two sizes too big, and in spite of two pairs of socks were slipping abominably. I could feel the blisters rising on my heels, and as the skin of my toes wore through I thought almost with tears of the beautiful handmade boots that anyone with a grain of sense would have had made in London. I had to stop at last, for the corrosive ridges in my socks were beyond bearing; and when finally my nonappearance was noticed, Zamchiya came nimbly back to see what had happened and stood over me, not out of breath at all but gently concerned, and peeled me one of his beautiful, thirst-quenching oranges.

At the end of the last and worst ascent, scrambling in painful silence up ledges and crags, it was a shock to find ourselves on the very spot that we had reached on our first climb. Here were the clump of aloes, the survey mark, the blackened ashes of our fire. Peter and I sat down in silence under a rock. Presently Zamchiya collected and kindled some sticks,

and when we had breath we questioned him. It now transpired that he had never heard of any ruins and thought it was the summit crags we had wished to see. Whether he had really understood us I have no idea, but he being the man he was (if one can ever judge anybody) we believed he was speaking the truth. It did not greatly matter. We were gazing over the plains of his Portuguese territory, with the shadowy thread of the river distantly visible and the blue-smudged hills far off on the eastern horizon. These were what we had wished to see in his company, and when we had shared our coffee and bully-beef I took some photographs of the view as a preliminary to asking some innocent questions.

Did M'jenami, the name of the mountain, mean anything? "Oh yes," he said, "there is a meaning. It means . . . now let me see . . . 'the rocks that laugh.' " We pondered this for a while, not liking it much. There was, he went on, hesitating for words, a belief among his people that a great lion inhabited these rocks, and that was perhaps what made our guides unwilling. They were, of course, he said deprecatingly, superstitious. They had strong feelings against showing anything to white men, since everything ancient belonged to spirits, even these rocks, and they were afraid of what might happen if things were disturbed. Europeans were apt to disturb by digging. This was well known. They were always looking for gold and precious stones, and the people believed if such things had ever been buried in the earth, that they had been put there for good reason and must remain hidden. He shook his head indulgently over this idea, while Peter and I stared at him in fascination, searching for hidden meaning in his expression. We found none. That was why, he continued, he had thought it best to show us the mountain himself. He understood, if he did not share, these feelings, and would be sorry to see us misled.

A little shaken by this conversation, and silently wondering how many of the Chief's people remembered Russell, who had passed that way and hanged a headman while Zamchiya was a boy, we moved to the edge of the rocks and asked him to show us the limits of his territory. He considered a little, shading his eyes with his hand, then pointed to the tree-lined curve of the M'rongwezi. "As far as the river," he said, "if you can see it. I end there." And in the other direction, I asked, how far did he go? He shifted his ground and pointed to the northeast. "I go to that hill."

"That mound-shaped one, do you mean? Like an ant heap?"

"Yes, that one."

"What is the name of the hill?"

"It is called Guma."

I had a sensation as though my heart had dropped, and knew what extravagant hopes had hung on his answer. There was a silence, and we all gazed at the hill.

"Is that the native name?"

"Oh no, it is Portuguese. We call it differently."

"What is the native name?"

"It is Nyabánga."

We slowly took out our field glasses, praising the view. Peter and I did not look at one another. Seen through the glass it was quite a sizeable hill, symmetrical and without any noticeable feature beyond a large tree distinguishable near the summit. We turned away after a brief look, nervous as to how the conversation might develop; but Zamchiya had already gone back to the fire and was stamping it out methodically with his boot. He seemed mildly worried still that we had found no ruins and suggested that we should go down by a different way. This meant a long and agonising detour, in which eventually nothing to me seemed desirable but to fall with a cry on the ground and give up the struggle. Down

we stumbled through rocks and thorns and the abominable grass, which concealed endless pitfalls and closed at times triumphantly over my head. I seemed to float at last through a trance of fatigue, my body falling forward as though through deep water and my limbs propelled by a power outside myself. There were light-headed moments when I told myself, and believed, that an influence sustained me which came from Nyabánga.

7

THE APPROACH TO NYABÁNGA

THE camp was very quiet without Michael. The cook and Shorty were on their best behaviour, nobody whistled or sang or did target practice, Jack was better; and after M'jenami it was wonderful to spend the next day doing nothing. I washed my hair and read *Edwin Drood* while Peter fished peacefully for barbel. With Shadow away the birds were noticeably bolder, and a small donkey which seemed to belong to nobody had wandered up from the river and was grazing along the sweet grass of the bank. I had been a little dubious about sleeping out by myself, since my bed was a good way off from the tents and the nights were dark; but everything had been quiet and reassuring and I had slept the sleep of exhaustion beside the fire.

On the second night, though, I was startled broad awake about midnight by a stealthy sound which my ears interpreted as someone tripping over the washing-up bowl. This large enamel object was always to be found lying somewhere in the grass, surrounded by sundry bits of the cook's equipment, and the sound of its being shifted was unmistakable. My first thought, as I sat up in bed with a start, was that Shorty and the cook must have sneaked off to a beer-drinking without permission, and had stumbled tipsily over the thing in the dark. After a time, however, as there was no further sound,

I concluded that they had found their way to bed, and I lay down again. Just as my muscles had relaxed and I had begun to drowse, the noise was repeated. This time there was no mistaking it. The big bowl had been pushed aside by something and had touched another object with a light clank. I raised myself cautiously on one elbow and played the beam of my torch over the camp. The battery was a new one and the beam strong, but it showed nothing. No one was stirring: the camp was as still as death. The fire had died down completely, and after listening uneasily to the silence, I got out of bed and tried to coax a flame out of the ashes. It revived soon enough, for the trench was still red-hot under the surface and I built it up with wood to a bright blaze. Now I could see more clearly, and assured myself that there was nothing there. The *munts* had not stirred from their tarpaulin and bushes and grass were motionless. I got back into bed and lay awake for a while, hearing a stealthy sound from time to time as though something were nosing about among empty tins, but I was convinced by now that it could be nothing more than one of the skin-and-bone kaffir dogs that we sometimes saw, taking advantage of Shadow's absence to do a little opportune scavenging.

In the morning, making his way through the bushes behind the camp, Peter stumbled over the front half of the donkey, lying clotted with blood and almost hidden in the grass. The hind quarters and legs had been eaten completely; even the bones were gone; the ribs stuck out from the tatters of hide and flesh. We stood round the sorry spectacle in amazement. From the look of the grass it was evident that the body had been somehow dragged through the camp, disturbing the cook's muddles in its passage, and been taken to this discreet spot to be devoured. It seemed extraordinary that dogs, how-

ever hungry, could accomplish such a thing, and we were mystified afresh when as the morning wore on they began to appear in timid ones and twos, skirting nervously round the bushes and appearing almost too frightened to approach their meal. How had these small and skinny creatures killed it? They made progress with the carcass during the day, but far less than they had managed during the night, and the head, shoulders and forelegs remained uneaten. The dogs disappeared at sundown, and the third night was quiet and without incident.

We had been expecting Michael all that day, but he had not returned, and we were wondering how long we should wait before crossing the border into Mozambique. Zamchiya had offered to show us the way when we were ready, and we were glad of this, being anxious not to do anything which might attract attention from the Portuguese. The nearest Portuguese native commissioner was at Spungabera, about thirty miles away as the crow flies, but news travels mysteriously in the bush, and a party of Europeans crossing the border without permission was likely to be reported soon enough. If Zamchiya went with us he would not only show us the way but by his presence allay suspicion in his own people. If he allowed us to camp in his Portuguese territory we should be accepted; if not, we judged it would not be many days before news of our presence reached Spungabera.

The pleasurable suspense of being at last within reach of Nyabánga was beginning to throw up sideshoots of uneasiness which I did not altogether like. I did not like the idea of the Portuguese, whose native administration was known to be severe. They might be unpleasantly interested in treasure and take a harsh view of foreigners looking for it. Nor did I care for the notion—indeed the more I thought of it the less I liked it—of accepting Zamchiya's help in an enterprise which,

if he understood it at all, would certainly appal him. He had impressed us all as a man of unusual quality, whom it was hateful to deceive, but of course we really knew nothing; it was equally possible that he had suspected us from the start, and was going with us for his own precautionary ends. We even canvassed the idea, sitting round the fire on this last night, that it might be prudent to take him into our confidence; but such recklessness was out of the question. What would Russell have said to such pusillanimous behaviour? We needed the moral stiffening of Michael's presence if we were not to be corrupted by feelings of guilty sympathy towards Africans, and his absence underlined yet another uncomfortable thought —that Michael, sooner or later, would have to be told.

He returned about three o'clock the next morning, crashing into camp in a blaze of headlights, with noise and shouting that brought us tumbling from our beds. He was so late because he had had a puncture twelve miles after leaving Hippo Mine, and having naturally forgotten to take a spanner, had had to walk that distance back to borrow one. He reported the area as being seething with game, as he had expected; he had even found hippo spoor round his bed that morning. He had shot a couple of buck and was feeling much happier. He was grimy and tired and had grown the beginnings of a beard, which he had decided not to shave off since it was his first and an object of great interest.

Even the beard was forgotten, however, when he was searching about in the bushes for something he had lost, and stumbled over the poor remains of our donkey. This was a lion kill, he said; how on earth had we managed not to know anything about it? We stood round the sorry fragments once more and I told him about the disturbances of the night and the kaffir dogs that I thought might be responsible; but he insisted that this was the work of a young lion. Dogs could

not possibly have done it, and a leopard, according to custom, would have left the uneaten half of the corpse in a tree, where it would be safe from scavengers. He was amused to think that I had been getting in and out of bed and mending the fire while the lion was patiently waiting in the grass, and said that it could never have happened if Shadow had been there. This was probably true, and I was glad that it was the donkey and not I that had been pulled into the bushes in his absence. In retrospect, the night had concealed a number of possibilities.

When we had all digested the subject and Michael had been fed, he hung up the buck by the heels in a tree and fell asleep by the fire, not waking even when his blankets began to smoulder and I was jerked out of strange dreams by the smell of burning. He slept so late the following day that we had to give up the idea of moving camp, and the afternoon was spent on the theory and practice of making biltong. This was a serious performance, and though I shall probably never need to do it again I like to remember how Michael made it and the gravity with which he performed the ritual.

First, he said, one cut strips of buttock meat, an inch thick and about two inches wide, and slopped it around in a cupful of warm water with three teaspoonfuls of pepper. It was soaked and moved around for about an hour. Then it was taken out, squeezed, and soaked for an hour or two in warm salt water. It was then dried, a handful of coarse salt was put in a basin, the meat dipped in this, and the salt well rubbed in. (This salting and peppering, he explained, was both to preserve the meat and keep the flies off it.) Finally it was hung in a tree in the shade for several days, until it was hard and dry. When it was black outside and nearly dry through it would be ready. The whole thing took hours and looked nasty, but Michael was pleased, and when we moved camp

next morning the biltong was carefully unhooked and travelled with us.

We moved in slow convoy, Jack and Zamchiya and I ahead in the Land Rover, Michael and Peter, Shadow, the *munts* and everything else piled high in the lorry. (I had asked Michael, as a concession to me and my funny ideas, to be specially nice to Zamchiya, Hla-Hla, and any other Africans toward whom we felt friendly: he had promised, in a teasing fashion, but we did not wish to try him too sorely by putting them cheek by jowl.) The Chief had been collected from his house early in the morning, and had loaded us with splendid presents of eggs and fruit. A basket as big as a cradle had been filled with oranges of that delicious and tangerine-like sort called *naartjes,* and at the last moment he had cut two small pineapples from their prickly stalks, growing almost on the ground beside his garden path. As we drove the lovely smell of all this fruit rose up from the littered floor of the Land Rover and was a pleasure in our nostrils.

After an hour of following a well-trodden track, we were seven miles into Mozambique and at the limits of the Chief's territory. We emerged from the bush on to a bare, open space and saw that we were no more than a mile or two from Nyabánga. It rose up in a steep cone of grass and trees, without any sign of rocks or habitation. We could not judge the height of the grass, but from this distance it looked fairly easy to climb; the trees were the usual scrub growth, the only conspicuous feature being the one big tree near the summit, darker in colour than the rest, which we had seen from M'jenami. In the midst of the open ground, trodden hard as rock by the feet of men and cattle, was a line of substantial open sheds with a corral at either end, which had clearly not been built by Africans. This was a cattle-dip, built on Portuguese territory by the Rhodesian Government,

we were told, owing to a mistake over the exact position of the border. The sheds concealed a deep trough, filled with a grey and evil-smelling chemical which discouraged ticks; the cattle for miles around were driven through it once a week. On the far side of this open area was a line of trees with a few green banners of banana showing among them, and it was here that Zamchiya recommended we camp, as the trees concealed a drift across a river. This seemed too good to be true, as indeed it was, for the river proved to be no more than a pestilent-looking trickle where cattle and goats were watered and some women were washing rags in a muddy puddle. The drift was a busy highway, with a constant coming and going of women and children; the whole place was bare, sordid, and public. When Michael arrived with the lorry he agreed at once that it was impossible to camp there; the water was dirty and insufficient and the place was totally lacking in shade and privacy. The only thing, it seemed, was to explore further, following the trail along the river until we came to something better. Zamchiya was willing to go with us, but seemed very doubtful as to what we should find. The road was bad, he said; and this, coming from him, should have made us cautious, but we were anxious to make camp while daylight lasted and impatient to get away from the distasteful place. We could see no harm in trying, and pushed on.

This was an atrocious mistake, as we soon discovered. The sensible course would have been to prospect ahead in the Land Rover, leaving the lorry at the dip; but this for some reason did not occur to us, and the two vehicles ground up a stony hill and dropped down into a narrow valley of dark rain forest. Here the trail was narrow, hemmed in by boulders and trees on either side. The river had disappeared in a leafy chasm, and we climbed in and out of slippery gullies, which in the rainy season must have been lively tributaries,

but which now were precipitous troughs of stones and mud.
There was no room to turn, so we could not go back, and
whenever we paused in dismay at what lay ahead the heavy
breathing of the diesel was close behind us. At length we
were brought up short by a crash and a shout; the lorry had
nose-dived into a narrow chine and was stuck in the bottom.
The Land Rover had scrambled out with difficulty, but the
lorry was too long for the width of the dip; it could not begin
to climb from such an angle, with its hind wheels still so much
higher than its head. There was nothing to do but unload it
and let the Land Rover try to haul it out with chains, and
this after several discouraging attempts succeeded after we
had cut armfuls of branches for the wheels and paved the
mud of the further slope with stones. It came out at last
with a huge roar of distress, and we tried not to think of the
time when we should have to return.

With every mile that we covered our hearts sank, for
though the river now had plenty of water in it and could be
heard among the rocks some distance below, we were still
held as in a vice in our narrow passage, hemmed in by steep
banks of rocks and trees, with not an inch of level ground
and no room to turn. When at last the trail dropped down to
the level of the river and we began to hope, the trail itself
broke out into such a nightmare stretch of rocks and boulders
that Zamchiya and I dismounted in horror, leaving Jack to
plunge and crash as best he could without having our extra
weight in the suffering Land Rover. There were three of
these stretches of hellish going, each lasting a quarter of a mile,
and when they were passed the ground began to fall into
gentler contours; and though the trail was still confined, we
moved easily. The road would soon, Zamchiya said, run into
a big drift of the Umzilizwe, and this we should not be able
to pass with safety. He would not be able to accompany us

any further, but thought that the place would make us a good camp. He had brought his bicycle in the back of the Land Rover, and on this he proposed to return to the cattle-dip, where there was a kraal which he was accustomed to visit regularly for the purpose of administering Chief Law. The only difficulty we had still to pass was a small bridge; it would bear our weight, he thought, though of course it had not been built to take vehicles.

He had no sooner spoken than we came to it, and got out to have a look at this last hazard. It was a flimsy-looking construction of tree trunks and branches, laid across the last of the narrow gullies that bedevilled the trail. Three sizeable tree trunks had been laid across from side to side, and across these again, lashed into place with creeper, was a thick, uneven flooring of stout branches. It did not look promising, but the gully was deep, and there seemed no possible way of going round. We unloaded the heaviest gear, and Peter, who had come up in the lorry and was in a state of loving anxiety over the Land Rover, took her over at a snail's pace while the rest of us stood by helplessly, holding our breath. The timber sagged and creaked but nothing broke, and we had now only to repeat the performance with the lorry. This, too, was unloaded, while Michael looked at the bridge and decided his strategy. We had run a great risk, he said, in taking the Land Rover slowly; if the bridge had given in the middle we should never have got out. The proper way was to take it at speed, so that the bridge hardly had time to feel the weight. Adopting this method one could get over practically anything, even with a four-ton lorry.

He reversed the lorry out of its litter of packing cases and had the road cleared. The diesel motor was roared to a deafening pitch, backed a little further, roared again, and then we were all scattered in the grass by the lorry's charge.

It went over with a sickening bound, landing triumphantly
as the bridge exploded behind it in a shower of timber.

It needed only this to drive home to us the folly of not
leaving the lorry behind while we reconnoitred. We had now
arrived at a place where we could reasonably camp, but we
were six miles further away from Nyabánga, cut off from
the trail by a broken bridge and more than three-quarters of
a mile of murderous rocks. Peter went off at once to look at
the bridge and was away a long time; when he came back
he announced that there was a possible bypass for the Land
Rover, cutting through the bush and taking the gully at a
less precipitous point, but he doubted its being practicable
for the lorry. He was wearing his most thunderous aspect,
as though he did not greatly care if Michael and the lorry
were immobilised for good. Michael, however, was as happy
as a bird, having within five minutes of arriving at this new
river seen a seven-foot crocodile with his own eyes; he
was now plunging noisily about in the reeds, devising cunning plans for outwitting the monster.

The river was not in fact a new one but our old acquaintance, the Umzilizwe, flowing fast and strong. The bank
on our side was extremely steep, a bare slope at a gradient of
one in four. At the foot of this the river had been roughly
dammed with stones and spread out to a width of forty or
fifty yards; it was not more than knee-deep but the current
was strong, pouring through the gaps in the dam into a
flurry of broken water. The ground on the far side was
level and easy, and the trail wound away into the further
hills, but we could see at once that it would be madness to
try and take the vehicles across. Even if the water were not
too deep the bed of the river was full of slippery boulders,
and the deeper pools on our side and the steepness of the bank
made it doubtful if we should be able to return. Fortunately

there was no need to cross; we were already uncomfortably far from Nyabánga, and had no wish to go farther. We were now, Zamchiya said, in the territory of a chief he did not know, whose village was a day's march further on and who spoke a different language. We would do better to stay on this side in any case, for the trail eventually led to Spungabera, and whoever followed it would sooner or later encounter the Portuguese.

We thanked him and said we would eventually return the way we had come and would hope to see him again to say good-bye. For the present we would camp on this excellent river, to rest awhile and take photographs of the country. We parted with mutual courtesies, and on our part a real unwillingness to see him go. He had proved himself so far a kindly friend, and his smiling face and gentle bearing rebuked any lingering thought of past suspicion. He mounted his bicycle and wobbled off, a dignified and sympathetic figure.

The new camp occupied our thoughts and energies for some hours, for the forest undergrowth made clearing necessary, and we all worked strenuously with hatchets and *pangas*. Shorty felled several saplings with great rapidity and hacked his way vigorously into the bushes, pausing only to make a protest because it was Sunday. This was a day, he sometimes remembered, when labour was disapproved of by his church; but on this occasion he contented himself with working fully clad as a Sabbath touch. He was wearing a clean vest belonging to Michael, and the seat of his pants, which as usual was split apart from cheek to cheek, had been modestly drawn together with a safety pin.

Before long the tents were erected in a leafy clearing under enormous trees, which spread hugely upwards like the roof of a cathedral. The sun could not penetrate here, and the

place had an air of almost chilly solemnity. Everything, from
the nearness of the river, was rank and green; where the trees
ended a forest of reeds enclosed us, and from the trees themselves fans of orchids spread fingers among the moss of the
high branches. It was like being in a cavern, with the sun
blazing at the entrance and on the world outside, where life
went on at a distance. There was no room in our dim interior
for the kitchen camp, which was set up in the grass on the
other side of the road, where it quickly became a centre of
attraction. At no time of the day was it without visitors,
usually women and girls who came with their water pots
and had a handful of eggs or a bunch of bananas to sell. The
cook came into his own, being the only one of our three
Africans who could understand something of the language,
which was no longer Shona; he held court on a crate of
bottles under the trees, bargaining for chickens.

He soon had several scrawny fowls in the dog kennel and
one or two others picking about in the road; Michael's biltong
hung in strips from a tree. The camp had an established air
and felt like home. We wondered at first why we saw so
few men, for nearly all the passers-by were women, but
learned that this was a feature of native life in these parts,
where the able-bodied males are rounded up for forced labour
by the Portuguese. The husbands and sons of these women
would be doing a three-year service, perhaps hundreds of
miles away, on the roads or in the mines; the chiefs each year
provided a quota of men as the price for continuing in tribal
authority.

Next morning Michael was up with the lark, concentrating
on his crocodile, which local information credited with taking
a goat a fortnight, with having already survived two rifle
wounds, and possessing great cunning. Michael was a little
worried about the bullet holes, since these might have dam-

aged the skin which he had already kindly offered me as a present; but he was full of optimism at breakfast, cleaning his rifle and studying his crocodile book, only too anxious that we should go off and amuse ourselves. This suited us well enough, for we were longing to return to Nyabánga, to form some idea of how best to explore the hill. We set off in the Land Rover, taking Peter's detour at the broken bridge and negotiating the gully at a shallower point without much difficulty. This new route took us through a group of native huts, which struck us both by their poverty and by their lack of squalor. It was the home of a single family, a small-holding; everyone was gone for the day except an old man of extreme age who lay like a dried-up corpse at the door of his hut. He moved nothing but his eyes as we went through, and at the last moment returned our greeting with a finlike movement of a hand. The hut beside which he lay, a frame of reeds and branches thatched with grass, was evidently the living room of the family; we could see inside, and it was empty. The cooking hut, a roof supported on poles, had a fire in it, the smoke creeping slowly through the thatch. Here were a few cooking pots of clay and a surrealist shape or two, scooped out from pumpkins into capacious ladles. Another hut was for storing water and contained enormous clay jars and the carrying pots that had not been taken to the river. A fourth hut, square in shape, was filled to the door with mealie cobs, and a fifth, not yet opened and smelling like the pit, was full of goats; we could see their beards and yellow eyes through the wattle. The striking thing about this place, which was as poor in possessions as any place could be, was the absence of all the dirt and litter that one associates with "civilized" poverty. Where nothing is bought and life is supported wholly on what lives and grows, there is no refuse; no empty tins, no dirty paper, no rubbish. The

maize of the mealies is eaten, the cobs are fuel. Where there is little, everything is consumed. The only things we saw which presumably had not been made in the kraal were the scraps of cloth round the old man's loins and the earth-coloured fragment of blanket on which he lay. The huts themselves, being made of branches and grass, were part of the hill, and their bareness gave the place a formidable dignity.

The cattle-dip when we arrived was deserted, but there was a battered lorry standing near the sheds, which we examined warily from a distance. It had a Portuguese licence plate, but there was nothing to indicate whom it belonged to or why it had come. We decided to climb the shallow, stony hill, which ran down to the dip, to examine Nyabánga through field glasses and for a time at least to keep an eye on the lorry. Russell's warning about native commissioners and their spies was never far from our minds; we had not seen another vehicle since we left Chikore, and were unwilling to approach Nyabánga with this unexpected phenomenon unexplained. We left the Land Rover at the bottom and went slowly up the eroded surface of the slope, which had been deeply corrugated by running water and pitted by the hooves of innumerable cattle. On the crown of the slope was a spinney of thin trees, and into this we withdrew for the sake of a little shade and in order to use the field glasses unobserved. Though there was no one to be seen, not even a child or a woman at the muddy stream, we had grown accustomed to the assumption that we were probably watched, and acted on it; we should see some stealthy movement sooner or later.

We sat for a long time in our screen of trees and studied what our eyes could tell us of Nyabánga. On a ridge between the dip and the rise of the hill the field glasses showed the thatch of a fair-sized kraal. This was either a small village or

a homestead bigger than any we had yet seen. No other habitation was distinguishable; so far as we could see the hill was neither cultivated nor inhabited; no mealie patch, no roof, no path was visible. There was not a breath of wind, and the grass and trees, so deceptively looking like parched savannah through which one could walk at ease, gave off a still and burnished shine, and the edges of the hill quivered like sun-struck metal. It should not be difficult, we thought, to quarter the hill by degrees, looking for anything that might be a burial mound; but since much time must always be consumed in getting from the camp to the cattle-dip and negotiating the abominable rocks, it would be necessary to find a way of approaching much more closely in the Land Rover. If we could take the vehicle part way up the hill the middle of the short day could be profitably spent, less valuable time wasted in coming and going. The physical difficulties of the climb seemed slight in comparison with the problem of explaining our strange preoccupation with the hill to Michael.

We lit a fire of twigs and made coffee, anxiously discussing the question of sharing our secret. Jack and Peter were less troubled perhaps than I was by the personal discomfort of keeping him in the dark, but they gloomily admitted all the practical difficulties. He could not be left indefinitely to hunt his crocodile while we disappeared daily to haunt this unprofitable place. His month's leave was nearly up, and if he were not to return to Salisbury without us we had got to work fast. Problem though he was, without him we should be barely able to communicate with our own Africans, and the thought of the Portuguese at Spungabera would be doubly uncomfortable. Besides, if we found what we were looking for on Nyabánga we should need all the help we could get; we should also need Shadow, who was the only efficient means we knew of keeping Africans at a distance. If we had to get

out of this territory in a hurry we should do it better for not being a man short. In sum, and in spite of the hazards of his incalculable reaction, the story had got to be told. We needed Michael.

Made drowsy by the heat and the complications of argument, we one by one dropped out of the conversation and, putting a stone or a knapsack under our heads, fell uncomfortably asleep. When we awoke the sun had travelled and a solitary man was standing beside the Land Rover. He was an African, but being neatly dressed in shorts and shirt with boots on he did not look like one of the local people. We gathered our things together and came slowly downhill, while he walked deliberately round the vehicle and appeared to be examining its licence plates. We greeted him with upraised hand and voices that sounded more friendly than we felt, but he gave us no returning smile and said at once in English, "Why you come?"

This did not sound like a purely social question, but Peter had the presence of mind to take it as such, and replied with affability that we were on holiday. The man frowned at this, and we could not tell whether he disliked or had merely misunderstood our answer. We stared at him in silence, and then Peter, beginning to suspect that his English was already exhausted, embarked on a further friendly conversation, waving his arms at random at the country, praising the beauty of the cattle-dip, and showing him his camera. It was soon apparent that he understood little or nothing of what was said and was less interested in us than in the Land Rover. We showed it gravely, opening the bonnet and inviting him to inspect the oily interior. He did not seem like an official, however humble, and we began to breathe again when he beckoned us across to look at his own lorry. It was battered, dirty, and empty, and from the few words of English that

he uttered we gathered that he was on his way to Chipinga. We could not learn where he came from; he may have been looking for company on the journey, and his air of frowning suspicion was perhaps no more than the reflection of his struggle with a foreign language. We pronounced the name Spungabera in a questioning tone, but he shook his head; and after some more frowning and staring asked us with pointed gestures to give him some petrol. Fortunately we had only a gallon in a spare tin, since he looked as though he were hoping for a large quantity, and this we obligingly poured into a crumpled container which he produced from the lorry. He offered us nothing in return and made no sign of continuing his journey. We left him at length, standing still and silent as we had first seen him, gazing moodily after us with a doubtful expression.

We went back to the camp with a troubled mind, anxious to ask Michael if he had seen this man, but as soon as we arrived at the river all thoughts of him were banished by a new difficulty. The crocodile had been given up as a bad job and Michael, presumably bored, had backed the lorry down the slope into the middle of the river. His intention had apparently been to give it a wash, but the current was stronger than he had imagined and the water deeper, and it was now wedged between slippery rocks, roaring its engine distressfully. He was not unduly worried, but was sitting in the cab as though on the bridge of a ship, shouting instructions to Shorty and John who were up to their thighs in water. He was unfeignedly pleased to see us, for he was sure that we could drag him out with chains. He had kept the engine running, since it had been incapable for a long time of starting without a tow, and he sent the *munts* scurrying to the Land Rover to attach him. Peter's face fell. He had long ago lost all confidence in the lorry, and was continually on

the defensive against any schemes of Michael's that involved the Land Rover; he did not want, as he put it, its guts pulled out in a futile attempt to retrieve Michael's folly.

There was no alternative, however. The Land Rover was backed down the slope, where it clung at what looked like an angle of forty-five degrees, and was harnessed to the lorry with a double length of chain. With Michael and Peter at the wheel both motors were revved up to a deafening pitch, the Land Rover shuddered and groaned and threw out clods of earth from its heels like a dog, and the rest of us waded into the water and pushed; but nothing happened. The lorry's nose was pointed downwards against a rock and the bank was too steep for the Land Rover to lift it. After much uproar and struggling the lorry was allowed to relapse to its stertorous breathing and Michael and Shorty, both wet through and with teeth chattering with cold, fought to dislodge the frustrating rock with a crowbar. The sun had now set and it was fairly dark; a bank of cloud, the first we had seen, lay across the moon; we worked by the Land Rover's searchlight. Out of the darkness on either side a group of silent figures had now assembled, women, boys, and old men. They stood at the top of the bank and sent up a faint cheer when the rock was finally prized from its foundations, the water swirling after it with a roar, and the lorry settled gratefully into the cavity. The extra strain imposed by this subsidence was too much for the chain, which at the next attempt broke in several places. The Land Rover rushed crossly up the bank dangling its fragments, and the lorry jerked its hindquarters sideways into a deeper and more comfortable position, where its lights continued to glow in and out to the rhythm of its heavy breathing. We had no ropes and no winch, and no amount of argument produced any better suggestion than that we should try to collect some extra

men in the morning. The lorry's engine, at Michael's suggestion, was left running, for if it could not be started again a
dead weight of four tons would be hopeless; but to this the
suffering mechanism was unequal; it had been running for
hours and no one had looked at the tank. As we crawled
wearily up the bank for the last time it coughed apologetically
and was silent.

Messages were sent out next morning for extra men, and
a couple of ragged ancients who had settled down with their
staves at the side of the road, determined to miss nothing,
assured us they would come; but after several hours of waiting
no one appeared, and while Peter was off in the bush on some
private occasion Michael removed the Land Rover's battery
and transferred it to the lorry. It did not succeed in starting
the lorry's motor, and when Peter furiously returned it to
its proper place the Land Rover would not start either. It
was pushed up the hill by hand until it recovered, then harnessed for a further attempt with pieces of rope and chain,
but to no purpose; the tremors induced in the lorry shifted
it with malicious skill into a worse position, so that it looked
even more surely doomed than the night before and as though
it must stay in the river until it disintegrated.

We began to take a sombre view of our quandary, for if
the lorry could not be moved, neither could the stores and
camp equipment, and all seven of us would depend on the
Land Rover. It would mean in effect the end of the expedition. Even Michael at last began to show signs of worry, for
he was due to report in barracks in a few days' time and did
not like the idea of leaving us in Mozambique in this predicament. He would take the Land Rover, he said, and go back
as far as Chipinga, where he could telephone his father and
ask for an extension of leave; he would also take the lorry's
battery and starting-motor, and if the battery would not

hold a charge, borrow or hire another, or in the last resort buy one. The thought of being left without any means of moving was not pleasant, but we could think of no alternative. Michael took Shorty and Shadow with him for company and, being busy calculating our probable losses, we saw him off without enthusiasm.

The next few days were spent in attempts to assuage a mounting feeling of frustration. Our time was slipping away; we were only seven miles from Nyabánga, and yet, without transport of any kind, we might as well have been fifty miles distant. To add fourteen miles a day on foot, in that heat, to the difficulties of exploring the hill itself would have fatally consumed the daylight hours. The shortness of the day, which was never more nor less than twelve hours, was a nuisance to which we never grew accustomed. If we had been camped on the very skirts of Nyabánga the day would have been none too long for the climb and descent, with some interval between for searching and rest; with fourteen miles of rough bush trail besides, the thing was hopeless. We mildly considered, as the hours passed, whether we should try to carry our water and blankets and sleep on the hill, but the unknown hazards and the darkness were intimidating. We could see our whole plan collapsing because of this folly of the lorry, and ourselves perhaps stuck in this place indefinitely, or until the Portuguese came. One thing at least emerged with unpleasant sharpness: as soon as he returned, Michael must be let into the story.

As a parting kindness, and to keep us occupied, he had extracted a promise from one of the local ancients to show us the haunts of several nearby crocodiles; but needless to say this guide never appeared, and our only visitors were women with water pots, incredulously amused at the sight of a white woman. We were not unduly sorry about the crocodile,

being absorbed in our own problems; it seemed more important to survey the country as far as we were able and to study Nyabánga from a distance. The best point for this was the crown of the nearest hill, which looked like a smaller version of Nyabánga, being covered with the same grass and stunted trees. It seemed easy, and there was no better way of passing the time than by climbing it several times by way of practice. We set off in the early afternoon of our first day of waiting, and had scarcely covered a quarter of a mile before we recognised an old and hateful illusion. The grass, which from a distance looked like sun-bleached meadow, was a dense forest of growth about eight feet high, springing up from a wicked confusion of earth and rock. One did not walk up the hill, one clung and scrambled, clutching at trees, stumbling in crevices, and all the time, because of the grass, maddeningly out of sight of one another. By the time we were two-thirds up the sun had set, and we had to tumble down again in a hurry. It was not an encouraging rehearsal for Nyabánga.

If it had not been for the frustration of being so idle and our manifold anxieties, the place we were in would have afforded infinite pleasure. The river itself, as we followed its course through gorges of rock, through festoons of creeper and dreamlike arcades of trees, was secretively beautiful; smooth volumes of yellow water poured and swirled between rocks on which butterflies rested, and monkeys fled shrieking before us in the high branches. The butterflies were large and flew with an air of languor at knee-level, settling on sequins of sunlight among the stones. The commonest were brown and spotted like guinea-fowl, and there were many of Chinese blue with stripes of black and yellow at the tips of the wings, and an even larger apparition of black velvet, which sailed idly before us as we advanced, as though offering itself to the

net. We saw few huts in our wanderings and fewer people;
only at the drift, when we returned, would there be a handful
of goats brought down to drink, driven by little boys with
musical instruments.

The sounds these made were monotonous and sweet and
carried on the still air to a great distance. One was an empty
gourd into which the player blew a hollow note. Another was
a child's approach to the idea of a fiddle, a bow of hardwood
notched from end to end and strung with a ribbon of grass.
One end of the bow was placed against the mouth, and while
the player sang through his teeth he stridulated against the
notches with a little stick, which carried a gourd full of beans
at one end like a rattle. It was music that might have been
made by a child playing in consort with a grasshopper. The
most ambitious instrument we saw was carried by older boys
and was clearly a prized possession. It was a little zither made
from a square of wood, the inside hollowed out for a sounding board and the keys made of iron nails, curved and flattened. When a curved point was depressed by a finger, it
sprang back into shape with a clear note, and since the nails
were carefully graded in length it was possible to play between five and a dozen notes of a faulty scale. The most
satisfactory tones were the ones most used, and three and
five-note tunes were varied endlessly. We heard one other
instrument besides these on a day when we waded across the
river and went for a long day's walk into the hills, but there
was nobody near it and we had to play it ourselves. We
found it in a clearing beside the ashes of a fire, and since the
ground was sprinkled with goat droppings, we guessed that
this was a place the herd boys used. The instrument was a
little hollow scooped out of earth, carefully lined with trusses
of dried grass. On either side a wooden trestle was fixed, about
three inches high, and across these several pieces of hard red-

wood, carefully smoothed and graded in length, had been pegged in place. The sticks for playing this xylophone or drum were lying across it, as though left for the next session, and we amused ourselves for a while in the shade by playing variations on its light, dry, curiously resonant notes.

As the sky piled up with incandescent cloud the haze on the distant hilltops vanished and their outlines took on the hardness of blue crystal. The children's music by the river, coming and going in the evening with their goats, was like the clicking of insects and the cries of birds, with the bell-like note of the zither, its surest one, repeated endlessly like the sound one hears in a cave of dropping water. An unseen bird high in our cathedral roof punctuated the theme with his own persistent statement, a loud, dry click like striking a key on a typewriter, followed at once by a long and liquid note. The whole chorus was complex and clear, heard through a limpid atmosphere that already carried the promise of coming rain.

The rain began at dawn the following day, splashing in sudden heavy drops on my face and spreading a noisy patter through the trees. I was wet through before I could get my blankets into the tent, and before it was light the hard earth of the camp had turned to mud. There was no wind; the rain fell in rods from a dark sky, unvarying in sound and volume for eight hours. Our fire hissed and steamed and was finally quenched; the road turned to slime and the slope leading down to the river became a slide. Our poor Africans crouched in misery under the lorry's canvas, spread over themselves and the stores, and we lay on our beds despondently through the day, rousing ourselves at intervals to eat depressing meals out of wet tins. The river began to rise, and by evening, when the rain stopped, was well above the lorry's axles, flowing fast under the body of the truck. The

moon came out among ragged clouds and I shivered in a wet bed by a dead fire, the trees dripping despondently on my pillow.

The next day was dark and threatening, with mist and cloud spread thickly over the valley. There was no wind and little movement; only the river was lively, pouring round and under the wrecked lorry; from time to time a cloud on the hill unfolded a long and weeping streamer of rain. We were too restless and anxious to wait any longer where we were, watching the lorry drown, and set off to walk to the cattle-dip to meet Michael. The air was still and heavy and full of moisture, laden with new and aromatic smells. Everything had come to life in the wake of the storm; great ants were abroad on the road in glistening armies, deploying their columns in complicated manoeuvres; the rustle of their feet on the leaves was faintly audible. Butterflies clustered like flowers on a fragment of carrion, and thick black seven-inch millipedes travelled recklessly before us on the path, transforming themselves into ammonites at a touch. The muddy chine where the lorry had had so much trouble was carved into new rivulets by the rain; we covered its slopes with branches, fearing for the Land Rover. It had been one of Michael's intentions to call on Hla-Hla, in the hope that he could send a tractor to haul out the lorry, but we listened for the sound of a diesel engine in vain. Only at one point, when we stopped to dig the clay off our boots with a stick, we heard women's voices at a distance, high and clear in the thicket like the voices of birds. We were sitting on a fallen tree and they were unaware of us, coming down the wooded hillside chattering and laughing; as they drew near we saw that they were carrying pieces of freshly cut timber on their heads. They saw us in the same instant and were suddenly silent, standing frozen like deer behind a screen of trees, and

neither spoke nor stirred until we moved on. Then the bird-like chatter broke out again, softly and cautiously, but so long as we were in sight they did not appear.

We spent several fruitless hours at the cattle-dip, not daring to go further for fear of missing Michael, gazing despondently at Nyabánga, now shrouded and remote in heavy cloud. We had been nearly a week in this place, and the hill itself seemed further off than ever. If only the clouds would break and the sun come out; if only the ground would dry and Michael return; if only the lorry were out of the river and all of us escaped from the cul-de-sac in which it had trapped us. . . .

But at this point the rain began again, spreading a network of rivulets over the road and making the going so slippery that it took several miserable hours to return, helping ourselves with sticks and grotesquely slithering about in clay and debris.

8

THE MAGIC AND THE HILL

BY the time it was fully dark an arena of clear sky had opened above us and the moon was rising majestically bright. It was once more nearing the full; everything was clear and strange under that marvellous radiance, reminding us of something nearly incredible—that we had already been a whole month in the bush. As we approached the camp we heard the jerky roar of the Land Rover crossing the rocks, and presently Michael overtook us. He was in good spirits; his father had obtained him a week's extension of leave, the lorry's starter motor had been doctored in Chipinga and its battery re-charged, and he had hired a mediaeval-looking contraption, which he said was a winch and which looked as though it had come out of a torture chamber. This heavy ratcheted machine was equipped with an old steel hawser and lengths of chain; only the rack was missing. He was confident that it would pull the lorry out of the river in the morning.

This was the occasion, as we dried our sodden clothes at the hissing fire, when we should have made a clean breast of everything to Michael, but a gloomy apprehension was still on us, and we said nothing. We did not share his trust in the ugly winch, and had a pessimistic feeling that if this also failed, and the only remaining hope was Hla-Hla's tractor, we might well be there for another week on the river.

It would be time enough to tell him when the future seemed
less hopeless than it did now; time was running out for all
of us, and we secretly blamed him for the wreck of the expedition. It was even a final exasperation that he had not
thought it necessary to call on Hla-Hla, so great was his
new-found confidence in the winch. The rain, he said, had
been a fluke; such a thing had never been heard of at this
season. An hour or two of sun and the ground would be dry;
he would winch the lorry out for us in the morning.

I was wakened again before dawn by sudden rain, but
it was less resolute than before and there were watery gleams
of sun an hour later. The winch was lashed with rope to a
stout tree and Michael and the *munts* slithered up and down
the disintegrating slope, replacing the starter motor and battery in the lorry. The engine, to no one's surprise but Michael's, refused to start. The winch was manned, but its
hawser proved too short to reach the lorry and there was
no other tree in a practicable position. The pieces of chain
that had come with the winch were contemptible and had
to be lashed together with pieces of rope. As soon as the
lorry was harnessed the ropes broke, and we spent some hours
in scouring about for native bullock chains, used for dragging heavy sledges and timber. These when found were in-
geniously hooked together and miraculously held, but as
soon as the winch was started it broke in two, revealing an
old encrusted break which in some remote age had been
incompetently welded. That was the end of the winch and
of our hopes for the lorry; we sat on the edge of the road
with our heads in our hands. This is a good position for con-
structive thought, and after a time two rather doubtful ideas
presented themselves. Michael would send a message to the
Portuguese chief, asking for help, and we three would go
back in the Land Rover to Hla-Hla. If Hla-Hla would send

us his tractor and the tractor could reach us, we had a chance;
but we also had a private and ulterior motive. If we could
find Zamchiya as well and he would allow us to camp in his
kraal at the cattle-dip, we might, even without the lorry,
be within reasonable striking distance of Nyabánga and could
pass the time of waiting in reconnaissance. We did not mention this to Michael, since our obsession with the hill would
need explaining, and we had a sufficient motive in the tractor.
Michael wrote a lordly request for fifty men, carefully printed
in Shona in thick pencil, and before we left we had the exquisite pleasure of seeing the note carried off in a cleft stick.
This was something we had never expected to see outside,
perhaps, the pages of Evelyn Waugh; but there it was, being
done as a matter of course, and the youth who had been
found to carry it forded the river and ran off with it held
at arm's length, like a banner.

When we had made the usual painful course to the cattle-
dip we found that it was dipping day, and the place was
crowded with cattle as though it were a fair. Herds were
converging on the dip from every direction, driven by boys
armed with bamboo poles. We watched them for a while,
surprised at the docile behaviour of the long-horned beasts,
which were driven one by one into a narrow passage and
plunged over head and eyes in the stinking trough. There
was much shouting but none of that orgiastic beating of
animals which is the horror of cattle fairs in European countries; a light whack with the bamboo was all that was needed,
and only the calves panicked and thrashed about, and had
to be guided out of the bath with poles.

So far as we could remember this was one of the days when
Zamchiya was due at the cattle-dip to hold his weekly session
of Chief Law, and it seemed sensible that I should wait for
him here while Jack and Peter went on to look for Hla-Hla.

Left alone at the dip, I made my way to the kraal we had seen from the hill; it was the only one we knew of, and we supposed it to be Zamchiya's, but only women and children were there and most of them fled at the sight of me. I tried Zamchiya's name on those that remained, but either it meant nothing to them or they were startled into speechlessness by my appearance, for however I tried the question they remained equally silent and amazed. There was nothing for it but to wait for the others to return, and I wandered off to a bare mound, where I had a view of the cattle-dip, and sat under the tree growing out of the crown of it, idly whittling a gourd I had picked up by the river. Here I was somewhat beset by little boys, who played an elaborate hide-and-seek round the foot of the ant hill, fleeing in terror whenever I looked or spoke, and then peeping out of the bushes, all eyes and smiles. Presently a man came down from the kraal and approached me. He looked handsome and prosperous, and had a pink knitted woolen cap on the back of his head. This he courteously removed when we were within speaking distance, and he asked me some question to which I could only reply by shrugging and smiling. He had no fewer than five gold rings on his fingers, and one of the rings was crudely set with a diamond. We could not understand one another, and after more smiling and gesturing we nodded a friendly farewell and he went away. He was followed after an interval by a woman who seemed not at all afraid of me but even extravagantly delighted with the encounter. She set down her water pot, the better to talk and laugh and wave her arms, and I responded as best I could, laying down my knife and pumpkin for the purpose. It was puzzling that neither of them seemed to respond to the name of Zamchiya.

When Jack and Peter returned it was with the good news that Hla-Hla's tractor was already on the way. It was a

powerful Ferguson and had good chains; if it could manage
the gullies on the trail the situation was promising. They had
also seen Zamchiya, who had made them a further handsome
present of *naartjes*, but he had seemed preoccupied that morning, and they had had a strong feeling that it would have been
unpropitious to ask about sleeping in his huts. If the tractor
failed, there was still this last resort; there was something
about Zamchiya's gaze which had made them uncomfortable.

As we stood talking the tractor appeared, manned by a
spirited driver in a raffia hat, and went boldly on ahead of
us down the trail. Jack had been looking at Nyabánga through
the field glasses, and now said that he would like to give the
rest of the day to exploring it on foot, having long had the
feeling that we should get very little nearer to it with the
Land Rover. If he could find a negotiable path to the summit
much time would be saved, and such knowledge as he could
gain would be useful later. He accordingly went off by himself, crossing the muddy stream in the direction of the hill,
and Peter and I drove hopefully after the tractor.

We found it where we might have known we should,
at the bottom of the chine. Its enormous wheels, armoured
with great corrugated tires, were churning up the sides of
the gully like butter, making sidelong rushes at the face and
sliding down again. The driver was full of resource and enthusiasm and was enjoying himself; he did not pause in his
plunging backwards and forwards until the whole of the
further slope had been reduced to a welter of furrows streaming with water. He then got out of the saddle, laughing heart-
ily, and beckoned to four old men who had appeared like
spirits with *pangas* out of the wood. Between them they hacked
down a quantity of brushwood and packed it thickly into the
slimy grooves, making a temporary surface of which Peter
took advantage in the Land Rover, tearing sideways up the

side of the chine like a crab; but it did nothing to help the tractor. This was clearly another case for chains, and we left the five Africans laughing and chattering over the plight of the tractor while we went on in the direction of the camp to see what we could find. Hla-Hla's machine had fallen into the trap like an elephant into a pit, but at least its engine was running and it was not up to the floorboards in the river.

When we reached the camp we stopped abruptly in amazement: the place was crowded with people. Michael was standing in a thick knot of men whom we had not seen before, and there was another group on the far side of the river. The Portuguese chief had come, having heard what had happened a full day before Michael had sent his message; he had decided to investigate, and had in fact encountered our messenger when he was only a few miles from the Umzilizwe. Michael drew us aside at once and warned us in an undertone that the proceedings were likely to be long-drawn and formal. The Chief was an important one, and protocol would have to be observed. It was particularly important, he said anxiously, that I should keep in the background, for the Chief would not care to be spoken to by a woman.

Peter and I withdrew discreetly under a tree, where we could watch the proceedings, and word was passed to the Chief on the other side of the river that Michael was now ready to receive him. A small old man now detached himself from the group and was ceremoniously lifted on to the back of one of his companions and carried in this position over the river, the rest of the company wading respectfully behind him. He stopped when he was a dozen yards from Michael and made a signal that he was ready to sit. Two of our battered camp chairs were now brought for the principals, and he and Michael sat facing one another at what seemed to us an inconvenient distance, but it appeared that this was simply

a matter of formality, since it would not be proper for them to converse directly. The Chief spoke into the ear of his eldest son, who bent solicitously to receive instructions and passed them on in turn to a lesser dignitary, who then transferred the message to our cook, who translated it into Shona to John and Shorty. They then, being fully conversant with the system of chain-communication suitable to a chief's dignity, passed on the message to Michael sitting in his chair, whose reply was conveyed back in the same manner. A conversation conducted in this fashion is a slow business, but such grave satisfaction was expressed on the faces of the crowd that one could not have wished to see it done more quickly.

The gist of the exchange, as we afterwards learned from Michael, was that the Chief was willing to help us out of our difficulty, provided that it was our intention to proceed afterwards to Spungabera and report our presence and our business to the Portuguese. He himself, he said, would be obliged to report the matter to the Commissioner of Native Affairs, and without this understanding nothing could be done, since he was answerable to the Portuguese and they were well known to be interested in strangers. This was a facer for Michael, but fortunately he was not troubled by scruples, least of all where the Portuguese were concerned, and replied gravely that we were indeed on our way to Spungabera, where we looked forward to paying the native commissioner a visit. In that case, said the Chief, would it not be well to take the lorry out on the further side, and carry the other vehicles over as well, and our stores, so that we could proceed on our journey? By a happy chance Michael did not agree to this, for though he knew nothing of our real plans, at least he knew that having crossed the border already without permission, nothing would be further from our thoughts than

Spungabera. So he said no, for the present we wished to stay on this side of the river, as he had Europeans from England in his party who had arranged to have private talks with Chief Zamchiya. This appeared to give satisfaction: the Chief conferred with his elders, and word was passed that they would need two shillings. Four sixpences were found in Peter's pocket and the money changed hands; it was not, we learned from our interpreters, to be regarded as a fee but for the purchase of a sacrificial chicken. There was some delay before the chicken was forthcoming; Michael and the Chief sat patiently in their chairs while the crowd conversed in whispers. At last a child arrived carrying a fowl by the legs, and the Chief announced that he and his elders would now recross the river. Before mounting his bearer, however, he passed a courteous message to Michael, inviting him to accompany them. He had taken a fancy to Michael, he said, and was willing that he should witness the necessary ceremonies from a distance.

Michael accepted after a momentary hesitation, caused by his fear of losing face if he waded through the river on his own legs; but it was no good thinking that Shorty could make a dignified job of carrying him, so he compromised by not removing his boots. The Chief was carried over dry-shod, preceded by his elders, with Michael floundering powerfully in his wake, and the rest of us gathered on the muddy banks above the lorry to watch developments.

Arrived on the other side, the elders withdrew with the chicken under a tree, and the Chief motioned to Michael to stand with him in a privileged group at a little distance. It was not possible, he said, still conveying his meaning through a chain of intermediaries, for a European to watch their magic too closely. The purpose of the ceremony was to draw power from the spirits of their ancestors who had

been devoured by the crocodile in this very river; it was to
the malign influence of the crocodile that we could attribute
even this disaster to our lorry. The elders by this time were
crouching under their tree; there was a brief squawk and no
more was heard of the chicken. There was muttering and
a weird singing that sounded like mooing, and then the whole
party slowly recrossed the river.

The Chief had brought thirty-four men with him, and
these were now divided into two groups. Twenty went into
the water on either side of the lorry and fourteen ranged
themselves on top of the bank. The twenty put their hands to
the lorry and waited, and at a signal from the Chief the others
began to sing. The song, as Michael translated it, began with
a rousing imperative "Let us show how strong our warriors
are!" and went on into swinging verses something like this:

> Ho, ho, men!
> Come on, men!
> We are not women,
> Heave. . . .

Each time on the *Heave!* the twenty shouldered the lorry,
and each time their combined strength urged it perceptibly
forward over the rocks. With each verse the singing grew
wilder and louder, and Shadow slunk in terror into the bush.
When they came to the final submerged rock, which was
immovable, the singers leaped in the air with huge cries, and
first the front of the lorry and then the tail were lifted clean
over it. It came out on the bank, dripping with weed and
water like a river monster, and was sung and heaved right
up the slippery slope. The crowd burst out into wild cheer-
ing and excitement and the lorry was patted and stroked by
scores of hands as though it too had a share in the achievement.

Michael made elaborate thanks through the proper channels and then asked what present he might make in return

for this kindness. For each of his men, the Chief replied, a shilling would be handsome compensation; for himself five rounds of buckshot would be acceptable. He was too grand to receive these things into his own hand and made a stately return across the river while we were frantically going through our pockets for silver. As a parting civility he invited Michael to bring "his people" to a party that he would give for us, with beer and singing, when we reached his kraal on our way to Spungabera.

The rest of the day was given over to modest festivities, for so stirring an occasion could not be relinquished lightly, and most of the Chief's people remained to celebrate. Tinned fruit and tinned beer (a poor offering, but they were accepted as rare delicacies) were doled out in small quantities, and when these were finished the heroes willingly posed for a group photograph. The power they had received from their ancestors was still working in them, urging them to further feats, and a dozen of them went off to the broken bridge and set about repairing it. The speed with which they accomplished this, cutting down trees and branches with hatchets and *pangas,* seemed to us no less magical than the rescue of the lorry; they were exalted in spirit and seemed capable of anything. We even thought of taking them back to the chine to lift out the tractor, but when Jack arrived at the camp, dusty and footsore, he announced that the thing had somehow got out on its own side; he had met it ploughing home in the direction of Hla-Hla.

Jack had his own news to give us, for he had actually been to the top of Nyabánga. It had been difficult, he said, but the thing could be done, though he doubted whether any of it would be possible for the Land Rover. He had followed false trails and been lost in some thorny thickets, but thought he might remember the route which had been at last suc-

cessful. The hill was bigger than we had thought and the bush very dense; after some mealie patches on the lower slopes there had been no sign of habitation. His climb was passed off as an "interesting walk," since Michael was with us, sipping an unaccustomed whisky in honour of the day's triumph, stretching out his great legs before the fire and basking in the return of mutual benevolence.

It had indeed been a wonderful day; the spell of ill-luck had been broken by one more potent, the lorry was safe, the bridge had been rebuilt, and there was nothing (except perhaps the condition of the chine) to prevent our moving camp the next morning. Never can the sacrifice of a fowl have been more profitable. And as if to set a seal on the day and mark it as one of plenitude, a girl arrived in the camp as we sat around the fire, bearing on her head a great pot of wild honey. She had brought it to sell, asking only a few shillings for the contents of the jar, which must have contained not less than sixteen pounds. She was an elegant creature of about seventeen, with ankles encased in bracelets of metal wire extending like greaves almost to the bend of the knee; her neck was garlanded with strings of beads and she wore a police whistle on a string. (She explained, when asked, that she was accustomed to play this instrument at dances.) She set down the pot at our feet and took off the covering of dried banana leaf, which had been tied in place with strands of twisted bark. It was full to the brim with honey, a gleaming mass floating with broken comb, and gave off a heavy smell of powerful sweetness. We tasted it at once with a spoon, lifting the dripping fragments to our mouths and crushing the fragile complex with our teeth. Wherever the spoon broke the comby surface the dark honey welled up like flowing topaz, bringing the dark bodies of drowned bees. It was stronger than any honey I had ever tasted, its sweetness

streaked with a lingering memory of wood smoke, as though
it had been taken that very day from the hive. We had seen
native beehives here and there, beautifully constructed cylin-
ders of curved bark fastened together with wooden pegs,
lodged high above the ground in a likely tree. I am not
clear why the appearance and taste of this honey was so
moving, but it seemed to contain a strong and mysterious
element, as though it were a part of the substance of life itself,
and we ate it in silence, passing the spoon gravely from hand
to hand. It was an absurd thing to burden ourselves with at this
stage, enormously heavy and the pot round-bottomed so that
it could not stand upright, but it had come like a final grace
on a day of blessing, and we gratefully put the silver in the
girl's hand.

The last undertaking of the day was to tell Michael everything that we had so far concealed, and to this my guilty
nerves proved unequal. I dreaded his reaction, could not tell
for a moment how he would take it, and feared that this,
and not the accident to the lorry, would be the ultimate un-
doing of the expedition. I was incapable of sitting quietly by
the fire, watching Michael's face while the story was unfolded, and retired cravenly into our tent with a book and
a candle, leaving the men to themselves and trying not to
listen to the murmur of voices.

They talked for a long time: I could distinguish Jack's
steady tones, with brief pauses when Michael asked a question, but I could not interpret the drift of the conversation.
There was no way of bearing the suspense but to be out of
earshot, and I soon blew out the candle, lifted the flap of
the tent, and wandered down to the edge of the moonlit river.
I have no skill in judging character on short acquaintance, and
though Michael's company delighted me and he seemed on
the surface to be as transparent as the day, I guessed that

there might be hidden reefs of obstinacy. His nature seemed to be one of innocence and good humour, with that reckless carelessness which comes from physical splendour and lack of thought. He was gentle in manner and full of intolerant opinions; there was much in him to which I was a stranger. His Rhodesian upbringing had filled him with simple bigotry, with a lordly belief in the white man and a contempt for the black that was total and instinctive; he had evidently responded with zest to police training. What we were proposing to do might affront or alarm him; he might be the wrong sort of person for such a venture, too disciplined, too puritanical, or both. Nevertheless some communion of sympathy told me that under the correct exterior lurked the instincts of a poacher.

When I came slowly back from the river it was all over. The three were at ease with their boots stretched to the fire, and Michael made only a dreamlike movement to make room for me, so deep was he in the discussion of the cunning strategy to follow when we had found the diamonds. He had responded wholly, as we all had in the beginning, to the glittering vision of Umzila's treasure and felt none of the misgivings that had worried us later. Africa was full of such hoards, he said; a few of them came to light from time to time, and people had had their throats cut who were caught looking for them. If any of the chiefs in this part knew of the treasure we would certainly be watched, and if our own Africans got any inkling of it they would be off into the bush in a flash; there was no act so dangerous as to violate a grave. He had some ominous stories to tell us of past prospectors, whose limbs had been hung like biltong from the branches, and was scarcely more reassuring when he recounted some anecdotes of the Portuguese police, with whose methods he was familiar; but none of these considerations

seemed to daunt him; he was as much our man as if he had
been a brother.

He knew something of African burial customs and was
able to confirm all we had learned from Russell and the missionaries. The undistinguished dead were simply put into
the ground and their graves forgotten; only a chief's resting
place would be marked by a mound and possibly a tree, and
would be tended for perhaps a generation. After that the site
itself would be forgotten by all but a few old men who would
keep the secret, and the place would be avoided and feared
as the abode of spirits. Nothing in our story struck Michael
as being in the least unlikely; what worried him (as indeed it
worried us to the point of not wishing to think about it)
was what we should do with the treasure if we found it. He
now saw the disaster of the lorry in its true light; nothing
could have served better to publicize our presence in the area;
it would be known for miles around that we were there,
and the news might already have reached Spungabera. If we
were to make our search before the Portuguese arrived, as he
was sure they eventually would, we had got to work fast,
and our first necessity was to camp as near as possible to Nyabánga. We could not camp at the cattle-dip, it was too public,
but we thought that by following the river a little further
along we might find a place with cleaner water, which for
a few nights at least would serve our purpose. From there
we could explore the hill, and if we found a likely spot would
dig as fast and as secretly as we could. After that, whether
we found anything or not we would have to get out, and
quickly; it would be madness to linger on the hill once the
news had leaked out that we were digging. If we found
nothing, a rapid get-away would still be essential, for apart
from the African reaction the Portuguese would not take
kindly to our unlawful entry, and we did not wish to be

escorted to Spungabera by the police. If, on the other hand, we were successful, the situation would be a thousand times more dangerous; there would not be a moment to be lost, and we would have to have a plan to cover our retreat.

We had given this a good deal of nervous thought, and it was a great relief to be able to discuss it with Michael, since he after all knew the country as we did not and, besides, was a policeman. The plan took shape round the fire that night as though we were planning the action of a crime novel. We would concentrate solely on the diamonds, which could easily be distributed among our pockets, and would make the best speed we could out of Mozambique and straight through, driving night and day, to Salisbury. Here we would take the first available plane, either together or separtely, ostensibly flying to London. Jack in fact would fly straight through, but either Peter or I, or both, would stop over in Rome, carrying the diamonds on us and getting the earliest flight we could for Antwerp. Friends with respectable contacts with the diamond market had told us, when discreetly questioned months before, that Antwerp and not Amsterdam was the centre. It would not be difficult to find brokers who were more interested in uncut stones than in their place of origin, and it would be perfectly proper to leave a sealed box in a safe deposit. Once that was done, we would make our way back to London at our leisure, and months afterwards if need be, if there had been no repercussions from the Portuguese or from Rhodesia, we could go back quietly to Antwerp and dispose of the stones discreetly through the regular channels.

It seemed very strange to be making such bizarre plans, sitting round a glowing fire in the leafy dark, and when panic occasionally ran through my nerves like a shudder I took comfort in the thought that it was probable, after all, that we should find nothing. Yet the possibility of success was also a

real one, and in the trembling firelight we felt very close to
it. It was a marvellous night, still and rather cold, and the
dazzling effulgence of the moon, which had reached the full,
pierced our cathedral roof with a thousand sequins. The
smoke from our fire rose up in a soft column, filtering slowly
through the leafy canopy to emerge with a ghostly radiance
of its own. Michael and I lay awake for a long time by the
fire, exchanging desultory and ever drowsier sentences, until
I dreamed that we were digging in an earth tunnel, in a cold
smell which I knew was the smell of bones.

Next morning early, anxious to lose no time, we left the
packing up of the camp to the boys and set out in the Land
Rover with food and water. It was our plan to make a preliminary survey of the hill, so as not to lose a day in moving
camp, and to shift to our new quarters the following morning.
We crossed the stream at the cattle-dip, passed the kraal,
which I had already visited, and bumped over the rutted
trail until it came to an end at a trampled and muddy
watering place. From here the grass and trees were too thick
for the Land Rover and we set out on foot, searching for the
threadlike trail that had eventually taken Jack to the summit
of the hill; but whenever we found one (and there were
many, criss-crossing through the high grass like the paths that
a colony of ants might make in a hayfield) it meandered aim-
lessly hither and thither, ending after half a mile at a tattered
mealie patch or petering out at a hole or a straggle of pumpkins. Once in the grass, we could not see the hill, though
whenever the paths led on to higher ground we caught
baffling glimpses of it, never the same and always changing
its position. It was not, of course, the simple feature that it
seemed, for no sooner had we climbed for an encouraging
distance than the ground would fall away into a tangled
valley, thick with thorns and reeds and knotted creepers

through which we struggled painfully, using our knives, before we could begin to ascend the hill again. Jack was determined to find his yesterday's path, which was somewhere in this malicious maze and which he had marked by knotting tussocks of grass, but Michael soon grew impatient of the search and was sure we should do better by fixing our position with compasses and cutting our way remorselessly uphill. We split into two pairs on this suggestion, Jack and Peter continuing their search and Michael and I plunging straight into the grass thicket. Our progress through this jungle was inconceivably slow, for even Michael was submerged, and we only occasionally caught a glimpse of the summit; so that when we eventually came out on the edge of an unexpected kraal the hill was nowhere to be seen, and we found we had lost our bearings altogether. The group of huts appeared as usual to be deserted, and as we wandered through it we noticed a peculiar feature. This was a circle of ground like a small garden, outlined by stones and enclosed by handsome trees. The ground was smooth and even appeared to be swept, and a flowering bush had been planted in the centre. Three metal tool-heads had been stuck upright in the ground under this bush, and a yard away from it some straight and forked sticks had been planted in the earth, forming a rectangle. We stood mutely staring at these strange signs, and the same discouraging thought occurred to both of us. Was it possible that we had stumbled on what we were looking for, and that this tended place marked an important grave? We were soberly considering this possibility when a young girl came out of one of the huts, appearing unpleasantly startled at the sight of us. Michael spoke reassuringly in Shona and she came a little closer, pleating the folds of her beaded kilt in her fingers. She understood him well enough and replied timidly, pointing with a long black arm and giving

us clear directions for the top of the hill, but when we asked her what the "garden" was she looked frightened and said (which seemed unlikely) that she did not know. Michael pressed his question, saying that the garden was pretty, and eventually, after glancing in every direction but ours, she ran away into the hut and fetched an older woman who might have been her mother. The woman listened with downcast eyes to a repetition of the question and replied in a musical sing-song voice that the garden marked the site of a big hut which had fallen down long ago. We asked who had lived in the hut but she did not remember, and as to the rectangle of sticks, they were apparently as much of a puzzle to her as they were to us. Somebody must have put them there, she said helpfully. Perhaps it was children.

This could have been the truth, but we were uneasy, for it if were not, we should make no headway against this bland concealment, and if it were indeed Umzila's grave, the thought of digging in a populated kraal was plainly ludicrous. We took careful note of the position of the place, exchanged courtesies, and went on in the direction of the hill.

The trail the girl had indicated was the right one; half an hour's further climbing brought us to the very spot that Jack had described, a clearing in the grass and trees that had been used for wood-cutting. There were several stacks of timber there, drying in the sun, and a small thatched shelter such as the herd boys used, in the shade of which we found Jack and Peter asleep. They had succeeded at last in finding Jack's fugitive path and had reached the top an hour ago, but had been too hot and tired to explore further.

From the open patch round the little shelter we could see across a panorama of hills, but on every other side the tangle of grass and trees enclosed us like a wall. When we had eaten and rested we began to skirmish about for a better view, and

digested the difficult nature of the summit. It was more extensive than we had supposed, and the trees, which were a scrub growth extending leafy branches out of the eight-foot grass, were dense enough to prevent our seeing anything, and at the same time not big enough to be climbed. I made several attempts, being the lightest of the four, but all that happened was that I found myself enclosed in a cage of leaves, and the lens-hood was scraped off my camera and swallowed irretrievably by the grass. Again we divided, determined to make some attempt to quarter the hill, each one of us cutting a path in a different direction; but after an hour of this arm-breaking work Michael and I had found only more trees, more grass, more thorns, and had torn our skin and clothes fairly extensively. Peter and Jack came back with something better: they had made their way to the one big tree we had seen so many times on the crown of Nyabánga, and reported that it was of considerable size, of a kind they thought we had none of us seen before, and growing out of a mound of striking proportions.

This was exciting news, and Michael and I were eager to see it for ourselves, but as usual there was no time for further search. It was past three o'clock; in less than two hours the sun would set, and half an hour after that it would be dark. We had no wish to be benighted on the hill, and it was important besides to find a better way down. Peter and Jack had lost much time before they had hit the trail, and Michael and I had made many wasteful traverses. We agreed that it was vital to find a way for the Land Rover at least through the bush surrounding the hill; otherwise, too much daylight and energy would always be spent in the toil of merely getting up and down, with no time left for searching, let alone digging. Jack had his own ideas of the best route to take, and so, as usual, had Michael. Once more we divided, so as

to cover the greatest number of possibilities, each pair heading for where we supposed the watering place to be, where we
had left the Land Rover. As it turned out, Jack's sense of
direction was the better of the two; he and Peter were back
at the Land Rover in little more than an hour, while Michael
and I got badly lost, spending two and a half hours following
false trails and cutting our way through cane-brakes, and
when we eventually reached level ground we were a couple
of miles towards the wrong side of the hill and had to do
some more dejected walking.

Michael was still fresh though he looked disreputable, but
I was worn out and my left foot had blistered, my hateful
boots having once more done their work. Our clothes had
been torn in several places and our arms and Michael's knees
were crusted with blood. We had cut ourselves stout sticks
on the way down, and with these and Michael's scrubby beard
and my dirty knapsack we made a pair of very sordid figures.
We trudged on doggedly, scarcely speaking now that we
were sure of our direction, and were presently startled to
see two strange Africans, also with sticks and also carrying
bundles, coming along the trail as though to meet us. Michael
raised his hand to pass them with the usual curt salute when
to our surprise they caught our hands and warmly wrung
them, laughing with pleasure and clapping our arms and
shoulders in boisterous greeting. Poor Michael all but reeled
with horror at the contact, snatching back the hand that
never touched a black one, but (for my sake, I think) swallowing the proper reply to such impertinence. He stood still and
listened scowling while the two men burst into a torrent
of conversation. His replies were short and I could see that
he was not pleased, but I had no idea of the extent of the
insult he was suffering until our hands had once more been
vigorously shaken and the travellers had gone their way.

"What was all that about, Michael? Who on earth are they?"

"Just a couple of—*munts*, on their way somewhere."

"But why were they pleased to see us? What did they say?"

"I'm afraid they took us for poor whites. They thought we were travelling on foot, as they were. They told us there were huts at the cattle-dip where we could sleep."

I was delighted with this glimpse of ourselves through other eyes, but Michael at first was anything but amused. He strode along, making me trot to keep up, murmuring "Poor whites!" amazedly under his breath. I could see that we presented a shabby appearance and anywhere else might well have been taken for tramps, but I had missed the finer points of the African's judgment. In the first place, Michael said, when he had calmed down sufficiently, it was unheard-of for Europeans to travel on foot. Only Africans did that, and those occasional lost characters, whom everyone despised, who scratched a living here and there in Africa and were contemptuously known and tolerated as "poor whites." The fact that I was the one who was carrying a knapsack, and had been limping behind Michael on the narrow trail, would have perfectly fitted in with this impression, for in the native world it is woman who carries the burdens. The rough staves we plodded with and Michael's beard had all been part of the picture, and consequently the friendly strangers had not been afraid of us. We both looked so travel-stained and I so footsore that in the kindness of their hearts they had been glad to tell us there were native huts ahead. When presently we met a string of women with water pots and one of them respectfully offered Michael a drink, he began to feel better, but a certain disenchantment with his beard dated from this incident.

9

THE DRUMS BEGIN

FOR our final camp we were determined to settle as near to Nyabánga as possible; provided we had water we did not care how little there was, nor how much the *munts* complained; now that Michael's authority was behind us there was not likely to be much trouble from that quarter. Both vehicles, creeping like snails, got over the bridge without accident, the heavy load of equipment going over by hand. Both were unloaded again at the chine as a precaution, and the Land Rover scrambled through on a bed of branches. The lorry gave us some anxious moments, for the furrows cut by the tractor were not yet dry and the wheels spun into the soft clay like butter; but after hacking branches until we were tired, somebody had the brainwave of using the barbecue; and this long-suffering object, which had made our toast and added a smoky touch to so many meals, was put under the back wheels of the lorry and brought it out of the chine with a roar of triumph.

We passed the cattle-dip and went on for perhaps a quarter of a mile, pausing every few hundred yards to examine the river. It was nowhere bigger than a trickle among ferns and stones, but it seemed cleaner, and we finally decided on a grassy hollow, well hidden by trees. There was a mealie field between us and the trail and the trees were large, so that we

had some hope of privacy, but we had scarcely dragged out the tents and begun to erect them than we saw a row of figures on the high bank opposite, squatting to watch us from a discreet distance. This was annoying but inevitable; nowhere was free from the nuisance of being spied on, and if these characters chose to sit there all day they would see nothing but the innocuous activities of the camp.

Michael's first care was to improve the water supply. The stream itself trickled from rock to rock in the depths of a leafy tunnel of palms and ferns, and by laboriously filling flour bags with mud and sand, he managed to construct a miniature dam to hold a tiny pool where one could fill a jug. This feat of engineering took several hours, which the rest of us spent in scouring around in the Land Rover, trying one direction after another for a route to take the vehicle on to the hill. We met with small success, for every trail ended in a thicket, and everywhere we went we were followed by boys. They gladly left their goats and cattle to follow us into the bush at a springy trot, and whenever we stopped to negotiate some obstacle, they clustered closely round us with chirping cries, waiting for us to provide the next diversion. We were further worried, as we lurched through the dense tangle, by hanging festoons of that evil bean which had already caused discomfort on one occasion. Here it proliferated, twining itself invisibly through the trees and sending down showers of stinging hairs whenever our bumpy passage shook the branches. We had taken off the top of the Land Rover for greater mobility, and the poisonous fallout, as light as disintegrated thistledown, floated into our shirts and up our nostrils. We were soon burning and scratching too much to know what we were doing, and beset as usual by boys, goats, and horned cattle, finally beat a demented retreat to the camp.

Michael had completed his dam, so that water could now

be fetched in modest jugfuls, and to his surprise had had a friendly visitor. This was a young native who had come wading through the grass and had greeted him by name, claiming to remember him from a visit he had once paid to Salisbury, where his brother had worked on Michael's father's farm. Michael did not remember him, but he was genuine enough, and Michael cunningly engaged him in conversation. When the usual questions had been asked and answered (we were no longer emphasizing the quest for ruins but were usually piously following the footsteps of my father, who had been either a missionary or a White Hunter) he asked him if it were true that the Zulu people had once been known in these parts. He had been told, Michael said, by a man at the cattle-dip that this was so, but did not know whether to believe it. Yes, said the young man, that was certainly true; a Zulu chief who had been defeated by his brother had been exiled to these parts. He had brought his followers with him, mostly women, the widows of his warriors, and these women had married the local men and the chief had prospered. He had even grown rich and lived to a great age, and was buried, the young man believed, not far away. "Oh, where?" said Michael, trying not to look interested; but this the young man said he did not know. Somewhere hereabouts; the old men would remember; somewhere not many miles from his old kraal. He did not know where the kraal had been, and Michael was chary of pressing him. He gave him a small present from our stores (corn flakes, I think; we were always trying to get rid of them) and sent him on his way apparently happy.

We pondered this incident at our evening meal, after time and cold water had soothed our burning skins and we were able to hold a coherent conversation. It was good to find our story further confirmed; we would have liked to hear the answers to more questions if we had not been always afraid

of betraying interest. Would the young man repeat Michael's questions to his elders? Would they eventually reach the ears of the Portuguese police? We hoped not, for the Portuguese by this time had become bogies, and whenever we heard a sound which might have been (but never was) a jeep, we stopped talking and strained our ears to listen. We were not reassured by Michael's confident proposal that if they came we should "surround them and take the bolts out of their rifles," for what the Portuguese police would be doing while we performed this manoeuvre was never made clear, and we did not share his confidence that such a *coup* would be the end of the matter, even if it were possible.

We went to bed early that night, before the little greenish-grey parrots inhabiting our trees had quite done fluttering and shrieking; they seemed disturbed by the fire, and kept up a quarrelsome racket in the high branches. At last all was quiet; the moon was rising slowly, already on the wane, and we fell asleep before it had dissolved the darkness. I do not know how long we slept in peace, gathering our energies for the morning; it was perhaps midnight when we were all awakened by a yell and I sat up in bed, my teeth chattering with shock. But it was not the Portuguese, nor any human, but only a small lemur-like animal with a long tail, a night-ape, parading the high branches over my bed. The darkness vibrated with the cry, and as soon as the silence flowed back, it did it again. It was a murderous sound, expressing the night-ape's tenderest longings of love, and so, no doubt, most melting to his kind; but to human ears it was the noise a sheeted ghost might make in a graveyard to dismay travellers; a yell of menace, the shriek of an afreet. The wretched creature repeated the performance tirelessly, at intervals of about a quarter of an hour, until even Peter, who normally slept through anything, was shouting from his tent "For God's

sake shoot the bloody thing, can't you?" and Michael was
sitting up in bed with his rifle. We would all happily have
seen its body drop from the trees, but it was a creature of
darkness and invisible, crying its love in a secret fastness of
branches, and it was not until five o'clock, in the first faint
light when our chickens began to stir and crow in the dog
kennel, that I saw it run nimbly along a limb and take squirrel
leaps from tree to tree, silent at last like a ghost in flight from
the morning.

Cross and unrefreshed, we set out early in the Land Rover
to make a last attempt to get it up the hill. Only Michael now
believed that this was possible, but he was so positive in his
theory, and the advantages of success would be so great that
we thought it worth spending the morning in a final effort.
He was sure that if we followed the course of the river to a
point where it seemed to skirt the foot of the hill and then
"cut fifty or a hundred yards straight through the bush" we
should arrive on an almost treeless and easy-looking slope,
which we had all seen and longed for in the distance. The
disastrous truth was, however, that on this side Nyabánga was
protected by a jungle valley worse than any we had tried,
and when we had hacked a course into it we sank finally
into a spongy morass of reeds and thorn bushes.

To get into this ridiculous position we had come down a
precipitous slope where in order to make the least progress we
had had to lever out boulders and fell saplings. We went on
because it was even less practicable to go back. Michael,
manfully slashing ahead, was badly stung by the fiendish
buffalo bean which hung in festoons in every tree and had
made every inch of this swampy jungle its own. We soon
saw why, in spite of the oozy richness of the soil, there were
no tracks in this tangled waste, no mealie patch, no pockets
of cultivation; it was wholly subjugated by this torturous

plant, which in every direction spread its invisible net. At
last we saw an open space in the thicket, and Peter, who by
now was driving the Land Rover like a tank, crashed head-
long through a thorn brake to reach it. He did not see that
the thorn branches over his head were laden with creeper,
and his violent passage precipitated such an explosion of
buffalo bean that the air became thick and golden with
floating hairs. They covered the Land Rover, drifted in our
nostrils, and enveloped Peter wholly as in a shower of pollen.
By the time we had followed him out on to what proved to
be an old mealie patch on the far side of the thicket, he was
already tearing at his arms and neck and stamping about in
a fever of blasphemous misery.

It is a property of this loathsome plant (which is also,
with justice, called the Nessus bean) that nothing but time
can bring its victims relief. For a hideous hour the itching and
burning are acute, and scratching, which no poor wretch in
his transports can resist, raises the irritation to a mad pitch.
None of us suffered so abominably as Peter, but we were
all scalded, and writhed in grotesque contortions around
the Land Rover. We tried swabbing our skins with water
from our bottles and rubbed ourselves with oil from the skins
of *naartjes*, but neither brought even the illusion of relief. We
were in no state to go on, yet could not stand still, and to
an unaffected spectator the scene must have been quite as
diverting as those on the walls of some mediaeval churches,
with the damned writhing like maggots under demons' pitch-
forks.

There were spectators, of course. The noise of our progress
through the valley must have been heard a mile off, and now
that we were through the worst of it and had come to an open
patch to which there were paths, first boys with goats appeared and then two young men, who watched our plight

with enjoyment from a little distance. The younger of the two was perhaps seventeen; he had a gentle face and carried a homemade zither. After watching us for a while in silence he struck a tentative note and then another, and eventually played a plaintive four-note tune, as though prompted by our contortions to some accompaniment. The other was unusually handsome, with the proud bearing and features of the Zulu. He approached us presently with an air of amusement and told Michael, who was either less afflicted or more stoical than the rest of us and was recovering his dignity, that nobody went into the place through which we had come because there was an evil plant in it. Whenever they themselves were stung they plunged into the river or covered themselves with mud, but neither remedy was much good; one could only bear it and wait. This we were doing to the best of our ability; poor Peter was crimson from head to foot and looked like a man in a fever. We were glad to ask for directions for getting out, and the youths obligingly led us into the thicket for some way, to a point where there was a distinguishable trail, and suddenly left us, vanishing silently into the fronded reeds.

It was now midday, and we were still far from our hill, which appeared and reappeared mockingly at a distance, serene and bright under the vertical sun. We now knew finally that there was no way of helping ourselves with the Land Rover, and that the hill would always defeat us until we approached it on foot. The day was too far spent for another attempt, and we were in no condition to make one. We were thankful at last to reach the watering place and to bump our way over the difficult trail to the camp, where we washed in cold water and changed every article of clothing.

A message had come in our absence that brought Michael

to a standstill, for he was always careful in matters of bush etiquette. The camp was not, as we had supposed, back in Zamchiya's territory, but on a spur of land in the jurisdiction of another chief, towards whom we had failed in courtesy by not asking his permission. The message said simply that the Chief, Chiquoqueti, had heard of the presence of strangers, and the implication was clear that we should take him a gift and pay him an apologetic visit. Peter and Jack were still only convalescent from their sufferings, so when we had eaten and rested and cautiously brushed the carpet of hairs from the Land Rover, I went on this courtesy visit alone with Michael. We were hard put to it to know what to take for a present, for we were down to our last bottle of whisky and were regretting several that had already been given away. Spirits and shot are by far the most coveted gifts, since Africans are not allowed to buy either, with tins of beer or fruit a poor second. Our beer had all been finished at the lorry festival, and most of our remaining shot was for rifles, which a chief would not possess, so we packed some tins of apricots round our feet, hoping that it was true (as we had been told) that this chief, though renowned for wisdom, was a very poor one.

We went up the stony hill above the cattle-dip and came soon enough to a small and dilapidated kraal where a very old man in khaki shorts was dozing outside his hut. This was evidently Chiquoqueti himself, for he bolted inside as soon as he saw us coming and sent out two of his sons to ask our business. Michael told me to stay where I was, in the Land Rover, since he did not wish to make matters worse by approaching the Chief with a woman, and I sat unobtrusively in the shade while he and the sons went through the conversational preliminaries. When the Chief emerged he was evidently in full dress, consisting of an army winter overcoat. It

was of an obsolete pattern and almost threadbare, but the buttons had been polished to the last dazzle of perfection.

The conversation was long, and from first to last the Chief's manner was forbidding. He was not pleased to see us and received Michael's apology in silence. He did not refuse the tins but would not look at them, and Michael had the impression that the prime cause of his displeasure was our coming without warning, catching him off his guard in a state of undress. He was a fine-looking old man and I longed for a photograph, and this was eventually permitted, though he would neither remove his coat nor relax his disapproving and suspicious expression. We came away with the feeling that he believed not a word that had been said, and had formed an impression of us that was deeply unfavourable.

After this chilling interview we cheered ourselves by visiting the large and properous-looking kraal that we had once supposed to be Zamchiya's. We now knew that it belonged to my old friend of the pink woollen cap; he had come to the camp while we were on the hill and had left a request for four gallons of petrol. We had not much to spare, but we needed fresh meat and a couple of *pangas,* since both of ours had been lost by Shorty on wood-cutting forays, and this seemed an opportunity for bargaining. Our friend was a man of importance, by African standards a highly prosperous farmer: he had twelve wives and fifty-six children, and himself never needed to raise a finger.

He came out expansively to meet us, snatching off his woollen cap and holding it with ringed hands against his breast. The women and children dawdling about the huts, each one languidly occupied in some unexacting task—fetching water, stirring a pot, shooing chickens—backed respectfully away at his approach, keeping out of range of the eye of authority. One of the younger women was hugely pregnant

and walked with the backward-sloping gait of the precariously
balanced. Others had babies bulging from a cotton satchel;
most of them had naked children at their heels. One was the
fat young woman who had talked to me so effusively at the
cattle-dip, but in her husband's presence she neither raised
her eyes nor returned my greeting. The kraal was tidily
kept and had an air of discipline; everything in it reflected
the personality of the master. He radiated natural authority
and that innocent charm that one encounters only in those
who have never had a moment's doubt of being in the right.
Maside (for that was his name) was delighted to be visited,
and even seemed not to mind that one of his guests was of
the despised sex; he made special remarks to Michael for my
benefit, and as they were translated watched my face with
an expression of eager vanity and politeness. It now transpired
that his approaching me on the day that I had been waiting
on the ant-hill had been due to a belief that I was lost and a
desire to offer help and hospitality. I thanked him through
Michael, and he shook his head, laughing. It was nothing, he
said; I had seemed to be alone, and this was difficult country.

He showed us his cattle with great pride; there were rather
too many of them, but they were in fair condition. He should
have more, he said, but wives were dear in these parts and his
family had impoverished him. For some, he said, opening his
eyes wide, he had paid the equivalent in cattle of fifty pounds.
He began pointing out his wives to us as he spoke, quoting
the price of each as a measure of the cost of modern living.
Michael, running a disparaging eye over the group, suggested that he had paid too much for some of them, and with
this disobliging remark Maside agreed. It could not be helped,
he said; things were exorbitant.

He showed a strong bargaining vein when it came to business, laughing and shaking his head at Michael's suggestions

and making impudent calculations on his fingers. But the performance was largely for pleasure; he sold us a goat for a pound, which was about right, and went up to a kid and two *pangas* for four gallons of petrol. On this he had perhaps the better bargain, for petrol was not to be got within fifty miles; but having displayed cunning he showed an oriental desire to appease us with presents. He sent a girl into one of the huts for a handsome calabash and placed it in my hands; it was new and unused, of a capacity of about four quarts. Then he shouted a command to the fat wife, who obediently crawled into the pigeon house, and emerged again backwards after an anxious struggle, holding a large beaky black-and-white fledgling. She approached slowly, eyes cast down, tenderly carrying the bird like a precious vessel, and knelt to offer it up to her husband's hands. He placed it at once in mine with a gallant speech; apparently Michael had told him it was my birthday.

The pigeon was quiet and did not seem to mind handling, but we were next invited to climb up a ladder of branches to inspect the corn loft, which was a thatched barn on legs, eight feet from the ground; and with the bird in my hands I found the ascent difficult. The floor of the barn was woven of springy branches, and the cobs of maize were stacked in rows to the roof, as orderly and beautiful to look at as a well-stocked library. Maside had already sold his surplus at a good price, and what we saw was the coming year's supply, enough to feed his numerous wives and children.

Not all the family was at home at this time: the grownup sons were mostly absent, working for the Portuguese, and some of the daughters had been disposed of in marriage; but the population of the kraal was still impressive, and the wives in their dark kilts and bright beads were, though a homely lot, pleasing. I asked permission to photograph the family, and this

was received with pleasure by our host. He clapped his hands and gave a brief command, and they all disappeared at once into their separate huts. They were gone for a long time, while I chose a spot and set my camera and Michael talked to Maside and fondled the pigeon. When they finally emerged it was evident that they had gone to immense trouble and had ruined their appearance. Each was dressed in a hideous and ill-fitting cotton-frock, of the deplorable kind that hangs in bunches at the back of every kaffir store in Africa. I had often examined these when we had had occasion to go into a store for bully-beef or paraffin, and had been appalled at the shoddy material and crass workmanship supplied to Africans; the two handkerchiefs I had bought of the same cotton had run their bright colours into a sorry mess at the first touch of water, and I had been relieved when Hla-Hla told me they were not Lancashire goods but had been manufactured in Rhodesia.

The wives now ranged themselves with their children under Maside's orders, the few sons who were at home standing in a row on either side of their father. A Portuguese felt hat was brought for Maside and the family's finery was complete. Every vestige of beauty was blotted out from the group, and I knew that I had taken a grotesque picture. The taking of it, however, was received as a compliment, and we parted from Maside on excellent terms. It did not strike us until later that it was odd he had not asked us what we were doing; indeed he had not put to us any of the usual questions.

The following morning we left camp early, taking food and water and leaving the Land Rover under the trees at the watering place. We followed Jack's route, which he had marked with knotted grasses and bent twigs, and got to the

top of the hill in under two hours, having lost ourselves
only twice. It was a still day with pockets of mist in the hol-
lows; the grass was moist and untrodden, cold with dew.
There seemed to be nobody about, not even herd boys, and
the silence, though reassuring, was oppressive. We were all
uncomfortably conscious of the shortness of time, for in two
days Michael's extended leave would be up, and we were
painfully on the alert for the Portuguese commissioner. It was
strange that we had been left in peace for so long, but we
knew that this was only a matter of time, and that when we
returned to camp he might be there before us. So long as
we had left no mark on the hill and had not begun to dig,
there was no reason why we should not stick to our cover
story, which though eccentric was harmless; but once we
had begun tunnelling the pretence would collapse, and we
would have to work fast and get out quickly. Many considerations pointed to these two days being the last we could
spend on the hill, for our repeated climbing was constantly
watched, as our own Africans, who gossiped at the cattle-dip,
had already reported; they themselves were openly uneasy
about it, and their recent questions had driven Michael to
invent improbabilities.

We made up our minds, since these last two days were
all that were left us, to devote the whole of the first to searching the hill, in particular to examining the mound with the
big tree. If we found nothing to disturb our guess that the
mound was what we were looking for, we would cut a
trench into the side on the second day, and make new plans
according to what we discovered. If this misty silence continued, it might augur well; we might, if need be, be able to
work through the night, and if the Portuguese police arrived at the camp they would not find their way up the hill
in a hurry. At all events, and if the hill yielded nothing, we

would still have to leave the area as quickly as possible. Our clues ended here. Nyabánga was the end of the trail that had defeated Russell.

Arrived at last breathless and sweating at the wood-cutter's shelter, we stretched ourselves on the hard ground and watched the last tendrils of mist dissolve from the hill. The blood was beating in our ears and we did not speak; but after a heavy-breathing silence first one of us sat up and then another; it was not our hearts making the whole rhythm. Somewhere below the hill we could hear a drum.

We had not heard a drum of any sort since we had crossed the border, and the beat we now felt rather than heard, tentative and muffled as though speaking with deliberate discretion, was quite different from the cheerful drumming of the beer-drinking. It began with heavy, slow, portentous thuds, which after a pause went into a light irregular staccato passage, followed by silence. After an interval which seemed endless but was really about a quarter of an hour, the heavy drum spoke again, and the light passage was repeated. "They're sending a message," said Michael.

We listened with apprehension, watching his face, but he could not read the drums and shook his head. All he could distinguish after the third passage was that the same message was being repeated, and presently it was taken up at a distance, by another drum on the further side of the hill. The heavy beats were simply an alert, an announcement that a message was being sent, and the second drum had received it and was passing it on. It might have nothing to do with us, but in the still air the distant thudding had a tone of menace, urgent, yet deliberately covert.

Startled out of fatigue, we scrambled to our feet. Whatever the meaning of the drums there was no time to be lost, and we hurriedly separated to quarter the hill. My way was across

the top to the north face, and after studying the tops of such trees as I thought I should recognise, I plunged into the grass. Again I had the sensation of walking underwater through a heavy forest of weed that closed over my head. As far as I could judge, pausing occasionally to look upwards to the surface, the grass in places was nearly ten feet high, and there seemed little hope of ever seeing out of it. At the level at which I forced a laborious passage it was laced together with the debris of past seasons, and the matted stuff dragged hard against my thighs. It was difficult to cut and I dragged it apart with my hands, pausing at each step for further unravelling. The trail I made was a narrow corridor, which at least I should be able to retrace, but it was futile to imagine that much of the hill could be examined by this method unless one pursued it for days, making a maze of ant-like runs over the whole surface. By the time I reached the north side the sun was blazing vertically down out of a white sky and seed pods were cracking open in the heat with a papery rattle. The grass was less dense here and I could see out of it in places, but nowhere was there a sign of a trail, a mound, or of anyone having passed this way for years. I took scraps of paper out of my pockets and impaled them on thorns as I went along, marking my passage, and they hung there motionless and ridiculous, like fragments lodged in the weed at the bottom of the sea.

We were out of sight of one another for perhaps two hours, and all this time the drums murmured their monotonous tattoo. Sometimes the sound was screened by a fold of the hill, and I could hear nothing but the dry rustle of my own progress; but sooner or later the old vibration would assert itself and I would catch a faint beat from a new position. This continual losing and finding of the sound was a disturbing sensation, as though one were hiding and being repeatedly

discovered, and in the end my ears grew so weary of listening to the drums that I could not tell if I were hearing them
or not.

At last I heard the distant shrilling of a police whistle, the
signal we had agreed on for returning, and made my way back
through my grassy catacombs to the first meeting place. The
others had covered far more ground than I had, my area having been even denser than theirs, and they had found nothing
to compare with the mound with the big tree. The species of
tree they had not been able to identify; they had not seen
one like it before, and it was the only one of its kind to be
found on the hill. It was an evergreen, not unlike an ilex, with
small, hard, dark-green leaves, which when broken gave off an
aromatic smell. It was growing out of the top of a fair-sized
mound, and from its central position appeared to have been
planted. The place was thickly surrounded and overgrown,
and except for the openings in the grass that had been made
that morning there was no sign of any trail or visitation. All
this was suggestive enough in a place where we had found
no other mound, not even an ant hill, but there were other
curious features which seemed significant. This tree, the
biggest on the hill, could be seen for miles; it was Nyabánga's
only distinguishable mark, and we had seen it from as far away
as M'jenami. The mound itself was a little below the crown
of the hill, facing across the plain to Umzila's country. It was
the only spot on the hill where, without climbing or lifting
oneself in any way, one looked over an open sweep of forest
and bush, leading the eye straight to a gap in the far hills,
beyond which lay the shadowy curve of the M'rongwezi. It
was thus the only place on Nyabánga from which one looked
straight as an arrow into Umzila's country, to the very river
on which he had built his kraal. It also—and this again seemed
to be more than chance—was the sole point from which the

western edge of M'jenami was seen in coincidence with the outline of a sister mountain, M'jervasi, the two standing like fortresses on the fringe of Umzila's country, enclosing it to the southwest in a rocky frame. If Umzila's grave were indeed on Nyabánga, it was from here alone that his spirit's eye could gaze on its old home; and here the mound was raised, crowned with its tree.

We stood there for a long time, gazing at the writhen roots and the hardness of the mound under our feet, suddenly aware of the task that lay before us. There was no longer any doubt in our minds that this was the place, and we probed in imagination into the stony ground, splintering the tree roots, tunnelling the clay, to the dark cavity we could almost see, the sense of it was so powerful. It was a forbidding obstacle, and the atmosphere of the place—our imaginations were no doubt at work, but who knows?—intimidating. Under our feet, perhaps six feet down, perhaps more, a skull might be gazing upwards from empty sockets, unmoved after seventy years of that rich darkness, secure in the age-old protection of fear and magic. What business had we to disturb him? None, we knew; yet all four stood rooted to the mound, staring downwards, as though our feet were held by an invisible magnet. When at last we broke away, closing the divided grasses to cover our tracks, we became dimly aware of the drums again, monotonously muttering, and woke out of our dream to consider present problems. We would dig the mound tomorrow, drums or no drums, and prepare a speedy retreat from Umzila's country.

We met no one, not even a child or a goat, on the way down; except for the drums, which spoke always at a distance, the bush was unusually quiet. We followed one another in single file and in silence, through the maze of hairlike paths

which at last, after so many errors, we were beginning to learn, and came to the watering place a good hour before sunset, to find the Land Rover surrounded by thirsty cattle. This was the hour when the herd boys brought them in droves to the muddy shallows, from miles of burnt-up bush where there was no juice in the grass and the stream beds were all dry; a convivial hour that the youths enlivened with simple showing-off, with walking on their hands and tinkling and blowing on their musical instruments. We had watched them often, laughing at their antics, which were sometimes aimed at us as a heaven-sent audience; but this evening they were quiet and seemed to avoid us, watching in sombre groups from the slimy bank.

As we rocked our way over the bumps of the homeward journey we discussed all possible tactics for the morrow. The ideal thing from a practical point of view would have been to take John and Shorty with us, since five men dig faster and further than three, and they were both of them strong and skilled with pick and shovel. But it was too great a risk. Used as they were to Michael's authority, there was no knowing how the fit would take them when they realised (as they eventually must) what we were doing, and Michael shook his head at the suggestion. No white man's order, he said, would weigh in the balance against superstition, and we should be fools indeed if we risked their running away and telling some garbled story in the villages. They had already asked too many questions for his liking, and the stories he had told them had been so far on the safe side of truth that it was better not to disturb them. We would leave the boys busy with packing up the camp and would be as secret as possible with the digging equipment.

This was another difficulty. We had little enough in the way of digging tools and did not wish to be seen with them

on the hill. The heads of the mattock and pick could be taken off their shafts and hidden in knapsacks, with the handles carried as sticks or strapped to the rifles; but the spade was so constructed that it could not be dismembered and defied every attempt at ingenuity. We examined it carefully that night, but it was obvious that once we took it apart we should never reassemble it; it had got to be carried whole or it would be useless. It was decided at last that the thing should be wrapped in a blanket and carried in a bandolier. So disguised it presented a curious appearance, not unlike a large and ungainly banjo, and was hidden under some sacking in the Land Rover. The *pangas* were normal equipment and could be carried openly, but when everything had been put together for the morning—tool heads in knapsacks, rifles, *pangas*, water bottles, cameras (we were always supposed to be keenly photographing scenery)—we were appalled to find them so heavy. We took out the tin of bully-beef and the coffee, resolved to make do with water and a handful of biscuits, and I rejected the heavy snake-bite outfit which I had so far painstakingly carried over every inch of ground, haunted by the idea that once I abandoned it somebody was certain to be bitten; but these minor adjustments made no appreciable difference, and we sighed to think what we should sweat under tomorrow.

All the time we had been busy with the tools, John had been lurking in and out of the shadows, waiting for an opportunity of speaking to Michael. What he wanted was a *squeret*, or advance on his wages; he needed, he said, a pound. This would not have been unusual in a place that offered the means of spending money, but here, with no store within miles and no meeting place beyond the deserted cattle-dip, it seemed peculiar, and Michael asked the reason. "Sorry, Boss, can't say." John was respectful but firm, and all Michael's

questioning and cajolery failed to move him. "All right," said Michael, "I shan't let you be a fool with your money unless you tell me what it's for," and stalked off to his tent with a displeased expression, quite sure that John, who was a confiding character, would presently follow him. But he did not; and when Michael came out of the tent again he saw John slipping unobtrusively out of the camp with a bundle. He brought him up with a shout, and John came reluctantly into the firelight with his hands behind him. He had been on his way to the cattle-dip to sell his clothes.

"What the hell are you going to do that for? They're your best ones, aren't they?"

"Yes, Boss. I need that pound."

"Tell me what you want it for and I'll give you the pound now."

"Very sorry, Boss. No." And the tedious argument was gone through all over again, with John respectful, apologetic, immovable.

A pound was a serious proportion of his weekly wages, which according to custom would be paid in a lump when we returned to Salisbury, and Michael was afraid that he had got into some silly trouble with the local inhabitants, or was being swindled. But it was no use. John meant to have that pound and would not say why, and after a further struggle Michael gave it to him.

We had hardly settled round the fire for a drink, remarking with relief that the drums were at last silent, when the cook appeared and asked for an advance. He, too, wanted a pound, and the only reason he would give was that it was "for something important." Michael was adamant, but Jack produced the money out of his pocket: it hardly seemed worth while at this stage having trouble with the cook. When Shorty, however, appeared with a wheedling expression, cap in hand,

hair meekly parted down the middle, asking for a pound, Michael's impatience exploded, and he took Shorty behind the lorry for questioning, which he did by the simple expedient of offering to kick him. This practical technique of persuasion was only too familiar, and Shorty gave in. If Boss Michael would kindly refrain from telling the others, he should know the story.

It now leaked out that while we had been on the hill the local witch doctor had sent a confidential message to our Africans. Since they were strangers, he said, he wished to do them a kindness, and would allow them to buy, for a pound a bottle, a secret and powerful medicine. The valuable property of this medicine was that, wherever the owner of it happened to be, it would make him aware of any danger that threatened him. Complete protection lay in the bottle itself, for even against an intending murderer one teaspoonful of the medicine was effective. Conveniently enough, it was the victim and not the murderer who took the dose; the magic made him immune from every harm. There were two footnotes, so to speak, to this information. One was that the witch doctor would not like to say that this was a safe area, where harm was never done to unwelcome strangers. The other concerned the medicine, which as well as beneficent had malignant properties. If any man to whom it was offered refused to buy it, for instance, it would attack him; wherever he was in the world, in whatever company, its baneful influence would follow and overtake him.

Michael had seen quite enough in his lifetime of the effects of magic to know that argument was useless. John's Christianity, the cook's sophistication, even Shorty's allegiance to the Dutch Reformed Church would avail them nothing. They were possessed of the virgin faith which moves mountains, and the witch doctor (by now, no doubt, filling his little

bottles with muddy water) had the formula for setting it in motion. He said every blasphemous thing he could think of about the witch doctor, making Shorty's eyes revolve with anxious terror, and came back to the fire with the news that he had given him the money. We would have "scoff" early that night, to leave the boys free to visit the witch doctor and purchase their immunity from evil. They might need it, he said soberly, before we got out from here. It would be nice if we ourselves could have had a bottle.

This idea seemed to the rest of us worth pursuing, but apparently it was out of the question. Witch doctors kept prudently clear of Europeans, and were rarely seen by them. They enjoyed a power equal if not superior to that of the chiefs, did considerable good as faith-healers among their own people, and could hardly be blamed if they ran a few profitable rackets. Wasn't it the same, Michael reasonably said, in Harley Street? We considered this carefully over our whisky and had to admit that, given a public as pure in heart as the witch doctor's and as innocent of doubt, there were no lengths to which a skilful practitioner might not go. The simplicity of the idea was almost beautiful.

Still, there were aspects of it which were not reassuring. Had the witch doctor thought it out for himself, or was there something afoot which had suggested this brilliant and profitable sideline? From what, tomorrow perhaps, would the medicine protect them? From the Portuguese, or the wrath of Umzila's spirit? This was a disagreeable line of thought, and we had not pursued it long in the dying firelight when once more, at no great distance, the drums began.

The pattern, so far as we could judge, was the same as before: heavy booming thumps at regular intervals, followed by silence, followed by the light, rapid, complex staccato message. We strained our ears to listen, and after the second or

third repeat heard a muffled answer a long way off, like an echo, and then the two seemed to speak at the same time, to overlap in muttering counterpoint and to fall silent together. After a time we could not tell if there were one or two drums conversing, or even three; the far one was so faint that we might have imagined it; in the silence an ominous pulse beat in one's ears.

With the boys gone, the camp was dark and quiet; we had nothing more to say and went to bed. The drums continued to beat alone until midnight, coming up from the pillow more as sensation than sound, so that one constantly raised one's head for a moment to listen; and at midnight the night-ape loosed his opening yell, adding his banshee voice to the concerto. We slept fitfully, waking to the night-ape's screams and to sudden silences, and at three o'clock to the boys' return, which was drunken and noisy. The final silence was a long time coming. When at last it fell the little doves were beginning to sound and the first grey light was prefacing the morning.

10

THE DIG

THE dawn was cold; a milky river of mist had flowed into the valley and was slowly weaving tributaries round the hill. The summit was hidden; trees and grass were heavy with chilly dew. Maside's kraal and the watering place were deserted; it was as though all life and sound had been drained away, and we moved in a world which we alone inhabited. Our packs were heavy and we climbed in silence, checking the knots of grass, the bent twigs, the private arrangements of sticks and stones that were our landmarks, and which led us faithfully through our complex channels. None of our signs, so far as we could see, had been moved, but here and there, where we changed direction or left one gully for another, there were strange ones beside the path, which we had not made. Handfuls of grass had been knotted together, forming a standing figure suggesting a totem, with a style and flourish which was none of ours. Some were mere knottings, others were like a grassy sketch of a corn-dolly; it was clear that someone had followed the trail since we had and at key points had left mysterious signals.

We reached the top in an hour and a half and sat for a moment to rest by the wood-cutters' shelter. It was past nine o'clock, the sun still invisible; our shirts were wet with sweat and the cold dew. There was no movement in the air

and no sound anywhere; none of those small noises, cries of herd boys, voices of women at the water, which normally floated up to the top of the hill; even the drums were silent, as though the glacier of mist had been a river indeed, spreading a chill of silence along the valley.

There was no sign that anyone had followed our trail from the summit to the mound; there were no knots or symbols here, and Shadow went before us with drooping tail, making distasteful leaps through the wet grass. The mound itself was undisturbed, the grass as we had left it; however closely our movements had been followed and our route marked, this final place at least had been avoided.

The point at which it seemed best to open a trench was on the lower side of the mound, facing downhill. By tunnelling here on the level and going straight in, we hoped to get to the centre at a depth of eight feet, using the slope of the hill to our advantage. We spoke as though we knew exactly how to do it, but I suspect none of us, except perhaps Peter on his farm, had ever tried to dig a trench in his life, and we thought enviously of Russell's mining experience. He and his confederates had trenched and cross-trenched the whole of Umzila's kraal, which years of use would have beaten to rocky hardness, with the floors of the old huts as durable as cement. We were faced with a mound which had never been trodden, which only time and the tree had together fortified; but at the first blow of the pick we exchanged glances; the mound was as hard and as strong as a stone sepulchre.

It was decided that the three men should take turns at the digging, working in twenty-minute shifts, one digging, one resting, and one shovelling. Shadow and I were deputed to keep watch, since in the silence and the mist it would have been easy for spies to approach from any quarter, and what

share we might have taken in the digging (we were both willing) could have been nothing but a nuisance. We spoke in whispers, aware that in this still and moisture-laden air the least sound carried to a distance; but as soon as digging began precaution was useless; the blows of the pick could have been heard a mile off. Shadow and I set off on our cautious rounds and I climbed a shaky tree which served as a lookout; but nothing stirred, and we heard nothing but the thud of the pick and the pebbly scrabble of shovelling. The mist was dispersing slowly, growing pearly and luminous under the diffused sun; vapour drifted out of the trees in shreds; it would soon be hot.

The surface of the mound was cement-hard and had been worked by ants, which was alarming, for although no other ant hills had been seen it was always possible that this was a solitary citadel; we had seen many as large in other parts of the country. The galleries were old, however, and after a few inches they disappeared and the pick broke out impacted clay and pebbles. The trench went in between two major tree roots, which held the mound in a vice of knotted arms, but when it was two feet deep and about four feet long more roots appeared, driven downwards through the clay like a portcullis. These were attacked and splintered with mattock and *pangas* and levered out in pieces with the crowbar, Michael and Peter throwing out the debris between their legs like dogs and Jack clearing the earth with a shovel behind them. We were still too near the outer surface of the mound to be examing the refuse with great attention, but an unfamiliar sound on the spade made Jack pause and probe in the loose earth that he had just thrown. There was something there all right, a fine potsherd, curved and smooth as on the day it was fired.

The others came out of the trench and we all examined it,

passing it from hand to hand in speechless excitement. It was a piece of a native pot, and the curve suggested that it had not been a large one. It would have been natural to find such a fragment if we had been digging a hut, but here, three feet below the surface on this uninhabited hill, how could it be other than significant? The three signs of a grave that Russell had repeatedly sought for had been a mound, a tree, and (as evidence of occasional pious observances) a beer pot. The mound and the tree were all that we had had so far, and the potsherd seemed like magical confirmation. From the curve, we judged it too small to have been a water pot, and there was, besides, no water on Nyabánga. This steep dry summit was in the highest degree unlikely ever to have been inhabited. Why then should a pot have been left or broken here? Could it not have been one of the beer pots that Russell had mentioned, placed on the mound years ago for the old man's spirit? Umzila had been dead about seventy years, too long for there to be any likelihood of recent observances; but twenty or thirty years ago perhaps, before the roots and debris of thirty seasons had added to the mound or the ants carried their structures over the pyramid, the surface would have been lower, and at the level from which the spade had thrown up the shard a pot of beer might well have been set in the grass.

We returned to the trench and sifted the earth with our hands, and in the trodden floor, as well as in the loose earth thrown away at random, we found several more fragments. They were all of the same thickness and colour and belonged presumably to the same vessel, but too much was broken and lost to reconstruct it, and since the edges were all of the same colour as the surface, we could not tell whether the pot had been broken that morning by the pick or had lain for many years in separate fragments.

The detail was not important; the fragments themselves were food to the imagination, and the diggers returned to their work with fierce energy. In the course of another hour the trench was deepened, so that even Michael was hidden to the shoulders, the pick flashing regularly upward into the sunlight and thudding down into the hard clay so that the leaves trembled. It was killing work: after twenty minutes each crawled out of the trench and lay sweating and speechless on the grass, glad to relax his aching muscles until another shift was gone and he must begin shovelling. We were all thirsty, the men from labour and I from anxiety and suspense; when the heat of noon was on us we had emptied our water bottles. We were all by this time subject to a strange ebbing and flowing of illusion, as though our eyes had moments of abnormal vision and could see through stones and earth to the mound's centre. At such times the mind's eye pierced clear through the barrier of earth to the inner chamber, where Umzila's bones lay couched in their airless burrow, already shaken by the tremors of our assault. The men dug like demons, believing at such moments that each next blow would open a crumbling hole into the final cavity and that we should fall on the dark mouth with crowbar and mattock.

But this hallucinated state was not constant. As blow after blow dislodged always harder earth or bit with a jarring shock into iron-hard roots, fatigue and despair would blot out the inner vision, imposing instead a conviction of solid rock and earth, impacted without a crevice to the hill's foundations.

As the hours passed and the hardness of the earth increased with the pains of fatigue, this hopeless vision became more frequent; the difficulties of the trench were now so extreme, allowing no room to turn or swing the pick sideways, that it finally became obvious that it would have to be widened before we could go further. Michael climbed out of the trench,

complaining of pain in his shoulders, and Peter, who had been wrapping pieces of rag round his blistered hands, went in with the mattock to widen the head of the trench. He had not been at it many minutes when a chopping blow dislodged a fall of earth, revealing what looked like a fragment of stone wall. He gave a shout, and we crowded over the edge of the trench to see. He was scraping with the head of the mattock at what appeared to be a vertical surface of old brickwork, or rather, a dark-coloured dry-stone wall laid in regular courses, smaller and smoother than those we had seen at Masingo, but not dissimilar.

Our hopes soared once more, and the next hour was spent in heavy digging and shovelling at the head of the trench in an effort to widen it sufficiently to uncover the wall. The trench had now penetrated well in towards the centre of the mound on a downward slope, and at the head was partly roofed in by the roots of the tree. We had arrived at a point where, if stonework existed to sustain and protect a cavity, one would expect to find it; we could not be more than a couple of yards from the centre. It seemed impossible to dislodge the stones without having more room to move, but time was slipping away and the tree roots buttressed the trench like iron stanchions. Sweating and exasperated, but sure like the rest of us that his blows sounded hollow, Peter attacked the face of the wall with extra fury, smashing some stones and breaking the shaft of the mattock.

This was a disaster, but we still had the pick and the crow-bar, and were too much excited to care. The end of the crow-bar was thrust at a downward angle into one of the crevices, and the three men brought their combined weight to bear. At this moment Shadow, who had wandered off unnoticed into the bushes, suddenly barked, and I sprang up in panic, guiltily aware that the watch had been forgotten. I could not

find him at first and searched anxiously through the grass in several directions. The men were so intent on their levering that they had not heard him, and I was on the point of going back to raise the alarm when I heard the rustle and thud of Shadow pouncing, and in the shaking grass found him gaily absorbed in the pursuit of some small animal. This was a dereliction of duty and shook me badly; he had been left on guard by Michael at the back of the mound and was as bad as I was. Who might not have crept up unseen while I lay face downwards staring into the trench and Shadow deserted his post in enormous boredom? I called him sharply to me and returned to the mound, to find the men standing back from a heap of rubble. They had levered the wall apart and could see what it was: no wall at all but a freak accretion of clays. It now lay in shattered debris at their feet, disclosing rock which not even the tree had fissured. Could it be that this earth had been undisturbed for centuries?

At this we sat down on the edge of the trench in silence, and presently said what was uppermost in our minds. Strangely enough, it was not that we felt we had followed a blind alley. I believe the magnetic sensation of being on the very roof of Umzila's chamber was stronger in all of us at that moment than at any other time, and the taste in our mouths was the bitter taste of frustration. Our tools were inadequate, that was the first admission; and the second was that we needed more time and more men. "If we had five or six *munts*," said Michael, "and worked in shifts, we could tunnel right into the bloody thing in a day."

"Not with these tools," said Peter; "look at the mattock. What we need is an experienced miner and a charge of dynamite." Jack glanced at the rock and said nothing; I guessed he was thinking of Russell.

"If we could come back later," said Michael, "with the

right stuff, and a team of *munts* for digging, and a power drill. . . ." Nobody replied; we knew the answer to that. "The hell of it is," he concluded, "I shall have to start for Salisbury in the morning."

"We shall all have to start," said Jack. "If three of us can't do it, what chance have two?" We relapsed into silence, thinking of the week lost with the lorry in the river, and the nightlong drumming, and the Portuguese commissioner.

"How long do you give it," said Peter at length, "before the local gentry come up and examine the hill?" He was rewrapping the sodden bandages on his hands and looked exhausted. We gazed at the devastation, and our hearts sank.

"I think we ought to cover it in," said Jack, but even as he got stiffly to his feet and stooped for the shovel he knew that it was hopeless. Tons of soil from the trench had been shovelled downhill and lay spread in trampled heaps over a wide area. The mound itself was hideously cloven, tree roots had been cut and thrown aside, branches broken, the grass hopelessly trampled. There was no concealing what we had been about, and as soon as we were off the hill we knew the word would go out that we had been digging. If, as we were still strongly inclined to believe, we had found Umzila's grave and were even now within a few feet of the treasure, our situation would be perilous. If we were wrong, the fact of our digging at all would be highly suspect, and we would be wise to get out at once, without waiting for questioning by either the local chiefs or the native commissioner. Our best hope was, since the sun was already low, that no one would care to go on the hill after dark, and that our activities would not be discovered before morning. By that time we would already be breaking camp and would be over the Rhodesian border in a few hours. As it was, we should have to move quickly; we were dismayed to find it was five o'clock and

that there was only an hour of daylight. We had no wish to add to our misfortunes by losing ourselves in darkness on the hill.

We gathered our tools hastily together, having given up all idea of covering our traces, and set off without loss of time for the downward trail. The men were numb with fatigue and often stumbled, and I was too heavily burdened to be able to speak. We slipped and scrambled down through grass and thorn, searching for our private signs as the light failed, thanking Heaven we had thought to bring pocket torches. We saw no one. It was dark before we reached the area where had left the Land Rover, and our wavering beams anxiously raked the bushes. It was there at last, hidden and safe under the screen of leaves, and we fell into it with relief. We would have been glad to move without headlights but this was impossible; in the moonless dark the noise and glare of our passage seemed outrageous.

We could not hope to return to camp unseen, but it was a shock when, in the moment of catching a glimpse of our own fire, a drum began to beat like a sudden signal. We lurched into camp and switched off the engine to listen. It sounded much nearer than before and seemed to come from Chiquoqueti's kraal. This time there was no staccato message, only the heavy rhythmic monotonous beat, pulsing away in the dark between brief pauses.

Our boys had been watching for us and seemed disturbed. They were plainly relieved when they heard we were leaving in the morning, and set about packing their gear by lantern light. Shorty, Michael discovered, had already finished his bottle of magic medicine. It was obvious they did not like the drums, but would not comment on them. Michael had asked them the night before if they could interpret them,

and they had said they could not; all that they claimed to know was that it was not a beer-drinking.

We were all depressed by the final admission of failure, and this ominous drumming was the last straw. We washed by candlelight and packed our clothes, all of us jumpy and more or less exhausted. It was useless to tell oneself that the drumming might have nothing to do with us; our nerves thought otherwise; and we all remembered Michael's stories of the disturbers of graves whose limbs the natives had hung like joints from the trees. We were on edge, and I came very near to frenzy when Michael in the goodness of his heart decided to cheer me up with a sprightly joke. He ran the Land Rover across the mealie field in the dark, causing us all to stop in our packing and listen, and then lifted the flap of my tent and in an urgent voice announced the Portuguese commissioner. I pulled on my shirt in horror, calling to Jack and Peter, and rushed out into the darkness with a torch to find Michael benignly smiling at the success of his jest. The relief of finding it was not true was so great that my eyes filled with tears, and it was some little time before I could laugh appreciatively.

But this fourth-form joke did something for us after all, for it broke the tension and made us all confess a craven relief. There were compensations in not having our pockets stuffed with diamonds, and I felt a thankfulness that surprised me. Now that all was over except departure, I knew how unequal I should have been to the fears and strains which would have had to follow success. I am a bad smuggler: excitement suffocates me. Conscience is a treacherous thing, and mine behaves badly whenever there is serious danger of being found out. I should have loved the diamonds, but could have wept with relief to know that I had not to fly after all to Antwerp, perhaps alone, and get them through the customs.

Our last evening together in camp was emotional. The drums went on, sometimes near at hand and sometimes far, and although they worried us we confessed to one another that we should have felt a thousand times worse if the diamonds had been hidden that night in one of the tents. It was maddening to have failed, but there was also a cowardly comfort in not being guilty. At least this was what we told ourselves, stretching our aching legs before the fire and circulating the last bottle of whisky. It is easy to deceive oneself in the face of failure.

"I wonder though," said Michael, after a long silence, "if we couldn't come back in a month or two, before the rains. With dynamite, I mean, and a miner's drill. I don't like to think of all that stuff lying buried up there forever, doing no good to anybody."

"What would you do if you found it?" We had discussed all this before, but the subject never palled. We all had stealthy plans for living in luxury.

"Well, first I should leave the police. Not until we had got the diamonds out, of course. I'd probably be the best one to fly them out of Africa. On my police pass, naturally. We could all meet afterwards to divide the loot, somewhere in Europe."

We protested chivalrously that this would not be fair. Things went ill with policemen found heavy with swag; the risk would be greater for him than for a civilian.

"Well, but what about you?" he said, nodding to Jack. "It wouldn't be a nice thing for you to be caught, now would it? Think of the publicity."

"The thing," said Peter, "is not to be caught at all. I don't believe anyone would suspect Jack. He looks so respectable." They all three, I thought, looked as disreputable as one could wish; Jack and Peter had not shaved for days, and Michael

for more than a month. All our clothes were torn and dilapidated and Peter had lost most of his buttons, so that his
stomach was exposed. Still, there was yet time; we should
have had a chance to clean ourselves in Salisbury.

"You could come to Europe later," Jack said to Michael,
"when we'd all lain low for a while and made the right contacts for disposing of the stones. Having left the police, of
course; I may be wrong, but I think that would be advisable."

"Would you dispose of them *all?*" I asked. "Couldn't I
keep just one? Not having it cut, you know, that mightn't
be safe; but I should like to keep one medium-sized one, in
a soft leather bag. It could be regarded as an investment."

"I don't see why she shouldn't have it properly cut," said
Michael kindly. "An uncut diamond looks like an old pebble."

We sighed to think of the calabash of pebbles, but it was
a comfortable sigh, soothed by fatigue and whisky and the
heat of the fire. The drums were still muttering, and it was
growing chilly.

"Of course," said Peter, "one of the most satisfying things
of all would be to do something for Zamchiya. Not a handful
of diamonds, perhaps; that would be dangerous, and I dare
say he wouldn't accept them. But a nice account opened in
Salisbury for his sons' education? Do you think he'd accept
a bequest from some rich Europeans?"

"It would depend, I think," said Jack, "on whether he
suspected the source of their generosity. I would imagine a
chief has to be pretty careful."

"He'll suspect all right," said Michael, "as soon as he hears
of that bloody great hole on the hill. And so will everybody
else. I should like to be a fly on the wall in the D.C.'s office
when the news gets to Spungabera."

But I was already concocting an explanation of the hole,
for though I did not care what Chiquoqueti thought, or the

local inhabitants, or the Portuguese for that matter, the thing that lay heavily on my mind was the kindness of Zamchiya. In a lesser degree I was uneasy about the missionaries, for they were the sort of people who would be shocked by expedient lies, and we had told them plenty. I was determined that when we were over the border we should visit them both, and tell them one more ameliorating lie to make my conscience comfortable. We would of course have been pursuing our search for ruins on Nyabánga and, having finally seen a mound that suggested earthworks, have carried out a little exploratory dig. We would unfortunately have found nothing but a few potsherds, which we could innocently show them. On Nyabánga, we would say, we had drawn a blank, but we were sure there were ruins to be found in this part of Africa. It is best to leave behind an impression of probity.

That night we slept lightly, for the drums continued as long as darkness lasted. We were up before sunrise, snatching a hasty breakfast while the tents sagged and came down, while beds were stripped and dismembered and boxes piled in confusion into the lorry. We had expected to wake dejected, sour over the failure of our adventure, but instead were buoyed up on a wave of absurd elation. Nothing on earth was so wonderful as to be going home.

Already the African landscape looked a trifle thin, as though we were remembering rather than seeing it, and as the vehicles ground their way out over the mealie field and I took my last look at Nyabánga, I could not grieve that I should never see it again. It had defeated us, as it had defeated Russell.

Though our pockets were light, I did not feel empty-handed. There are satisfactions which, if not as durable or as saleable as diamonds, are worth having; and in these I felt rich, though I could not have said for the life of me

what they were. Instead of the calabash of diamonds, which had for so long obsessed us, we were leaving Mozambique with a fledgling pigeon and a pot of wild honey. The pigeon went to live with Michael in Salisbury, and the honey has long since been eaten; but I still have the pot and the shard.

Besides, there is a residue—the unlikely debris of an ambiguous experience—and I sometimes hear the echo of Umzila's laughter.